Violence in Media and Society

Violence in Media and Society
Literature, Film and TV

Edited by
USHA BANDE
ANSHU KAUSHAL

RAWAT PUBLICATIONS
Jaipur • New Delhi • Bangalore • Hyderabad • Guwahati

ISBN 978-81-316-0433-5

© Contributors, 2011

No part of this book may be reproduced or transmitted in any form or by any means, electronic or mechanical, including photocopying, recording or by any information storage and retrieval system, without permission in writing from the publishers.

Published by
Prem Rawat for **Rawat Publications**
Satyam Apts, Sector 3, Jawahar Nagar, Jaipur 302 004 (India)
Phone: 0141 265 1748 / 7006 Fax: 0141 265 1748
E-mail: info@rawatbooks.com
Website: www.rawatbooks.com

New Delhi Office
4858/24, Ansari Road, Daryaganj, New Delhi 110 002
Phone: 011 2326 3290

Also at *Bangalore, Hyderabad* and *Guwahati*

Typeset by Rawat Computers, Jaipur
Printed at Chaman Enterprises, New Delhi

Contents

Acknowledgements vii

Introduction 1

1 The Necessary Burden of Violence and the Compulsive Search for Peace: Subcontinental Realities of Being-in-the-World 17
 Jasbir Jain

2 'Violence' in Creative and Critical Acts 33
 Avadesh Kumar Singh

3 Violence in the Age of Empire: An Indian Consideration 42
 Rajesh Kumar Sharma

4 Innovative Strategies to Counter Domestic Violence: Exploring the State and Community Responses in Karnataka and Gujarat 50
 Veena Poonacha

5 One Hundred Years of Violence 66
 José Sol Lucia

Contents

6. Functions of Violence: A Study of Caste Violence in David Davidar's *The House of Blue Mangoes* — 81
   P.K. Kalyani

7. Terrorism and Violence: Chitra Banerjee Divakaruni's *Queen of Dreams* and Kiran Desai's *The Inheritance of Loss* — 96
   T.S. Anand and Manjinder Kaur

8. Violence in Indian Literature: Some Thoughts on Domestic Violence in Kiran Desai's *The Inheritance of Loss* — 114
   Silky Anand Khullar

9. Nuances of Gendered Violence: Shashi Deshpande's *The Dark Holds No Terrors* — 125
   Jyoti K. Singh

10. Partition Violence in Jyotirmoyee Devi's *The River Churning*: A Gendered Perspective — 138
    Seema Malik

11. Violent Women in Fiction by Women Writers — 149
    Usha Bande

12. Victims of Violence: A Study of Three Stories from Tribal and Dalit Writing — 164
    Usha Bande

13. Power–Violence Nexus: Girish Karnad's *Tughlaq* and *Tale-Danda* — 177
    Vineeta Kaur Saluja and Shibani Basu Dubey

14. A Study of Chaplin's Film *The Great Dictator*: Violence as Irrational, Laughable and Avoidable — 185
    Shyamala Vanarase

15. Power Rangers: Violent Media and Violent Children — 203
    Anshu Kaushal

Contributors — 218
Index — 221

Acknowledgements

We hereby express our gratitude to all the contributors who have made efforts to submit their papers despite their tight routine and also waited patiently for the book to appear. Thank you all for lending us your precious words and voice on this important issue. "'Violence' in Creative and Critical Acts" by Avadesh K. Singh published in *Critical Practice* has been reprinted. We wish to acknowledge the permission granted by Prof. Singh to reprint it.

Introduction

Violence requires no introduction; but a book on violence does, precisely because violence is so ubiquitous, persistent and relentless that it cannot be contained in the limitations of a book and hence the choice of contents needs to be explained and maybe, justified. Besides, violence is a reality – a lived reality – that is experienced; words cannot put across with any amount of intensity, what is experienced by the psyche. Yet, when a writer moves fairly methodically from one act of violence to another, the general severity of the result both illustrates and emphasises the premises about our society and its most threatening problem. Edward Bond, the playwright, when censured for loading his plays with violence, said, "I write about violence as naturally as Jane Austen wrote about manners. Violence shapes and obsesses our society, and if we do not stop being violent we have no future. People who do not want writers to write about violence want them to stop writing about our time. It would be immoral not to write about violence (Bond, 1977: 3)."

Paradoxically, these words of Edward Bond, which seem to justify violence, are in fact a tirade against the cult of violence and the erosion of the sense of humanity in man. Violence, aggression and cruelty have become a way of life, if one were to analyse the contemporaneous incidents of rape, arson, killings, bomb explosions and terrorism which are reported daily in the media. What, indeed, reaches our eyes/ears is far less than what actually takes place, and goes unreported. It shows the mind – desensitised for whatever reason: profit, hatred, political or racial fanaticism, or some sick fancy of standing above or beyond humanity.

Mallika Sarabhai's brilliant piece of activist theatre staged a play "V for ..." showing the surfeit of violence that has desensitised people to sights and incidents they should be appalled by, but aren't. The performance was not meant to project any political programme or ideology but was staged with the express aim of provoking the audience out of its flaccid complacency. In an interview Sarabhai maintained that "Violence exists in us all," and it is not only the "hooligans" who are guilty of it, but even we, "the so-called 'educated', 'cultured' people" who are guilty of violence. For the past few years violence has been increasing and the quantum of aggression has brought a sense of insecurity in the ordinary citizen's life. It is particularly sad and alarming for a country given to the ideal of non-violence to seek solutions to problems by *himsa,* violence.

Violence is a complex thing. It has many faces. What we see around us is its external manifestation – internal wrangle, communalism, caste-ridden tensions, violence against women, the neglect of children and so on. Apparent physical violence generally leads to killings, loot, arson and frenzy which destroys the unity and harmony of society. But, the latent and structural violence leads to far more harm, cutting into the vitals of the country. There is large-scale exploitation of children, cruelty to the girl child and the down-trodden. Women themselves, as a group, face violence of both types – physical and structural. While physical violence is accompanied by rape, assault and physical torture, structural violence leaves a psychological scar on the victim. The third kind of violence is generated by forced forbearance and erupts occasionally to do spiritual harm to both – the victim and the victimiser.

The condition of being a victim presupposes the existence of a victimiser or an executioner. It is linked inextricably with power and violence – physical or psychological – and is perpetuated due to slavery or prejudices through aggression or oppression. Victim–victimiser syndrome can be political, historical, sexual, social, economic, existential or psychological. In whatever form it be, it is perpetuated by creating a myth of the superior and the inferior, the powerful and the powerless, which is further supported, directly or indirectly, by the society, the government and the educational pattern.

The institutionalisation of the process of victimisation has power dynamics at its basis by which the "power elite," to use C.W. Mills' term, subjugate the powerless. There is, thus, a binary power structure, one side dominating and the other dominated. This is known, in sociological parley, as power-relationship. Though power-balance is subject to recalibration, and is always in a flux, it creates the dual myth of powerlessness and omnipotence. When in Mulk Raj Anand's *The Big Heart*, Bibiji screams at Munoo: "What right has he to join the laughter of his superiors?" or when in Shankara's novel, the caste Hindus object to the name Mohan which a pariah chooses to give his son, we see the power-relationship operating through the caste system; when the Indian masses readily accost their native overlords and later their British masters as *Mai-Bap,* we see its psychological manifestation. Here, the colonised (or the powerless) transfer to their masters "the feelings of dependence, the prototype of which is to be found in the affective bond between father and son (Mannoni, 1956: 158)." Raja Rao's description of England as India's "foster mother" confirms the identification of the colonial ruler with parental figure.

Resistance to the discourses of the privileged include deconstruction of the given socio-cultural construct, overcoming the negative self-image perpetuated by the dominant class with regard to the oppressed and the juxtaposition of alternative visions which take group rights and historical injustices into account. What Emma Goldman tells women, can well be repeated here as a case for all the oppressed. Exhorting women to rise up and make efforts for their liberation, she says:

> History tells us that every oppressed class gained true liberation from its masters through its own efforts. It is necessary that woman learn that lesson, that she realize that her freedom will reach as far as her power to achieve her freedom reaches. (Goldman, 1972: 78)

Camus' famous injunction "neither victims nor executioners" recognises the existence of violence embedded in the historical process and the necessity to say the compelling "no" to the power-relationship. Significantly, every "no" to the outside forces means a "yes" to the self. This "yes" suggests an affirmation and awareness; it becomes a voice of protest and reform and leads to progress; it is a harbinger of change. Foucault's analysis of power points out that challenge to power does not necessarily come from outside but from calling into question "the mechanism of the constitution of subjectivity." Foucault's concept of power as both productive and pluralistic can be seen in some of the essays contained in this study. On one hand power can be supportive of different forms of power, while at the same time producing sites of resistance, struggle and change. Foucault defines all power as producing resistance; resistance to power can produce 'new truths' that may be called 'counter discourses' and these 'counter discourses' oppose the dominant truths or 'reverse discourses'.

When we talk of "violence in the historical process," we do not always mean violence which entails physical harm or assault. Even verbal insults or the tendency to deny someone his fundamental human right can be termed violence. The question of intentionality is vital in understanding the nature of violence or aggression. One may be violent in many subtle ways ... causing mental pain or suffering to an individual, or harming someone's reputation. Elaborating on it J. Krishnamurti says, "we kill people's reputation with a word or gesture; we wipe people out through gossip, contempt and defamation. The cruelty, the hate that exists in ourselves is expressed in the exploitation of the weak by the powerful and the cunning (Krishnamurti, 1977: 166)." Thus, when individuals are deprived of social benefits and are rendered more vulnerable to sufferings than others, there is the case of violence and consequent victimisation. In its multi-disciplinary and trans-disciplinary character, violence can be defined as 'violence by' and 'violence against'. Violent behaviour generates conflicts between two entities, the aggressor who victimises and the victim who suffers. In this sense, violence acquires the proposition from 'microcosm to macrocosm'. In its macro form, violence generates caste and communal riots, ethnic clashes, group conflicts, mob violence and terrorism. Novels of partition or of political violence and victimisation like Amrinder Kaur's *Lajo* or Taslima's *Lajja* depict violence in its 'macro' form when mob frenzy leads to death and destruction. During such situations both the entities become victimiser and victim, simultaneously. The horrendous acts of violence or tendency towards crime in Arvind Adiga's *The White Tiger*, Tarun Tajpal's *The Story of My Assassins*, Siddharth Sanghvi's *The Lost Flamingoes of Bombay* are eloquent examples of violence prevalent in the psyche of the nation.

In the current milieu, films depicting violence provide an immediate stimulus to fiendish behaviour in impressionable minds. Children, adolescent and even some mature people get the message that violence can be a method of solving problems. The lasciviousness and aberrations in films and even on the small-screen is too much for a society to absorb and yet remain sane and healthy. Unless we cry halt to this tendency, it will be difficult to contain its outcome – out of which the propensity to violence is only one.

It is, indeed, the function of society to produce goodwill and fellow feeling. But when society itself is morally diseased, how could it restrain the individual? Nobel Laureate William Golding, the British novelist, opines that when the restraining hand of society is removed, an individual reverts to his 'savage' nature. In a statement to the American publishers of his novel *Lord of the Flies,* he described the theme of his novel as: "an attempt to trace the defects of society back to the defects of human nature. The moral is that the shape of a society must depend on the ethical nature of the individual and not on any political system however apparently logical or respectable."

Though some sociologists and theologians believe that aggressiveness is rooted in man's psyche, the humanist psychologists contend that violence, aggression and destruction are not intrinsic to man. B.J. Paris, studying the tenets of Horneyan psychology puts it thus, "destructiveness, aggression and a need to be omnipotent are not part of essential human nature; they are defensive reactions to what Abraham Maslow calls 'basic threats,' that is the fear that basic needs will not be fulfilled" (Paris, 1994: 217). In today's context, with greed mounting high, we have scant respect for other persons. This possessiveness is termed 'cannibalism' by psychologist Eric Fromm. Man is insecure because he measures himself through his materialistic possessions. "If I *am* what I *have* and if what I *have* is lost, who then am I?" (Fromm, 1977: 96) The answer is, 'nobody'; in that case you are a defeated, dispossessed individual, a being who has lost touch with the inner self – with the core of his being.

Probably W.B. Yeats had a foreboding of this. In his poem 'The Second Coming,' he says, "Things fall apart/the centre does not hold." The *Centre* is not outside us; it is a sense of the human connection, more precious than any fanaticism. What we have lost today is 'the human connection,' resulting in the crumbling of the personality structure and the rise of strange, inchoate cult of violence. The way to change society is to begin with the self.

Evolutionary thinkers like Montesquieu, Morgan, Spencer and many others believed that violence is linked to 'savagery' and primitiveness. Once the human mind becomes enlightened, the society would become civilised and the problem of violence would be solved. Montesquieu argued that this would be a movement from the barbaric to civilised society. While Comte suggested a transition from a theological to a scientific society, Spencer averred that once the society moves away from its militaristic character to industrial type, the problem of war, skirmishes and violence would vanish. The theories propounded by the forces of rationality raised hopes in the human mind. Modern scientific approaches tried to counter the existing religious and metaphysical philosophy to salvage human beings from the obscurantist belief systems that gave primacy to the other worldly approaches to gain peace of mind.

But modernity and science have had their pitfalls and could not solve the problem of violence. A school of thought emerged in the early twentieth century that may not be called anti-modernity *per se*, but which saw and understood the ill-effects of too much science and modernity. Levi Strauss studied the tribal communities and found that their social structures have a well-developed culture and cannot be termed 'savage'. He, therefore, defended their social and cultural norms and raised his voice against the colonial approach to liquidate pre-modern societies to make them 'modern' and 'civilised.' Mahatma Gandhi perceived the problems modernisation would create by dislodging the common man from his age old institutions, uprooting the poor from their soil or their traditional occupations. In a bid to make the poor 'civilised' and part of the development process, we have added more to the misery of the common man. Not only have we been violent to them but have also introduced them to violence and taught them survival through violent means. We have created many a 'Balram' of Arvind Adiga's *The White Tiger*. In a perceptive article published in *The Hindu*, Vandana Shiva focuses on the violence of globalisation. "We thought we had put slavery, holocaust and apartheid behind us – that humanity would never again allow dehumanizing and violent systems to shape the rules by which we live and die. Yet globalisation is giving rise to new slavery, new holocaust, new apartheid. It is war against nature, women, children and the poor" (Shiva, 2001). Vandana Shiva goes on to discuss how technologies of war are becoming the basis of peacetime production, how herbicides, pesticides, genetically engineered crops are putting stress on societies, ecosystems and life.

"Witness the events of our times, which are now front page news. Cows in Europe being subjected to Bovine Spongiform Encephalopathy (BSE), millions of animals being burnt as foot and mouth disease spreads due to increased trades, farmers in India committing suicide in thousands, the Taliban destroying their heritage by vandalising the Bamiyan Buddha, a fifteen-year-old Charles Andrews Williams shooting his classmates in a Californian high school, ethnic cleansing" (Shiva, 2001). What the author said in her testimony at the Women's Court, South Africa in 2001 holds true today and we can add a lot of new things to it. Thus, advances in technology and science, globalisation and multi-nationalism have created both direct and indirect violence. There is a vast difference in the Indian global approach and the present concept of globalisation.

The question that looms large before us is: Can we control violence and aggression? Abraham Maslow, the humanist psychologist, once said that we need is a little more primitiveness and a little less taming. When the world was on the brink of entering the 21st century, thinkers, philosophers, scholars and ideologists were trying to find out ways and means to make the world a better place to live in – a world not stalked by violence and aggression, but made livable by the cherished values of non-violence, love and peace. Since aggression and violence are not intrinsic to human nature, as some social psychologists and anthropologists contend, it is possible to change the present crime graph. But then, the proverbial question looms large, "Who will bell the cat?" How and who could be trusted to bring in transformation? Law-enforcing agencies? Preachers? Moralists? Or man himself? The moving finger stops at *man* himself – yes, only the individual man and woman can bring about inner transformation.

Examples abound in world history of great men who conquered evil by love and sympathetic understanding. The Bishop's magnanimity towards the culprit in Victor Hugo's *Les Miserables*, Lord Buddha's affectionate dealing with Angulimal, the notorious criminal, King Shivi's healing touch to the wounded bird and many more stories, anecdotes and incidents are pointers towards the fact that humans do place a negative premium on aggressive traits. When Jesus Christ forbade his disciple from using violence to counter the mob and warned, "Those who use the sword shall perish by the sword," he gave the great lesson of non-violence. Gandhiji's use of the weapon of non-violence and unaggression against the brute-force of imperialism provides a befitting example to forward our thesis that the expression of anger and aggression can be controlled. A leaf from the social structure of some of the primitive societies still existing on the surface of this earth can display how tribals control violence.

In our culturally oriented language the word 'primitive' brings to mind the word 'savage,' and savage connotes something ferocious, cruel and uncivilized. That is because our language equates the 'primitives,' the 'tribals' with the primates, the predators who are instinctively violent. But anthropologists, who have stayed with and studied some gatherer–hunter societies, away from mainstream civilisation, have great admiration for the methods tribals have evolved to control aggression. For example, the Eskimos, living in the most difficult environment and in the most inhospitable lands in the world, consider violence and aggression as repulsive. Not that they have no ill-temper or quarrel. There are squabbles between individuals or groups but these seldom result in fights or violence. The traditional manner of settling disputes is by contestants' "assaulting" each other with reproachful songs. With song and music the attack is mounted by the victim on the victimiser. The other party too replies with music and songs much to the delight of the onlookers. After a while anger subsides, tempers cool down and the suffering party withdraws, satisfied of having avenged the wrong.

Among the East Greenland Eskimos, a singing contest is the traditional means of resolving disputes. Even the murder of a relative may be avenged by starting with reproachful songs and ending in applause; here is the gist of what an anthropologist recorded once:

> Since skill in singing is greatly admired, and the artistry of the performer so absorbs the interest of the audience, the cause of the contest tends to be forgotten, and the focus of attention is entirely upon the wit and skill with which the contestants attempt the ouster of each other. He who delights the audience most and receives the heartiest applause is declared the winner. Singing ability, indeed, equals or outranks gross physical prowess, and brings great prestige.[1]

Among some of the tribes of the Australian aborigines, quarrel takes the form of talking and talking all day long, throwing spears or boomerangs with such accuracy that they miss the mark and do not hit anybody. W.E. Harney, who lived among the aborigines of Arnhem Land, gives an interesting account of native fights. These aboriginies would fight all day, with plenty of running about and talk. They would scuffle one another but there was very little bloodshed. Although they threw spears and boomeranged about, nobody was seriously injured. In fact, the talkers are not the fighters, they are the protectors. They keep the combatants away. The combatants roar and shout but they are never allowed to face each other. After some time, tempers cool off and peace is restored.[2]

Another tribe of central Australia named Pitjantjatjars has a singular method to clear aggressive drives. They fight 'ceremonially,' following the rule of turn and turn about. The fight clears the air and there are no grudges. Once the quarrel settles the dispute, the fighting parties assist each other to receive first-aid.[3]

The Pygmies of the Ituri Forest of Central Africa have an interesting practice of shouting and inviting the entire community to partake in a quarrel even if it is a domestic quibble. Colin Turnbull lived among the Pygmies for three years and found them unaggressive both emotionally and physically. They may get angry, slap children or quarrel over some issues but anger is short-lived and quarrels are evanescent. In fact, Turnbull points out that their occasional outlets of anger are designed to provide 'insurance' against intentional, calculated aggression.

In our country, too, some of the tribal societies studied by anthropologists show remarkable signs of non-violence. The

Todas of the Nilgiri Hills are a pastoral tribe who live in amity with each other. They have their primitive weapons like clubs, bows and arrows which they take out only on ceremonial occasions. Likewise, the Baigas of Satpura region are unaggressive and friendly. An Anglo-Indian anthropologist, Verrier Elwin records some interesting incidents he encountered when he stayed with the Baigas. During the Second World War reports trickled in about the traumatic war events. An old tribal woman came to Elwin, wondering how God equalizes things. Their sons and daughters die young of hunger or disease or the attack of wild beasts. The sons and daughters of the English could grow old in comfort and happiness. But God sends madness upon them, and they destroy each other, and so in the end their great knowledge and their religion are useless and we are all the same.

This does not, however, mean that the tribals know no violence and that they are the 'noble savages'. They, too, have their ill-tempers, vengeance, witchcraft and murders. But, as many case-studies have shown, the early societies, who had to counter inhospitable Nature, had learnt the art of amity and co-existence. They can be ferocious and unscrupulous. Among the Kung Bushmen of Africa, if a quarrel becomes heated and someone shoots a poisoned arrow at another, wounding a member of the other party, hostilities cease immediately. Then they start a 'trance dance'. Everyone, including the rival parties, joins the dance, which signifies a kind of ritual healing of wounds.

In our culture, we too, have been instructed to practise methods to control our aggressive tendencies, not through philosophical treatises or didactic literatures but through small everyday proverbs, anecdotes, songs and games. Tulsidas' *Ramcharit Manas* records how during the Shiv–Parvati wedding, the bride's party sings songs hurling reproaches at the bridegroom's party which everybody enjoys. This method of giving vent to fear for the future of the daughter prevails in some parts of the country even today. Such folk songs are sung with impunity at weddings.

One folk tale, upholding the wisdom of controlling aggressive behaviour, shows how a merchant coming back home after twelve years discovers a young stranger in his bedroom. In anger, he takes out his sword to kill his wife and the man. But, suddenly he notices the words he had got written on a plank in his bedroom, "when angry, count up to ten." He takes control of himself, wakes them up and discovers, much to his joy and surprise that the handsome young man was his little son, he had left behind twelve years ago.

Various marshal games, sports competitions, riddling contests to solve disputes were probably ingenuous devices invented to discharge the aggressive forces within us. The 'quantum leap' from his biological heritage to his cultured form, has landed the *Homo sapiens* on precarious grounds. His behaviour is now dominated by his culturally learned responses, than by predetermined reactions. Aggression, Eric Fromm says, is a biological given construct. But, the biologically programmed aggressiveness is not malignant. It is life serving and adaptive and reflected in his instinct of 'flight or fight' for survival. The harmful one is the malignant aggressiveness, characterised by cruelty and destructive tendencies.

In his much acclaimed novel *The Lord of the Flies*, William Golding shows how the children stranded on an island create hell instead of heaven. These are British children, coming from so called 'cultured' homes. Struggle for power leads them to quarrels, quarrels to fights and from thence to killings. On the contrary, a Belgian physician Dr Alphonse Van Schoote, while travelling among the islands of Melanesia came to know of a real-life story. A group of children was inadvertently left on one of the islands. The elders, after leaving them on the island went out, planning to return to pick them up. But, a storm kept the elders away for some months. When they came to the island finally, fearing the worst, they found the children in a state of amity, cooperation and coexistence.

During his tour of India in the late 1980s William Golding was asked why his children in *The Lord of the Flies* created problems when other fictional children are recorded to have pulled on well (*Kidnapped, The Coral Island*). To this, Golding replied that he was tracing man's fall from Grace. Man is a moral being, the Nobel Laureate said, but he has lost his original nature somewhere along the journey. Is it culture and civilisation, then that makes us vicious?

If one looks at the crime graph today with cases from minor thefts to the bigger crimes of rape, murder and organised violence of all kind, one wonders if we were not better off without the corroding social environ?

II

The articles contained in the present study look at violence mainly from the perspective of literature but the few articles on films, television, and those approaching violence from theoretical angle contribute to find patterns of violence in diverse ways. The concept of violence is not so facile as to be understood in the course of a book. There are 'kinds' of violence and the literature surveyed here is only a minuscule part of the forms of violence that has infested humankind.

The articles analyse various facets of violence and offer diverse perspectives on this much-debated word. Violence is present all around us and is clearly discernible in acts of terrorism, domestic violence, socio-economic injustice, physical and psychological violence, caste violence, gender violence, to name a few. The anthology proposes to show how violence perpetuates society in its myriad forms, some articles doing so by analysing certain literary texts. It also includes articles which establish the fact that many a time violence is necessary to overhaul a decadent social system and can at times be treated as laughable and irrational, and thus avoidable.

Violence does not always carry a negative connotation. It is legitimised when it occurs in the form of a protest to perpetuate an important social change. Jasbir Jain analyses *India's Bandit Queen* by Mala Sen, Michael Ondaatje's *Anil's Ghost* and Sorayya Khan's novel *Noor* and deliberates on the necessity of violence for the continuation of culture and civilisation. This kind of violence is beneficial for social health as it destroys negativity, giving way to more positive emotions.

The 20th century has been the most violent in the history of mankind. Violence acquired countless forms in the past century and became more destructive in effect with the progress in science and technology. Jose Sol in his essay "One Hundred years of Violence" argues that socio-economic injustice has been the greatest act of violence in the past century, an act that has ruined innumerable lives leaving no possibility of change ever for its victims. Ironically, socio-economic injustice and democracy work hand in glove in the present social structure of the world order. Another factor that contributed greatly to violence in the last century is the fractional interpretation of the concept of nationalism. This category of nationalism criticises, rejects and does not even hesitate to eliminate anything that goes against its spirit. The only way to rise above it, he says, is to promote a harmonious co-existence of diversity.

Avadesh Kumar Singh in his discourse "'Violence' in Creative and Critical Acts" takes ahead the argument of Roland Barthes by suggesting that creation of a literary text and its criticism are not possible without doing some violence to the text. He delineates four stages of violence in the creative act and the fifth stage occurs during the process of criticism. However, this violence is devoid of any negativity for it encourages the author and the reader to make an effort towards understanding the infinite reality.

Rajesh Kumar Sharma traces the origin of violence to history and finds its roots in the authority of the state and the notion of sovereignty. Violence is 'real', he says, and hence devastating. Language, money, law, history and morals play major roles in generating and perpetuating violence. Violence can never be sporadic or symbolic. It has a pattern. Once we recognise that pattern, we can understand and control it.

The issue of gender violence gained prominence after various women's movements protested against gender inequalities which are at the root of such violence. Veena Poonacha's article documents the responses of the state/community to violence against women and provides information about innovative strategies adopted by the government and non-government organisations of Karnataka and Gujarat to tackle gender violence. These organisations have done a commendable job in creating networks and structures within limited means to provide support to victims of domestic violence.

T.S. Anand and Manjinder Kaur focus on unpredictable acts of terrorist violence anchored in the national and international arena. Analysing Chitra Divakaruni's *Queen of Dreams* and Kiran Desai's *The Inheritance of Loss*, the writers expose the physical and psychological agony that the innocent civilians have to undergo as a result of terrorist activities. Terrorism sets in motion other kinds of violent acts like racism and communal disharmony which create a feeling of alienation in one's own motherland.

Literature reflects all the forces which shape the world around it. Silky Anand's article throws light on the works of various Indian English writers in different genres and the recurring pattern of violence in their literary creations, especially so in the literature of the first half of the twentieth century. The writer then goes on to study Kiran Desai's *The Inheritance of Loss* and examines the debilitating effect of domestic violence on an Indian bride.

Conflict is inherent in all kinds of social organisations. It is not viable to get rid of this ubiquitous phenomenon. P.K. Kalyani takes a look at the positive aspect of violence without any suggestion to encourage it in any form. David Davidar's *The House of Blue Mangoes* depicts violence as it takes place against varied backdrops, not as despicable but as necessary to bring about a positive social change. Conflict allows pent up feelings to find a vent and is cathartic in effect. Ironically, conflict can also contribute to restoring balance and order to a socially disintegrated civilisation.

Shashi Deshpande's *The Dark Holds No Terrors* is a poignant narration of a woman suffering silently in a callous and insensitive patriarchal society. Jyoti K. Singh examines the variety of forms that gender violence takes in every phase of Saru's life in this novel. Saru's story exemplifies Simone de Beauvoir's remark: "One is not born, but rather becomes a woman" as she journeys from one form of bondage to another, unable to seek respite as a daughter or a wife.

In their article entitled "Power–Violence Nexus in Girish Karnad's *Tughlaq* and *Tale-Danda*" Vineeta Kaur Saluja and Shibani Basu Dubey take a look at the two works dealing with Indian history to see how the greed for power is inseparably linked to violence. Muhammad-bin-Tughlaq's reign is one of misplaced zeal and mindless violence. He eliminates his father, brother, the Sheikh, Ain-ul-Din, his half brother Shihab-ul-Din and even his much-loved stepmother. But in the end he turns a spiritual wreck! Similarly, Bijjala, the king of Kalyan acquires the kingdom by murdering the king. But ultimately he is eliminated by his son Sovideva and the rebels in a violent overthrow. The bloodshed that follows is infernal and neither the king's liberal approach nor Basavanna's teachings can save the situation. Girish Karnad opines that both the plays depict our contemporary society and asserts that what existed in the 12th and 15th centuries still continues in different garbs.

Shyamala Vanarase presents a unique viewpoint by exploring Charles Chaplin's depiction of violence in his motion picture *The Great Dictator*. The film treats violence in a hilarious manner, though the message that is conveyed through it is rather a serious one. The greatest pursuit of life is happiness and human beings can create their own chances of happiness by living in harmony. A peaceful coexistence, free of any kind of greed eliminates chances of violence in the world. The film prods us to look at violence as something that is irrational and laughable and thus avoidable.

Anshu Kaushal's article on violence in media focuses on the children's psyche exposed to violence in TV and video games. These games have taken out the thrill and physical aspects of playing outdoors or even the traditional indoor games. Kaushal recounts the incidence when the popular 'Pokemon' games affected around 600 children with seizure in Japan and the parents' reaction and concern. The present gun-culture among school children the world over – this includes India as well – is leading children towards crime.

Usha Bande takes a look at the other side of the picture by analysing women who act violently and turn victimisers instead of remaining passive victims of violence. Her article studies two novels and two short stories by contemporary women writers and tries to examine the psycho-social factors which compel women to turn against their inherently submissive nature. The women in these texts adopt violence as a weapon to retaliate and take steps to counter the atrocities committed on them by men who are products of an inflexible patriarchal society. Physical and psychological brutality against women has wounded their psyche and, at last, they have begun to strike back. The roles may have reversed, the scores may have begun to be settled, but violence *per se* still exists and leaves many questions unanswered.

A totally different picture emerges when Bande explores three short stories from Dalit and tribal backdrops. The women in these stories try to speak out and get severe punishment. Jaabaali has the 'audacity' to slap her molesters which results in her gang rape. These are her own people – the Dalit youth of the Basti; Thaurani Devi tries to lead a life of dignity for which she has to pay with her life; Phoolkunwar has the guts to say 'no' to the advances of the high and mighty of the village and is burnt alive. The question that Bande raises is "Can a subaltern speak?" And if yes, at what cost? Are the established social forces ready to tolerate female-headed households? How violence stalks these women and takes its toll is a point for further consideration.

It is an irony that while one face of globalisation views the world as a unified entity, its other face has made the society more inward looking and divisive. Fundamentalists and communal forces are exploiting the caste, class, gender, kinship and religious sentiments for their sectarian agenda. Chauvinistic forces are promoting the gun-culture that disrupts normal, everyday life. Literature is taking the fight against violence in its own way, and though proverbially, the pen may be mightier than the sword, the challenges are overwhelming and only an inner change in the human beings – the homo sapiens – can redeem this world.

Endnotes

1. This information has been condensed from two articles published in *The Tribune*, Chandigarh. See Usha Bande, "Can Violence be a Way of Life," *The Tribune*, June 7, 1977 and "Taming the Beast Within," *The Tribune* (Sunday Reading), January 31, 1999.
2. See Usha Bande, "Taming the Beast Within," *The Tribune* (Sunday Reading), January 31, 1999.
3. Information culled from Ashley Montagu, *The Nature of Human Aggression*. New York: Oxford University Press, 1976.

Works Cited

Bond, Edward. *Bond Plays: Two*. London: Methuen, 1977.

Fromm, Eric. *To Have and To Be*. New York and London: Bantam Book, 1977.

Goldman, Emma. "Women's Suffrage," in *Anarchism and Other Essays*," qtd. by Sheila Rowbottom. *Women, Resistance and Revolution*. London: Penguin, 1972.

Krishnamurti, J. *Commentaries on Living*, ed. D. Rajagopal. New Delhi: B.R. Publications, 1977.

Mannomi, O. *Prospero and Caliban: The Psychology of Colonization*. Trans. Pamela Powesland. London: Methuen, 1956.

Paris, B.J. *Karen Horney: A Psychologist's Search for Self-Understanding*. New Haven: Yale University Press, 1994.

Shiva, Vandana, "Violence of Globalization". *The Hindu*, March 25, 2001.

1

The Necessary Burden of Violence and the Compulsive Search for Peace

Subcontinental Realities of Being-in-the-World

JASBIR JAIN

Any consideration of violence places one in the midst of much larger questions than the acts of physical violence or of mass destruction which surround us from all sides. One finds oneself confronted with a mind-boggling range of connections and roots. What is violence? What is the *nature* of violence? Can it be rooted out and eliminated from modern life? Are the reasons for violence temporary fits of passion and anger or are they rooted in issues of social justice and equality, in issues of power, control and individual assertion? Is violence the expression of frustration and despair or is it the expression of power and greed? Or is it mere/sheer survival? What is the relationship of violence to nature? And how is it affected by the faculty of reason? These and endless other questions crop up and I have been thinking of the connections it has with life, tradition, religion and literature, amongst a whole lot of other things. The present article hopes to debate the necessity of violence for the continuation of human intensity, moral growth, challenges, in fact what we refer to as civilisation and culture. I have taken up three different texts from the subcontinent which deal with the long-term effects of the various expressions of violence for the purpose of analysis. These are: *India's Bandit Queen* (1991), a biography of Phoolan Devi constructed by Mala Sen, which is more documentation than imagination but takes up both sexual violence and economic exploitation; Michael Ondaatje's *Anil's Ghost* (2000), which is concerned with both, the violence resulting from terrorist activities and the violence born out of colonial governance in the aftermath of a colonial regime; and Sorayya Khan's novel *Noor* (2003), which deals with war, poverty and terror which filters through memory from one generation to another.

The Existential Requirement of Violence

The word 'violence' does not always call forth negative associations. As an adjective it often expresses deep involvement, intense emotion or passion and at times the overcoming of the rational by the irrational. Violence is often done to one's feelings, sense of propriety or of balance. Even noise can qualify for the adjective violent. It is closely related to violate, thus the incursion of any privacy, right, freedom, independence, territory and the like would be a natural fallout. The word 'violate' immediately calls to one's mind the act of rape or an atrocity which infringes upon the rights of the individual. Other words which follow this trend of associations are volcano, volcanic burst, dynamic force, energy, vehemence and the like. Anger, power, assertion, fury follow close on them. Kant's theory of dynamic force is constituted upon the principle of the coming together of two opposites, like attraction and repulsion. Amongst the methods of violence one can turn out a long list but to begin with words like torture, cruelty, denial, isolation, an act of brutality which causes pain or deprivation, qualify as acts of violence.

The antonyms are defined by control, civil, decent, courteous, mild, considerate, rational and the like. This polarity at once makes it clear that the contest is between the oppositional categories of control and freedom;[1] that there is a perpetual dialectic at work between the different parties which aspire to achieve power over a common object; that it is not for nothing that nature reflects positive fallouts of volcanoes and earthquakes. Cain and Abel have inhabited the world together as have the Kauravas and the Pandavas. Shiva resorts to his *tandav nritya* and even the mild-tempered Krishna has his version of the *tandav*. Why do religion and myth reflect an ongoing cohabitation of opposites?

Just as violence, beginning with the very act of creation[2], and the dismemberment brought about by it, manifested even in the act of a human birth, needs to be accepted as an existential reality for being-in-the-world[3], there is the search for peace which follows a parallel course in human history. Aware of the possibility of failure, conscious of the control which non-human agencies exercise over human life, men have, time and again, continued to dream of peace and harmony, tranquillity and happiness. They have practised asceticism, sacrificed for causes which possessed them and have been martyred for not submitting before tyranny or imposition of the wrongful authority.[4] All concepts of courage, heroism and morality are connected with or have been formulated in the face of challenges, as forms of resistance to tyranny. It is difficult to define the methodology of power. Who is a tyrant – the father who uses force or the mother who uses persuasion? It is difficult to say.[5] Does this mean that one has necessarily to stretch oneself to resist the boundaries, to push them further?

Again, most change, specifically social change has been brought about by revolutions and rebellions. In recent human memory the French and Russian revolutions are an evidence of this. Closer home we have had our own revolutionaries both during the freedom struggle and after independence. The Naxalites and the new category of 'terrorists' (a description forced on all revolutionaries by the power-wielders) are also dreamers who clamour for change, or freedom, or rights and socio-political space.[6]

Given this reality one needs to face at least two major questions: can we imagine a world without violence and if we cannot, because of the necessity of growth, can we do something to make its face more human? The real problem is to reconcile personal interest and individual claims with those of the larger community, to be able to transcend short-term gains for the fulfilment of a long-term dream. A task well-nigh impossible given the conflicting needs of different societies, and even more than that, the lurking presence of mortality, which chases human life. Strangely enough, both the act of violence which seeks to capture, destroy or possess and the act of heroism which seeks to resist it revolve round the fact of human mortality. Only those who are mortal seek different routes in search of the immortal, to make both life and death meaningful.

India's Bandit Queen: The True Story of Phoolan Devi (1991)

Mala Sen's reconstruction of Phoolan Devi's life cannot be viewed merely as a biography. It does not attempt to trace the life course of a great hero who progresses, through countless hurdles, to either a martyrdom or success. Phoolan Devi is a woman, whom most of us have read about and discussed without the necessary empathy or understanding. Her contesting the elections, becoming a Member of parliament and then later being assassinated, leaving behind her a tale of which the storyline is muddled and confused, do not form part of the narrative.[7] I read the work as the story of a victim, a woman who can be seen as a representative of countless other women who struggle continuously against atrocities committed on their bodies, and whose real-life happenings contrast sharply with the idealistic cultural presentations of marriage, family and kinship ties. The sole possession of such women is their body which also never wholly belongs to them. Fathers and husbands bargain over it and the possession or pride of a man, may give them some temporary protection. This is not merely a sexual body; it is also a body which puts in physical labour and requires food.

India's Bandit Queen works at another level. It comments upon the gross inequalities in society and the hegemonic patriarchal structures which are reinforced by the caste system. There is also a comment upon the 'voting power' of the upper classes (xix). Mala Sen's 'Introduction', as it traces the history of thuggee, is obviously catering to the non-Indian reader in its evocation of the Raj tales, but manages nevertheless to comment upon the origins of lawlessness.

> On either side of the river lie the badlands of central India, some 8,000 square kilometres of bandit country, inhabited by people who have, for centuries, been contemptuous of the state but remain fearful of God.
>
> The land yields little. Erosion is severe. Each year thousands of hectares, nearly 20,000 acres, are lost to the ravines that scar this wasteland …. Earth that was once arable falls into the river …

In this desolate landscape of sand and thorn, people have for generations, settled their own scores, taken their own badla – revenge – killing and maiming in the name of God and justice. (Introduction, xxiii)

But the choices are not always as simple as they may appear to be. Hidden under this tale of revenge, there is also a tale of longing for peace and belonging, tender, short-lived attempts at building up relationships and compromises with the demands of reality. On the one hand it is the tale of a woman who is married young to a man far older than her and is scared of him. The marriage runs an uneven course. She is reduced to the status of an abandoned wife. Earlier also she had been an unwanted daughter, being one of four sisters. Her father and his family are continuously persecuted and thwarted by his brother Biharilal and his son Maiyadin. The family quarrel adds both to their poverty and unhappiness and there seems to be no end of the litigation in sight.

Eleven year old Phoolan is claimed by her husband Puttilal shortly after their marriage on the pretext that he needs her at home and the threat that if she is not sent he would take another wife – thus brushing aside the earlier agreement that she would be claimed only after three years. Puttilal is a hard man and she is afraid of him. Fear makes her fall ill. When her father comes to fetch her, he is insulted and humiliated (45). But being young, and naturally high spirited, Phoolan retains her sense of fun (47). She has wit and humour and is both mischievous and rebellious (43). She is not the kind of person who is capable of submitting to injustice passively for long. The making of a future 'baghi' is writ large over her sensitivity to injustice. Suresh, an upper caste man, tries to molest her and when she protests, she is framed as a disreputable person of doubtful character. Strict morality, concepts of virginity and fidelity go ill with the social attitude to women which views them as mere bodies who can be exploited in a variety of ways and for a variety of purposes. Family ties, marital relationships, kinship systems, caste-divisions all find ways and means of harassing them. Her father tells her that they cannot afford to fight the upper caste people. The biographer observes that the middle-class feminist movement simply passed them by: "a woman like Phoolan Devi – or hundreds of thousands like her, scattered throughout the villages of India – felt no affinity with nor were aware of the movement .... The women were the victims of a 'fundamentally' feudal society" (54).

Back again to Puttilal, who by now has acquired a third wife, (Phoolan had been his second wife, after the death of the first), she is subjected to beatings and starvation. Violence as a method of retaliation seems the natural outcome of this violence of possession, so pervasive in everyday life. Later, tossed from one dacoit gang to another, she also experienced torture in the police cells, and the framing of charges through the production of false witnesses. The system is both flawed and heartless. These violators of law are people who have failed to find any help in it.

The narrative covers a period of ten years, from 1983 to 1993, but within this period, it constantly moves backwards to capture moments of self-reflection, realisation and the need to find ways of survival. But even as the linearity of narration is interrupted to fill up the details regarding Phoolan's childhood and marriage, and develop her character in order to provide a link with her later behaviour, the story remains one which concentrates on the present. It is a string of moments – of frustration, of insight, of consciousness, of the need to survive, moments of compromises and helplessness. Ten years after her surrender, in 1993, she felt lonely and abandoned, and expressed the feeling 'it would have been better to die like a dog in the ravines than to live like a rat in this hole ...' (244). Summing up the living legend that Phoolan had created around her, Mala Sen writes: "From the Hindu point of view, a woman of her status, born into a community of fishermen and abandoned by her husband, was meant to be submissive. Her defiance of the social order needed to be curbed" (245).

Literature, documentary or social history? *India's Bandit Queen* is all three for it demonstrates the connections between life and literature and placing woman centrestage explores the origin of violence and its continued perpetuation through tropes of poverty, deprivation, physical abuse, social injustice, betrayal and treachery, in fact the manipulation of law to engender violence, to render civil life ineffective. Revenge and jealousy and the whole lot of factors listed above are all the fallouts of this power struggle and the illogicality of its pursuits.

Anil's Ghost (2000)

The ending of *Anil's Ghost* leaves behind a lingering sadness. Its memory haunts one. The title is actually realised fully only in the last four chapters as one by one the different strands which govern the different narratives are brought to a conclusion.

Set against the background of the civil war in Sri Lanka, *Anil's Ghost* is a complex narrative as it explores the past, not only in terms of human atrocities and mass murders, but also in terms of tradition, the Buddhist culture and of relationships, national and family histories, lost loves and missed opportunities. The present is deeply rooted in the past both in terms of political realities and personal relationships. As the novel works its way through fear and destruction, through acts of violence, a saga of missing people, bomb blasts and broken bones, the past comes forward to yield its ghosts. Surprisingly, the brutality, even of this level, does not destroy the human capacity to search for truth or for a meaningful existence. Instead one realises that the human ability to sacrifice is summoned from its hidden recesses in order to demonstrate the integrity of human desires and values, qualities which are necessary for the continuity of life in the larger setup of political conspiracies and mindless power. The struggle is uneven, it is not even rational; but it is necessary and has to go on.

The scene which really shocks one and remains to haunt the reader is the moment when Gamini realises that one of the seven dead bodies he is preparing a report on, is that of his brother Sarath, "Ever since he had picked up the third photograph, all he could hear was his heart banging". Slowly he comes to the present:

> There were things he could do. He didn't know. There were things he could do perhaps. He could see the acid burns, the twisted leg. He unlocked the cupboard that held bandages, splints, disinfectant. He began washing the body's dark-brown markings with scrub cotton. He could heal his brother, set the left leg, deal with every wound as he were alive, as if treating the hundred small traumas would eventually bring him back to life. (287)

One by one he recalls the history of every scar which Sarath had acquired during his boyhood days, he recalls their relationship, and the memory of Sarath's wife whom he had also loved.[8] And with each memory his brother's character rose before his very eyes, a man "who in his sarong would stroll into the garden or into the verandah with his tea and newspaper. Sarath had side-stepped violence because of his character, as if there had never been a war within him". As he looks at his brother's body and washes and tapes up the wounds, he recalls the hundreds of other cases "where every tooth had been removed, the nose cut apart, the eyes humiliated with liquids, the ears entered .... It was they went for in ..." Sarath's body was dressed in a shirt with giant sleeves: "Gamini knew why. He ripped the sleeves down to the cuffs. Below the elbows the hands had been broken in several places" (288–290).

Immediately one is able to connect it with the message Sarath had sent Anil. He had managed to send her the skeleton of Sailor, the skeleton which had called her attention to the violation of Human Rights, which had led her to an intensive research regarding soil conditions. Had the man died where he had been buried? Was it an age-old skeleton or a more recent murder? Whose body was it? Could the face be reconstructed? Weeks and weeks are spent in watching Ananda reconstruct the face. For in this skeleton, whom they call Sailor, lies the possibility of framing a clear case against the government. They needed to identify him in order to have a victim, before they could go ahead with charging the government (176).

But when the face is reconstructed it is a peaceful one: it embodies peace not a personality. It is the Buddha in him. That is how Ananda wants the dead to be – at peace, not unhappy, or in pain, or struggling. It was not a face anyone would be able to recognise. But even then the search continues. And they succeed. Sailor was a man called Ruwan Kumara, a toddy tapper, later a miner and a rebel sympathiser (269).

Anil's next move is to seek an appointment with a friend of her father's, who is in the government, with the idea of seeking justice. But the meeting turns into an interrogation. She is put to test, and the skeleton of Sailor is confiscated. She is almost put through a torture chamber, the air-conditioner is turned off and interruptions from the audience distract her. Anil persists in the face of all odds:

"What I wish to report is that some government forces have possibly murdered innocent people. This is what you are hearing from me. You as an archaeologist should believe in the truth of history.

"I believe in a society that has peace, Miss Tissera. What you are proposing could result in a chaos ...

"The skeleton I had was evidence of a certain kind of crime. That is what is important here. '*One village can speak for many villages. One victim can speak for many victims*'." (275)

Anil is stripped off all the evidence she possessed, her notes, papers, slides, everything. Sarath could guess that they would halt her at each corridor level, and remove vials and slides, humiliate her and make her undress and dress several times. Somehow, he manages to get the confiscated skeleton back, smuggles it in, warns her to be quick in her examination and advance her departure by a day and half and to leave before dawn the next morning. And he pays for this with his life. Gamini's vigil by Sarath's dead body holds the story not only of two brothers in love with the same woman, but of a man in love with a cause. Sarath's death raises several questions. And the foremost of these is: is it worth it? This resistance to falsehood, tyranny and ruthless authority; this manipulation and suppression of both national and human concerns?

Anil's departure marks one ending; Sarath's body in Gamini's hands a second; the third is marked by the assassination of the ageing President Katugala. The bomb explosion kills more than fifty people and "shredded Katugala into pieces." There is yet a fourth ending – the Buddha statue which is smashed and reconstructed by Ananda. He worked on restoring the "composure and the qualities of the face" (302).

Finally the statue is ready to go in for the Netra Mangala ceremony and amidst the chanting of the *slokas*, Ananda and his nephew climb upto the face. With the eyes yet unformed, he was not the Buddha. The task is performed with patience and persistence, the shape chiselled, the colours filled in, and with the vision restored the statue is complete. But the face is no longer that of a god, distant and composed, it is a human face with "a pure sad glance". Ananda as he remembers his wife, also remembers Sarath, whose cotton shirt he is wearing even at this moment, realising fully well that he (Ananda) and "the woman Anil would always carry the ghost of Sarath Diyasena" (305).

Thus, the novel has four endings, each embedded into the other and all of them coming together to create some meaning and justify the struggle against the violence which denied human values. The novel comments upon both the futility of violence and the necessity of resistance. Why do Anil and Sarath resist? Why does Gamini continue with his work at the hospital? Why does Ananda make Buddha human? Perhaps the answer to all these questions is the need to keep the human alive. And the quality of the human is vested in love and compassion, truth and sacrifice.

There is also the political question of terrorism, the separatist forces, the guerilla warfare and the triangular civil war, which has its own complexities and has a great deal to do with the inability to recognise the right of minority groups and, more importantly, the continued adherence to a colonial pattern of governance which has outlived both its utility and relevance. Even though the British have left, their pattern of governance has been incorporated without any consideration for the concepts of equality and social justice. Indigenous patterns need to evolve and be homogenised with the aspirations of modernity outside the imperial–colonial context. But this is a question much larger than can be handled in this context. Nevertheless, it needs to be pointed out that the term 'terrorist' is relative. It is not fair to label all revolutionaries and resistance forces as terrorists without any sense of discrimination. The impulse behind the act of resistance, the 'need' for resistance and its contexts need to be examined. All resistance is not terrorism. Perhaps terrorism is only the irrational form of resistance, or worse still, it is an act of desperation, when all other channels have been blocked, for whatever reasons. Terrorism is also a relative term. And there are always two parties to it. Like the statue of Buddha, which has to be endowed with all-seeing eyes through a human agency, those in power also need to develop all-seeing eyes, not the eyes of Big Brother, but ones which possess compassion and understanding.

Noor (2003)

The step from a civil war to a full-fledged one is but a short one; it doesn't take long for one to change into the other. *Noor* is a novel about this step; it is also a novel about two cultures, two languages and two wings which are unable to fly together. Located in Islamabad, the narrative moves back in time to East Pakistan and the conflict which resulted in the birth of Bangladesh. But even as the narrative leaps back into the past through spasmodically revealed memory holes, surrealistic drawings, and dreams, it also becomes a counter discourse to the acts of violence.

Ali's family is an acquired one. His daughter, Sajida, is a child he picked up during the 1971 war, and who is the daughter of a fisherman. She is, at that time 'fiveandsix', and has lost all her family during the cyclone. Ali, having lost his childhood fiancée to death, has remained unmarried. This young man of twenty-three and the child come together to make a family.

Ali's mother who should rightly have been addressed as Dadijaan is called Nanijaan. Ali's son-in-law Husein, Sajida's childhood sweetheart, lives with them in accordance with the precondition of Ali's consent. There is a fourth generation, Husein and Sajida's three children of whom the youngest Noor is an unusual child, a mongoloid, who learns to speak late, walk late and is slow in every way. Her real talent lies in the drawings that she makes and the dreams that she summons. Her surrealistic bizarre drawings delve into the world of Sajida's childhood, seek to reach the dark depths of the past, of pain, suffering and deprivation and to present a world which absorbs contradictions and puts together a human alternative to the non-human world of violence.

The child's drawings fetch forth different fragments from the past – episodic in their nature. A fish boat, the cyclonic waves, a young child clinging to a tree in a snake like twist around the trunk, sights she has not seen in this life. Even before her birth, she had surfaced in her mother's dreams, announcing her strangeness. Noor with her constant demands becomes the cause of estrangement between her parents, evicts first her father from the room by crowding it with her presence (33) and later even her mother by claiming the whole bed as her own:

> Noor ka Bister,' Noor said one morning, pointing at Sajida's marriage-bed and making it her own. Where's Ammi's bed? (91)

There is violence of other kinds as a backdrop. Nanijaan's marriage has been put through the crucible of physical violence

(69–70), an overstocked ammunition depot had exploded on the day Sajida and Husein had got married (99), and then there is the violence of the war in Ali's mind. On coming home after the war, Ali had subjected himself to a hot searing bath, in order to cleanse himself of those visions which haunt him:

> He submerged his feet, and just like that, he relegated the screams to one drawer, the pit of dead bodies into another. Kneeling into the tub, the scathing heat turned his knees pink, and he put the rich colour of blood disappearing into a pit of mud into its own compartment .... (59)

Later, Ali recalls the dead bodies which floated around them during the war, the mass graves which they had to dig in the rain and slush. Ali lives with his memories, and one day, years later, Nanijaan asks him a direct question:

'You killed someone?',

...

'Who?'

'Who?' Ali answered incredulously. 'Is that what you think war is? Excuse me, before I shoot you, what's your name? So I can tell my mother when she asks?'

'You killed someone and don't know who?'

'No. I didn't kill some *one.*'

'More than one?'

'You need a number? More than one and less than a hundred? What did you bloody think I was going to do when I told you I was going there? ...' (147–148)

When Nanijaan asks him, 'How could it be that you could kill someone and not see them', Ali wanted to tell her that they could kill only because they couldn't see them. It was the anonymity of the victim that rendered it possible (150). The past is dug up through Noor's drawings and, after many years, Nanijaan's mind begins to think about Ali's time in the war in concrete visual terms as a time of violence. The past becomes a barrier between the mother and son. She wants to ask him several questions, but does not have the courage to face the answers. She would like to ask him:

What does it feel like, to kill someone? Where do you put that knowledge during the day? At night? Ah, sometimes, when it rains, you can't sleep for remembering! What does it feel like, to know you are the reason for someone's else's grief? (151)

He also has memories of a woman who was gang raped, but when directed to rape her he offered to clean her up instead (153–155). The war had turned Ali an atheist and a vegetarian. God and meat, both were off-limit, "God because nothing Ali had seen (or done) could have been divined by God; And meat because he smelled flesh in every manifestation" (156–157). War is not temporary; it never really gets over; the wounds never dry up. War does terrible things to all concerned. It never really is the past for it always remains in cultural memory. Everyday phrases bring the past alive – crows don't wait for the food to get cold, they swarm like vultures. The crows like the dogs often beat death when the dead lay strewn on the ground and were always there before the burying was done (171).

The motif of revenge is an undercurrent even in war, a kind of throttling the 'other' with the very sense of power he once possessed, and has used against others. Defeated soldiers are made to walk on the very mines they themselves had laid. War never leaves behind any victors, only agonising memories. The only stay against these memories is the love one can find in oneself for others, the kind of love which Sajida has for Noor, Ali has for his readymade family, the love which Nanijaan has for a granddaughter – Sajida – not born of her blood. Then there is human consideration, the compassion which compels Ali to pick up the starved fiveandsix year old child Sajida, a compassion which can turn into love and cross the barriers between East and West Pakistan, between the dark Bengali and the fair Pathan. Where does war find a place amongst them? *Noor* is the "First Pakistani English novel to focus on East Pakistan during the war of 1971" (*Dawn*); it is also a novel about violence where the violence of nature and of man are placed side by side.

The Compulsive Search for Peace

How does one live in a world full of violence, sustain oneself, grow and live in the world? Violence cannot be done away by a simple wave of a magic wand. Its very illogicality has a logic behind it. There are intimate relations between socio-economic structures, international power politics and human greed as they all conspire to create a violent world. Questions of identity, subjectivity and objectivity, the perpetual opposition between self and the other contribute to environmental imbalances. The dividing line between freedom and aggression is almost invisible. When does one's right to freedom encroach upon the other?

If violence is born out of transgression, martyrdom and sacrifice are also acts which move out of line in order to become effective. Some offer themselves to the act – while others do not. The three examples which I have taken from the subcontinent present different realities. Each documents some kind of a social reality. But while Ali, Sarath and Anil have the benefit of education, of economic support, of middle or upper class environments, Phoolan Devi is deprived of all of them. Violence in her case is also the product of narrowing down of concerns. It becomes important as to how we *relate* – relate to others, to traditions, to memory, to faith. Ideals are natural only if there is space for them to grow. They do not grow in barren land. The 'nothingness' of life can yield to 'something' provided there is a world of personal existence to interpret it, to experience the dread.

Violence also has roots in the past. Cultural memories, communal hatreds are all fed by acts of the past. Revenge or retaliation are acts located in temporal histories.[9] Is there ever a possibility of beginning afresh? To acquire the strangeness of first love? The capacity to remember *selectivity* combined with the inability to forgive perpetuate violence. I am often caught up in controversies within myself. Is it possible to forgive war crimes? To bury the past? To get rid of colonial histories, of the unequal relationships between cultures perpetuated by the lust for power? Again, what does one mean by the phrase 'the human face of violence?' I have used it and it does signify a meaning to me, but from where has the phrase come, how has it fallen into place? In itself, it is loaded with ambiguities and torn by contradictions. Would it suffice if compassion and concern were to be the end result of violence? Or that there is, at times, a legitimacy to violence, when it surfaces as protest? Or does it mean that the dynamism of violence is essential for human survival? I am not sure. But at times an act of violence is an attempt at extracting meaning from nothingness. Every shift is a *shift*, it shakes up, it rearranges; it is a part of dream being tagged onto reality.

Endnotes

1. Hobbes had imagined the state of nature as 'nasty, brutish and short', a condition which rendered the social contract necessary for life to continue. There has also been a constant contrast between the 'law of the jungle' and the 'rule of law' in the history of mankind. In our own living memory, we have seen how imperialism has flourished on the projected dichotomy between the civilised and the barbaric, not conceding any ground to the more moral approach of human and inhuman. Any civil society or community demands some kind of adjustment and defining of limits where individual claims are concerned.

   Further, I would like to point out here that the word 'violate' has several meanings, some of which mean 'break, infringe, transgress, treat irreverently, without respect'. Violation carries within it the meaning of infringement and non-observance of rules.

2. See *Hindu Myths: A Sourcebook Translated from the Sanskrit* by Wendy Doniger O'Flaherty, Harmondsworth: Penguin, (1975), 1978, for the various myths of creation, in the *Rg Veda*, *Brahmanas* and *Upanisads*, *Mahabharata* and *Puranas*. (25–55). Dismemberment, incest, sacrifice and dispersal are some of the routine courses.

3. The term has a reference to Martin Heidegger's concept of '*dasein*' which professes that 'the essence is in the existence', there is no existence in isolation – the 'needle implies the thread, the garment, the sewer, and the wearer'. Thus it rules out independent, self-contained structures and by describing the process as a being-in-the-world, conceives of a reciprocal, active relationship between the individual and society. Blackham in *Six Existential Thinkers* comments upon it as a recognition that the 'existence of others is not merely accidental, nor a problem for thought, but is a necessity of thought, is constitutive of my being and implied in it ...' (90).

4. Every religion has a history of martyrdom, crucification, asceticism, sacrifice and the like, whether it be Christianity, Islam, Hinduism, Jainism, Sikhism or any other. These acts of courage or sacrifice bring the communities together and work as sources of inspiration for other-centred behaviour.

5. Orwell in his essay, "Lear, Tolstoy and the Fool", commenting upon Tolstoy's act of renunciation, wonders whether he also abjured the principle of coercion, 'There are families in which the father will say to his child, "You'll get a thick ear if you do that again", while the mother,

her eyes brimming over with tears, will take the child in her arms and murmur lovingly, "Now darling, *is* it kind to Mummy to do that?" And who will maintain that the second method is less tyrannous than the first?' (Orwell 118).

6. More than three decades ago in a paper titled "Anger in Wilderness", I explored 'anger' as a positive emotion with reference to John Osborne's play *Look Back in Anger* (1956). Anger and violence are not always necessarily negative terms. They often integrate forces, create a challenge and provide a much-needed catalyst for the release of positive emotions.

7. Phoolan Devi was released on parole in 1994, and in 1996 she ran for a seat in Parliament on a ticket from the Samajwadi Party. In 2001 she was assassinated just outside her home. Phoolan Devi herself resented being portrayed as a victim. There are several versions of her and both caste politics and gender politics have been exploited by the media to depict her in a heightened manner. A Durga, a Robin Hood or a killer? An outlaw, ruthless and defiant, or a victim of poverty and persecution? Whatever the truth, there is no denying that she was the product of social injustice and of a general callousness towards the plight of women. And she had the determination to find loopholes in this repression.

8. Refer *Anil's Ghost,* pp. 251–253.

9. Sudhir Kakar, *The Colour of Violence* p. 22ff. Kakar comments upon the psychology of the riots and the feelings of communal hatred.

References

Blackham, H.J. *Six Existential Thinkers.* London: Routledge and Kegan Paul Ltd. (1952), 1956.

Kakar, Sudhir. *The Colours of Violence.* New Delhi: Viking (Penguin Books), 1995.

Khan, Sorayya. *Noor.* New Delhi: Penguin. 2003

O'Flaherty, Wendy Doniger. Trans. *Hindu Myths: A Sourcebook Translated From the Sanskrit,* Harmondsworth: Penguin (1975), 1978.

Ondaatje, Michael. *Anil's Ghost.* New York: Vintage, 2000.

Orwell, George. "Lear, Tolstoy and the Fool" (1947) *Inside the Whale and Other Essays.* Harmondsworth: Penguin, (1957), 1987.

Sen, Mala. *India's Bandit Queen: The True Story of Phoolan Devi* (1991). New Delhi: Harper Collins Publishers Pvt. Ltd. 1993.

2

'Violence' in Creative and Critical Acts

AVADESH KUMAR SINGH

The validity of applying a critical approach or theory to a certain creative work has been under constant questioning and skepticism for long. Such an attempt, according to traditionalists, would amount to deliberate distortion of text/creative work by the critic who would try to fit it in a certain work 'violently' or thrust that work in the mould of an approach, and in the process may either add something that the text never intended, or prune it of its essential stuff to suit the scope and acceptability of that approach. Conceding sufficient space for such concerns there is no denying the fact that it is fraught with dangers to apply critical/theoretical approach to a work. I, however, sound a caveat in my present endeavour against the prevailing fallacy regarding creation and criticism and lay ground for an argument that it is not possible to 'create' or 'criticise' without 'disturbing' something or the other. I don't claim to be absolutely original in my 'positions' which were already anticipated by Roland Barthes when he stated that criticism is an act of violence, yet this awareness should not undermine the extension of Barthes's position in a different direction.

It can in no terms be considered justifiable to even think of keeping critical/theoretical approaches for their own sake without considering their applicability which would imply their rejection and thereby end in dumping them in a dustbin of theoretical garbage. Moreover, it would be nothing short of subscribing to 'logocentricism' or 'phonocentricism' of the western metaphysics which always laid emphasis on 'individual' and creator/author and for centuries considered a critic a 'parasite' and critical exercise an encroachment by 'the other' till Roland Barthes (un) successfully dislodged the author from his/her high pedestal of centrality. Barthes like T.S. Eliot and the 'New Critics' enunciated the death of the author in his article "The Death of the Author" and even earlier when he said, "I that writes the text is never, itself, anything more than a paper I" ("From Work to Text" 79). As language refers to itself so it is disconnected from reality and "linguistically the author is never more than the instance saying I: Language knows a 'subject' not a person" ("The Death of the Author" 145). The moment writing commences, the disjunction between the author as a person and text occurs, and the author enters into his "death" (142). It is the death of the empirical author – who employs language to express himself. It "is the language which speaks not the author" (143), for the author fails in mastering the language. In the process of mastering language he/she 'surrenders' him/herself to language and becomes its servant. Barthes here marches a step ahead of Eliot in announcing the death of the 'historical' and 'implied' author as well. In non-existence of the implied reader, the text fails in finding a fixed meaning but a "plurality of meaning, an irreducible plurality" ("From Work to Text" 76). "The Text, for Barthes, "is not co-existence of meaning but passage, traversed, thus it answers not to an interpretation ... but to an explosion, a dissemination" (76). The meaning of the text exists in the system of rules and conventions – not in the text itself as believed for long. Thus, the meaning of the text is diffused and dissipated not centralised. He, however, admits that the author can enter by the back door as a 'Guest' like "one of his characters, as another figure sewn into the rug; his significance is no longer privileged and parental, the locus of genuine truth but rather ludic. He becomes a *paper author* (my italics) (78)"[1] Jacques Derrida is of the opinion that language is disconnected from reality, inclusive of the author's physical reality, remains outside verbal universe of the text, expelled the empirical author and denied the implied author too. The author enters by the *retroscena* in deconstruction because the very idea of 'decentring' presumes presence of centre before it was de-centred and thus follows re-centring. And, the moment we are in view of the centre, the author creeps in. Thus, Derrida at least succeeds in pushing the author to the periphery. Consequent upon this, critic and translator who were forced to decorate margins were brought into the elusive centre, though the mainstream has still not accepted them for it takes time to get social sanction. An age old hierarchy dies hard.

It is inconceivable to indulge in critical enterprise without doing some sort of violence to the work concerned. It is ironic – may be even tragic to some that violence and critical acts are inseparable, as Barthes called criticism an 'act of violence'. It is to be borne in mind that critical theories on most occasions succeed creative endeavours and creative artists of substance will never subscribe to the taste of theoretical approach (es). He/she is supposed to break away from tradition and subvert existing system, somehow, sometime in the course of his creative pursuit. Therefore, critical evaluation means imposition of a 'different' but not alien process. It is not alien because creative and critical exercises are subsumed in one and considered from a different perspective, the critical act is an extension of creative act – a stage ahead, a complementary and indispensable stage.

'Violence' is centripetal to critical exercise. As a critic lays his/her hand on a creative work to criticise or create meaning there begins a tug-of-war in intentions particularly between 'authorly intentions' and 'readerly intentions' to use archaic physiological terms. It is the reader-critic who sees the work as he/she wants to see it and the work becomes what this reader-critic intends it to be. As a text is in a state of suspended animation or 'dead' or at the most inactively alive, it becomes effervescent with life only when the reader-critic lends his/her pulsating touch and it comes to life only then. But the life (meaning) it attains is in direct proportion to the reader's knowledge of the system and conventions at his/her disposal as the structuralists would put it. A creative work is, but whatever it is, is not in itself outside it. Its 'beauty'/'ugliness' to a good measure depends on the way of viewing it. The creation of meaning is often thrust upon the text and in this process he/she creates his/her text different from the one created by creator/author whose organic living creation is creatively and constructively distorted, damaged and reconstructed.[2] Thus, creation of a new text outside the text rests on violence – gentle, invisible and creative violence which the text like a bride anxiously waits for its completion and fulfillment.

A polemical discussion of critical exercise in the preceding passage necessitates reconsideration of nature of creative process (as shorn of its traditional halo) – what actually invisibly happens when the creative act takes place, not the process of artistic creation in itself that defies being defined or confined in certain formulae even in our age of applied psychology and electronics. Here, furthering Barthes's position regarding criticism, we would see that creativity too is an act of violence from a different direction in the sense criticism is an act of violence. Various stages in the process of creation are characterised by continuous wrestling of intentions which can be projected with slight modification as thus:

(i) Experiential/perceptional intentions.
(ii) Systemic/linguistic intentions.
(iii) Authorial/writerly intentions.
(iv) Textual intentions.
(v) Readerly intentions.

In the initial stage the creator/writer wrestles with his/her experience(s) and perception(s). When a situation, event or experience real or imaginative, factual or fictional disturbs his/her 'psychological equilibrium', to borrow I.A. Richard's phrase, he/she strives to evacuate this state of psychological inequilibrium or agitation to re-attain, if possible, the former state and then to transport that state to his/her target readership through text. But prior to its textual formation the systemic intentions/linguistic intentions clash with experimental intentions. As creative articulation is possible only through the system which in case of literary creation is linguistic system whose limitations, artificiality and incompetence perpetuate violence, as the author tries to master perceptional intentions through it. The author surrenders him/herself to the linguistic system in the process of mastering it but the system does not remain unaffected when it transgresses other levels of intentions.

Language is artificial and it perpetuates artificiality as may be witnessed in the emptiness of the language of social transaction.[3] The greater the distance, artificiality, formality, complexity, nebulous and nascent state of mind or relationship or affair, the more would be reliance on language. Here I am far from suggesting that language breeds these complex problems and hence this system should be done away with a view to get rid of them. However incompetent, artificial and limited this system may be, it is the only articulating device that serves as social and mental 'safety valve' by giving outlet to surging complications. Nevertheless, as it deals with artificialities, complications/complexities and experiences real and unreal, 'bitter' and 'beautiful', it contracts some of the properties of these perilous problems and at times gets trapped in itself. It is even truer in our age in which language is symptomatic of hollowness, emptiness, unnaturalness, formality, and even hypocrisy to such an extent that it becomes 'undesirable', as T.S. Eliot voices for some of us, "I've gotta use words when I talk to you." Eliot is privileged to propose unspoken, unuttered, unwritten, natural and informal language of heart and gestures as R.P. Blackmur would propose for his poetic universe but it is inconceivable to banish this system at least at this stage from our world for social transaction.

It is also to be admitted that language/linguistic system as a medium of articulation suffers from limitations, incompetence and inadequacies. That is why the linguistic meaning wavers so much. It has failed in coping with demands of a newer idiom capable of expressing increasingly complex experiences, perceptions and realities rendered more complicated by every fleeting moment of explosion of new experiences, sicknesses, situations and sensations. The problem is aggravated by an individual's/writer's limited capacity of acquisition of the system and further problematised at the level of use of this laboriously acquired and culturally inherited system. Even the most eminent of the writers at their best can claim to have articulated only about a fragment of reality. (For instances, if a writer pours him/herself in volumes and volumes altogether on his/her mother then even at the end of his/her last volume there would remain something unsaid, and unarticulated about the mother. The writer would 'fiddle' with his/her experience/reality and monumentalise violence in text). The experimental and perceptional intentions are conditioned violently by linguistic system and then by authorial intentions and limitations and further by textual intentions – which constrain authorial intentions, its possible interpretation, its form and medium. Thus, the authorial intentions try to grasp certain experience or experimental intentions with the help of linguistic system and authorial intentions wrangle with textual intentions. And the ultimate synthetical issue of this continuous yet invisible violence results in creative work. Wallace Stevens seems to have expressed it exquisitely in poetic terms in his poem "The Man With the Blue Guitar":

> They said, "You have blue guitar,
> You do not play things as they are,"
> The man replied, "Things as they are
> Are changed upon the blue guitar. (265)

In the last stage, text goes through violent processes at the hands of reader.[4] Meaning is created through subtle persuasive violence of the text by competent reader-critic (Bloom's misreaders). Thus, the reader imposes his intentions on the text and creates his own text which is resisted by textual intentions (as discussed earlier) and at times he/she may react so violently to the text that he/she may reject the textual intentions and make his/her own text absolutely different from the text in itself. Thus, from the first to the last stage the whole process celebrates a series of systematic violence of a sort of other which creator/critic is not unusually conscious of because he/she is so continuously frequented by these violent operative processes that his/her sensibility becomes immune to all these invisible processes. This clash of intentions can be projected through the following scheme:

```
I      a   (Reality) Experiential/Perceptional Intentions    Vs
N
T      b   (Medium) Systemic/Linguistic Intentions           Vs
E
N      c   (Communication) Authroial/Writerly Intentions     Vs
T
I      d   (Articulation) Textual Intentions                 Vs
O
N      e   (Interpretation) Readerly/Critical Intentions
```

It is not difficult to locate 'violence' (shown by Vs.) in the above mentioned classification which is a divergent form of commonplace categorisation. Systemic, authorial, textual, readerly intentions and their inherent limitations commit violence as the two living agents, viz., author and reader try to capture apparently non-living agents and make them yield to themselves with varying amount of success (Barthes would say that it is the author who surrenders to language), as they try to infuse life on non-living agents. The first four stages denote violence in creative act and the fifth stage points to violence in criticism. It should, however, not suggest that there is greater violence in creative than in critical act. The nature of clash in intentions may vary from writer to writer and reader to reader and even from work to work and from moment to moment even in the some work. It is always the powerful agent or intentions which dominate and at times suppress or bypass intentions of certain stage. Nevertheless, it becomes evident that critical and creative acts are subsumed in one and critical act is an extension of creative endeavour which would remain incomplete and even meaningless if it fails in attracting critical attention.

Further, if we look at the diagram from different direction and use the word 'surrender'[5] in lieu of violence, we find that the whole process (creative and critical process) involves a series of systematic 'surrenders' in which the experimental/perceptional intentions surrender to linguistic intentions, authorial intentions surrender to linguistic intentions (in certain cases at certain points linguistic intention 'surrender' to authorial intentions), authorial and linguistic intentions surrender to textual intentions and the textual intentions ultimately surrender to 'readerly' intentions. (Here, the reader too employs the same system, which poses as a wall between one man (author) and another (reader), as earlier used by the author). Surrender too is a sort of violence, as both of these are based on outrageous aggression but violence in creation and criticism as used hitherto is devoid of its negative, unjust and unwarranted properties. Therefore, the term 'violence' or 'surrender' should not deter creative and critical striving which would merit more meaning and consequences if creator/author and reader/critic are continually conscious of 'violence' or 'surrender' in their respective endeavours. The 'beauty' of their endeavour lies in their straining urge to transcend their and the systemic (linguistic) limitations as they strive to embrace infinite reality through finite medium. Their fumblings and failures in their exercises results in something for them and for the whole human race as well as that even their so called success would have failed to provide them.

Notes

1. Michael Foucault, however, countered Barthes's argument and sought to re-establish the author. He says, 'A certain number of notions that are intended to replace the privilege position of the author actually seem to preserve that privilege" ('what is an Author?' 143). Foucault in his essay suggests that the author still lives in spite of numerous endeavours to kill him/her as his/her name is associated with a set of works which make it difficult to reject the author.

2. Robert Crossman asked Jacques Derrida about his puzzling dictum on his visit to Providence in 1975, "Is the text reader writes differently from the text the author wrote?" Derrida replied, "Oui." Derrida's response was 'Oui' again when Crossman counter-questioned, "Do the two texts have anything in common." Robert Crossman, "Is there such a thing as Misreading?" *Criticism and Critical Theory* (ed. Jermey Hawthorne), p. 2.

3. I state this with full awareness of risk involved in my statement. While highlighting weaknesses of language I should confess that language is the greatest wonder and the most indispensable invention of human kind whose very meaning and continuity relies on it. It may be artificial, inefficient and incompetent but it is impossible to even think of human civilisation without it. It is like Philoctetes whose foul-smelling wound made him unacceptable to society which can, however, not afford to be without him and his bow, his genius. It needs him to sustain itself and battle through trying times successfully. Also it has an ability to improve upon itself. Further it would again be unjustifiable to denounce language in its own terms. Language immolates itself symbolically, throws off its slough periodically and gets regenerated through self-annihilation not very unlike the phoenix which rises from its ashes – Perhaps.

4. Harold Bloom categorises readers as ordinary readers who 'read' and extraordinary readers like William Blake who 'misread' their predecessors to justify their own poetic endeavours. Reading is collective, passive, and sterile and dull; 'misreading' is individual, creative and valuable. Misreading, though deplorable in common sense of the term, is not a perjurious act in Bloom. (Harold Bloom, A. *Man of Misreading*, New York: Oxford Univ. Press, 1975). Bloom does not clarify as to why he uses the term 'misreading'. Stanley Fish appears to be right to use the term 'Reader-critic' (which I too have used for the sake of convenience and to avoid confusion). Fish divides readers into 'interpretative communities'.

Such community is governed by its own interpretative rules which determine 'right-reading' and 'misreading'. Fish does not state anything about the nature of these communities but believes that the meaning of text lies in the system and informed reader is well-versed in reading interpretative conventions in making their use. He states: "we do not have free-standing readers in a relationship of perpetual adequacy or inadequacy to an equally free-standing text. Rather we have readers whose consciousness are constituted by a set of conventional motions which when put into operation constitute in turn a conventionally seen object." Stanley Fish, *Is There a Text in This Class?* (332).

5. I use the term 'surrender' as employed by the Geneva Critics and then by J. Hillis Miller who share the position that poet surrenders his individual personality to collective personality of tradition. The critic thus becomes in Hillis Miller's words 'either prey' of the author's thought and allows himself to be entirely governed by it. This complete surrender of the movement of the author's mind is the starting point of the critical process (*Blindness and Insight*, 95).

Works Cited

Barthes, Roland. "From Work to Text". *Textual Strategies*. Ithaca, New York: Cornell University Press, 1979.

—. "The Death of the Author". *Image, Music, Text*, trans. Stephen Heath. London: Fountain Paperbacks, 1984.

Blackmur, R.P. *Language as Gesture*. New York: Harcourt, Brace and Company, 1952.

Bloom, Harold. *A Map of Misreading*. New York: OUP, 1975.

Crossman, Robert. "Is There Such a Thing as Misreading?" in *Criticism and Critical Theory*. Ed. Jeremy Hawthorne Baltimore. Maryland: Edward Arnold, 1984.

Eliot, T.S. " Fragment of an Agon" in *Complete Poems and Plays*. New York: Harcourt Brace, 1969.

Foucault, Michel. "What is an Author?" *Textual Strategies*. Ithaca, New York: Cornell Univ. Press. 1979.

Fish, Stanley. *Is There a Text in this Class?* Cambridge, Mass.: Harvard Univ. Press, 1980.

Miller, J. Hillis. *Blindness and Insight*. New York: OUP, 1971.

Stevens, Wallace. "The Man With the Blue Guitar," *The Collected Poems of Wallace Stevens*. New York: Alfred & Knopf, 1967.

3

Violence in the Age of Empire

An Indian Consideration

RAJESH KUMAR SHARMA

Violence as a Matter of Discourse

A discourse about violence must begin with a consideration of discourse as violence

When we speak of violence, we are constrained by the terms of a given discourse. The discourse may not allow the articulation of certain forms and instances of violence because those forms and instances may not constitute violence in it's connotation. A discourse imposes limitations even as it offers opportunities; it disallows, even as it allows, certain understandings of violence. Discourse is, in other words, in itself a field of violence.

But a discourse of violence may not be of much use if it is not equipped to address differences and encourage possible new understandings. It needs openness and dynamism to address the specificity of situations within which particular forms and instances of violence get constituted.

The sign of the 'global' is marked with ambivalence

One face of this sign is ideological-hegemonic. From this derive those 'global accounts' that are ostensibly coherent and claim to offer comprehensive understandings of general, universal applicability. But in the face of concrete, specific phenomena irreducible in their singularity, these accounts very often, expectedly, fail.

Do we then have no use for the sign of the "global"? Yes, we do. And that use is imposed on us by the reality in which we happen to live today. This is the reality of globalisation.

The other face of the sign of the "global" points to this reality and exhorts us to remember the history of the present as also to reread the present as history (not as only *past*).

The sign of the "global" has to be recuperated by critical engagement with both its faces. A global account of globalisation may be a contradiction in terms, yet it is an inescapable necessity. The question is how to reconstruct a global account of globalisation. Can we conceptualise globalisation as multitudinous, as globalisations?

The need to conceptualise the post-global

This involves to simultaneously *comprehend* and *critique* the global and reflecting on the global from a position within globality. For the global is the defining condition of both the present as history and the present as erasure of history.

The post-global, then, requires a new kind of metanarrative.

Perhaps we can rethink the metanarrative as the narrative of narratives. Not as the yet-to-be-unpacked history inscribed as *akash-lipi* (transcendental script) in *kaal-yoni* (the matrix of time), but as the tale of the telling of tales, the (hi)story of the making of (hi)stories. Obviously, this would be the 'meta' of deep materiality, not of the denial of materiality. And that means revisioning the metanarrative not as the junk of postmodernism but as the recovery of forgotten and being-forgotten originary global ecologies.

We have an obligation to remember the deep materiality of global ecologies. We have to understand ecologies as *home* sciences, as the sciences of *home* and also as stories of homelessness, of violated homes, of disinheritance, dispossession, disenfranchisement.

In fact, a post-global metanarrative may be the best way to comprehend the non-linear, rhizomatic structures of violence in our times. Indeed, it may even be the only way to strategic pattern-recognition.

The Question of Definition

Dictionaries are notoriously status-quoist when it comes to registering change. They continue to explain violence principally as the unlawful exercise of physical force causing physical injury or damage to a person or property. Decades after the exposure of previously unrecognised forms of violence permeating modern societies in the shape of disciplinary technologies, ideological apparatuses and discourses, violence continues to be officially defined in extremely restrictive terms. The reason probably lies in the enduring nexus between the state, law and sovereignty.

The conception of violence as the unlawful exercise of physical force is implicitly based on a certain notion of sovereignty. According to this notion, the state is the exclusive locus of sovereignty. The notion of sovereignty thus grants to the state the absolute authority to determine what constitutes, in the law instituted by it, violence and what does not. Obviously, the exercise of this authority would effectively exclude from the legal-definitional ambit of the term 'violence' those acts of violence that emanate from the state or from its accomplices. The first requirement therefore is to mount a sustained discursive challenge to the statist discourse of violence. The second is to look beyond the state and the law and grasp the ubiquity of violence in its myriad forms, such as economic, cultural and social, in the age of Empire (Hardt and Negri).

The World Health Organization, in its first "World Report on Violence and Health", extends the parameters of the definition of violence when it redefines violence as "the intentional use of physical force or power, threatened or actual, against oneself, another person or against a group or community, that either results in or has a high likelihood of resulting in injury, death, psychological harm, maldevelopment or deprivation". A positive consequence of such a readjustment of focus is the enhanced awareness of the range of violence, exemplified by the WHO's estimate that violence swallows nearly as many as 1.6 million people every year in our world.

The definition of violence put forward by WHO firmly brings into the picture "oneself", "a group" and "community" on one hand and "psychological harm, maldevelopment or deprivation" on the other. Both moves are of strategic import at a time when the juggernaut of globalisation rolls over and tramples unsuspecting selves (inflicting psychological disorientation through their naïve self-understandings), results in cultural genocide of varied scales and shapes visited on groups and communities that would either join or not join the juggernaut, and spreads new kinds of misery in the name of "development" while postponing infinitely the promise of distributive justice.

Development, as the world has learnt, is not an innocent word. In the interests of justice, a crucial distinction has to be made today between development as a set of economic activities specifically oriented towards people's empowerment and development as an obfuscating discourse which covers up the contemporary global *realpolitik* of predominantly corporate economic management.

Implicated in the above illustration is the essential question of language, which can both be the object and the instrument of violence. This is a question that has not been sufficiently addressed outside philosophy and cultural studies. In fact, the redefinition of violence by WHO at once exemplifies and fails to acknowledge the centrality of language to the question of violence in our times. It extends the definitional scope of violence but does not extend it enough to include the symbolic violence that is ubiquitous to globalisation.

Symbolic violence is not unreal violence. It is a very real violence. It devastates the symbolic structures of a community, the structures that organise its ethos in complex ways embedded in history and locale. It is the violence done to a community's ways of being, to its peculiar production of meaning-making and meaningfulness. Language, obviously, bears the brunt of symbolic violence.

But it is a peculiar paradox that language also catches, reflexively, the violence being inflicted on it, and lays it bare.

In our time, the perpetrators of this violence are usually assumed to be anonymous and faceless forces driven with the inevitability of what the Greeks probably meant by fate. In reality however, they are very much identifiable. They happen to take the form of institutions, groups and persons, characterised by a pathologically high sense of self-worth and potent self-identities (brand names included) to protect and project. But they weave such formidable illusions of complexity and inaccessibility that the *aam aadmi* (the famous "common man" of political speech-writers) is left eternally bewildered and awestruck. Pure inaccessibility is the logo of this new racism, the racism of the *democratic elite* in the globalising world's *developing* economies. Before this pure inaccessibility the *aam aadmi* is expected to stand in dumb, mindless awe.

By a perverse logic of democratic *representation,* a few persons and groups arrogate to themselves the right to stand in for all people. The ground of their special right to represent the *aam aadmi* is that that they are themselves not *aam aadmi* and hence must be the better qualified to understand the *aam aadmi's* wants and needs. The farce of their hypocritical position is utterly lost on them because they would not heed the murmur of language that often undercuts any manifest rhetoric. So they speak solicitously of reforms "with a human face", not seeing that their inept choice of metaphor ironically suggests, down below, a demon's torso: that of the demon of certain putative "reforms" in unreserved and horrid nakedness. And these *masters of representation* speak of the "trickle-down" effect of prosperity, smugly advertising their ritual trust in the hierarchical distribution of wealth. They also speak of "human resources" without any sense of history and hence without any trace of irony, gleefully disremembering the mass commodification of human beings, the mass dehumanisation, which has been deposited in the phrase by the Holocaust. Such history is strictly outside the range of their post-historical, contemporary sensibilities.

The wonder is that their rape of language goes unreported. Rather, their "malpronouncements" are received and disseminated like oracular utterances, to slowly become the foundational terms of the discourse of the country's new-found modernity. The general deadness to language aborts the possibility of a collective critical consciousness. In a country where most people still look up to the media for the highest standards of language competence, the absence of a society-wide debate cutting across classes gets conveniently identified as a trait of the national temperament, whereas a better diagnosis would reveal the moral and intellectual failure of those entrusted with the care of language. Between a systematic abuse of language on the one side and a general deadness to it on the other, the ground is prepared for the burial of history. Groundless language makes an easy playground for playing games with history.

There is a vital link between language evacuated of memory and history engineered, managed and reconfigured for the sake of compatibility with certain economic doctrines and regimes. Indeed, right under this link lurks the principal target of symbolic violence. If language is the house of Being, as Heidegger said, you can reasonably hope to bomb that house out of existence when you take aim and push the button.

Towards Pattern Recognition

"India is a young country of sixty years." Prime Minister Manmohan Singh's amazing declaration on the country's Independence Day in 2007 left many editorialists and columnists crooning a non-idea like a catchy Bollywood tune. So history begins afresh, albeit with not much of historicity left. Avant-garde disaster economists moonlighting as neo-liberal historiographers find sixty-odd years manageable to account for within the ideological format of the *new* world order. (Thousands of years of civilisation can unnecessarily mess up things). And it makes great practical and political sense too: with the threshold lowered (or raised?) to sixty years, history would now begin with *our own* man, Jawaharlal Nehru, whose bona fide *errors* can be surely owned up with a good conscience.

But the greater gains of the speculative move of neoliberal historiography are in long-term investment: when you push the unwieldy inheritance of history beyond the horizon of visibility, you are virtually clearing the slate of sedimented memories and preparing to raise single-brand shopping malls in places cluttered up with bazaars of civilisation where countless cultures rub old and dusty shoulders. You are getting ready to sell your heritage buildings to hotel wallahs to either recycle or demolish them. And the mercenary inducement does not always wait to find a good enough disguise; it can abruptly break out like a rash of chicken pox on the face of the neo-political. Hence, the Ram Setu affair is today a significant landmark not so much even in the epic of Rama's wanderings as it is in the short history of India's affair with neo-liberalism. When commerce becomes the pre-eminent criterion in all matters, you should not be surprised if there is tomorrow a survey of all places and structures of cultural and historical importance with the obviously *rational* aim of turning them into profitable enterprises such as leisure resorts and shopping malls. Time was when invading armies are said to have vandalised the world's libraries. Now that most libraries have gone digital, let the torches and hammers fall elsewhere. The sight of new invading hordes flashing their Harvard and London School of Economics degrees may not seem very threatening, but it is a very real sight. History repeats itself in many ways. And lest people should check it out, let it begin in 1947 only.

Even the Greek fates could not have been that vicious. They challenged the defiant man to discover and show his humanity at its best. The latter-day fates do not only erase memory and reconfigure history, but also literally brutalise people, practices, institutions and human relations. And all this in the name of a higher rationality inaccessible to *aam aadmi*. Factories and shops are closed down with the force of a law that has shed even the pretense of justice. Vendors of food and their hungry customers (who reportedly earn *as much as* half a dollar a day) are supposed to just shut up and disappear. When there is a hue and cry against judicial impropriety, a new propriety of studied silence and stonewalling comes to prevail. When a minister in the government does some loud thinking about the health hazards faced by the hard-earning young women and men in the BPO industry, the profit-makers howl in protest in their self-appointed role as defenders of lifestyle choices. What was considered to be immoral living just five years earlier becomes a lifestyle choice today – because someone is happily making a quick buck out of it.

Language, memory, history, law, morals. The symbolic violence of our times is evidently not random and sporadic. There is a pattern to it. To begin to recognise that pattern is to begin telling that tale of tales which awaits telling and which holds the promise of redemption *in*, as against *from*, history. To tell the tale is to bear witness, to suffer and to act – all gathered into one.

David Riches speaks of "the triangle of violence" which includes the perpetrator, the victim and the witness (qtd. in Strathern and Stewart). Depending on persuasion or threat, the witness, it is said, may incline toward the perpetrator or the victim. The triangular division of violence is as neat as any academic division can ideally be, but in reality there is also a zone of ambiguity in which the witness is also doomed to *be* both the victim and the perpetrator. In these times, we need to see ourselves precisely as such witnesses fortunately trapped in a zone of ambiguity. The least we can do perhaps is call upon ourselves to bear witness to our witness-status in that zone. That may open the way to a better understanding of our own victimisation as well as our complicity in victimisation. The comforting delusion that we are only witnesses, and hence not participants in the making of the history that is the present, is a rather fragile delusion, for no witness box can be a protection against the onslaughts of reality.

Works Cited

Hardt, Michael and Antonio Negri. *Multitude: War and Democracy in the Age of Empire.* New York: Penguin, 2004.

Strathern, Andrew and Pamela J. Stewart. "Violence: Conceptual Themes and the Evaluation of Actions." *Polylog: Forum for Intercultural Philosophy* 5 (2004) <http://them.polylog.org/5/fss-en.htm>.

World Health Organization. "World Report on Violence and Health." 2002 <http://www.who.int/violence_injury_prevention/violence/world_report/en/full_en.pdf>.

4

Innovative Strategies to Counter Domestic Violence

Exploring the State and Community Responses in Karnataka and Gujarat

VEENA POONACHA

Violence against women is one of the few cultural constants prevailing across geo-political boundaries. Historically, the many culturally sanctioned forms of gender violence such as, *sati* (widow immolation) and female infanticide in India, foot binding in China and female circumcision in parts of Africa, are the hardest to eradicate. There is always the additional danger of the revival of such retrograde practices – a danger made real by the resurgence of *sati* with the immolation of Roop Kanwar in Deorala, Rajasthan, more than a century after it was banned. The sheer brutality of some such instances may have the power to shock, but there are others that remain hidden from the public eye.

One such unacknowledged crime (that is often culturally condoned) is domestic violence, minimally construed as the physical, emotional, sexual, psychological and financial abuse of a woman in her intimate relationships. In the Indian social context, this definition of intimate relationships would include all the intimidating acts by the members (both men and women) of her marital family. This is not to deny the vulnerability of women/girls in their parental homes; but rather to turn the spotlight on one aspect of the problem, increasingly foregrounded in international fora (such as the World Congress on Human Rights, Vienna, 1994 and the Fourth World Conference of Women, Beijing, 1995) as a human rights violation, requiring state intervention. The UN Platform for Action emerging out of the Beijing conference requires an explicit commitment from governments to check domestic violence (along with other gender crimes), in their respective countries. In keeping with this commitment, the Government of India promises to enact the Domestic Violence against Women (Prevention and Protection) Bill.

The credit of placing domestic violence on the centre stage of national and international agenda goes to the women's movement. In their analysis, the aim of gender violence is to control women. Often condoned by society, it reinforces gender inequalities by curtailing a woman's rights and freedoms. This violence is sustained by ideology and enforced by the material realities of women's lives. They have fewer resources and entitlements in the family and community. The failure of governments to deal with the issue is increasingly seen as a denial of women's citizenship rights. Located within the broad parameters of the struggle, this article seeks to elaborate on the strategies that the various state and voluntary organisations have adopted over the past three decades to counter domestic violence and ensure protection for women affected by family violence. It specifically examines some of the innovative strategies devised to prevent domestic violence based on the findings of an exploratory study that was aimed at documenting state/community responses to domestic violence. The article thus develops as follows: (1) a brief description of the study, its methods and frames of reference; (2) the preventive and reactive responses adopted by the various organisations to deal with domestic violence; and (3) some of the innovative strategies used in dealing with domestic violence in Karnataka and Gujarat.

It is argued here that dealing with domestic violence is not easy. It requires measures that go beyond punitive action against the perpetrator through the prevailing criminal justice system, to include strategies that provide women with alternatives and raise awareness in the community against the crime. The ensuing discussion here, on the one hand, broadens the scope of human rights discourse; on the other, threatens some of the bedrock assumptions encoded within the discourse. This is because the human rights discourse, in its classical formulation, was largely construed as the relationship of the individual vis-à-vis the state and confined to the public space. Failing to acknowledge the hidden crime of domestic violence, the human rights principles that enjoin, the state shall not interfere in the private domain of the family and the legal system shall protect the individual from such intrusions. This breach of the conceptual public/private divide in the discourse generates a fear of the erosion of individual rights by concomitantly increasing punitive state powers. To an extent, this explains some of the reluctance of the criminal justice system to view domestic violence as a human rights violation; it also explains the resistance to section 498A of the Indian Penal Code criminalising domestic violence. It also explains the overwhelming resistance among legislators to institute a comprehensive bill to prevent domestic violence. The Protection from Domestic Violence bill tabled in the Indian Parliament in 2002 was full of loopholes. Instead of firmly pinning the blame on the perpetrator, it defined domestic violence as "habitual assault" and it enabled the perpetrator to justify violence on the grounds that he was merely defending his property and that of other members of the household (Sharma, 2002: 13; Karat, 2002: 8). Therefore, the various women's groups, lawyers and activists are lobbying to ensure that a bill that provides women with legally enforceable protection against violence in the home is passed.

The Research Study and Methodology

To identify and understand the preventive, conciliatory and punitive strategies, in these states, the study investigated through the use of in-depth case study method, ten organisations in each state. Further, on the premise that the effectiveness of the strategies could only be understood within the socio-economic and cultural context in which each organisation operated, the study examined the ideological underpinnings (specifically their ideas of social change and gender relationships) of each organisation. It also looked at the organisational structure, decision-making process, staff morale and intervention strategies. Such a framework was seen as necessary to appreciate the unique contribution made by each organisation to initiate social change. At the same time, it was hoped that such an in-depth analysis would enable us to avoid the pitfalls of making hasty generalisation or value loaded judgements.

Given this focus, the study did not explore the nature or extent of domestic violence; nor did it look into the interventions by the family or kin group in such situations. Seeking to examine the public response to what was largely construed as a private matter, the study confined itself to examining measures adopted by the government and the non-government organisations to complaints of domestic violence by women, or their family members or even outsiders on their behalf. From such a perspective, domestic violence comprised all acts of intimidation and aggression that forced a woman to seek redressal by breaking the silence imposed on her by patriarchal culture. She was seen as a survivor rather than a hapless victim of violence. This operational definition of domestic violence helped to delimit the research question; it did not necessarily include the culturally sanctioned forms of violence (such as unequal access to the household resources or other restrictions) unless challenged by the woman or other on her behalf.

The selection of organisations for the study was not random. The selection was based on a detailed mailed questionnaire carefully prepared after discussion with various experts in the field. Based on the responses, a typology of organisations and a scheme to classify different kinds of responses to domestic violence was prepared. In Karnataka, the organisations selected were from regions culturally disparate and included Dakshina Kannada from the west coast (with an admixture of different religious groups and communities); Bijapur from north Karnataka (with a deeply entrenched *devadasi* tradition, i.e., temple prostitution); Raichur from the north-east and Tumkur from the south (both with a sizeable Telegu-speaking population and problems of rampant alcoholism); Kollegal, further south with a large Dalit (i.e., socially marginalised group) population; and the state capital Bangalore which is today one of the fastest growing metropolitan cities in the country with the dubious distinction of having a high instance of domestic violence. Similarly, in Gujarat, the geographical regions selected include Ahmedabad, a historically significant city with a large migrant population; Valsad from south Gujarat; Bhuj, Kutch, which lies on the north west borders of India and Pakistan and has a sizeable migrant tribal population famed for their crafts; Anand in Khedha district, Central Gujarat known as the forerunner of India's white revolution; Jamnagar on the west coast of Gujarat with a sizeable Muslim population and Dahod Panchmal another tribal district. Each of these regions in both the states represents diverse socio-cultural and economic problems. The research process was based on participative strategies that derive from contemporary advances in feminist methodology. The data that was collected for each organisation may be summarised as follows: (1) interviews with the leadership to understand their ideological moorings; (2) interviews with the staff and the beneficiaries (if possible) to gauge their responses to the intervention; (3) participant observation of the activities of the organisation; and (4) an examination of all the available reports of the organisation (including cases, annual reports, brochures records, etc.).

Strategies to Deal with Domestic Violence

This study makes it apparent that there are varied and multi-layered responses to domestic violence, which are subsumed in the overall struggle for gender justice. These strategies may be broadly categorised as those that seek to prevent/eradicate domestic violence and those that react/respond to such instances. Encoded in these broad categories are a variety of responses, which may be delineated further on the basis of their target groups and their expected outcomes as follows:

Attacking the Roots of Violence (Preventive Measures)

(a)   *Through Research, Documentation and Dissemination*
- Developing a social analysis of violence through research and documentation.
- Understanding the extent and limits of the law and the criminal justice system.
- Ensuring that these theoretical insights are disseminated to the field staff and social workers of the organisations.

(b) *Through Intervention Strategies (that focus on the survivors of violence)*
- Neighbourhood vigilance to identify and monitor vulnerable families to prevent violence.
- Creating new options by developing skills (self confidence, employment, political consciousness, etc.) among vulnerable women.
- Creating economic opportunities for women.
- Empowering women with the knowledge of their rights.
- Providing them with information with the various government welfare programmes and helping them to access them.
- Providing women with the necessary socio-cultural space to conceptualise and articulate their issues.

(Focussing on the community and state)
- Sensitising the community and the bureaucracy about domestic violence.
- Media publicity given to the issue of domestic violence.
- Campaigning for gender-just laws and reform in the criminal justice mechanism.

Reacting to Instances/Issues of Domestic Violence

(a) *Through Research, Documentation and Dissemination*
- Documentation of cases and conceptualising experiences.
- Systematically documenting the procedural lapses in the criminal justice system.

(b) *Through Intervention Strategies (Focussing on the survivors of violence)*
- Extending emotional and material support to the survivor.
- Enabling her to access economic resources, information, etc.
- Shelter/Short stay homes
- Counselling
- Medical aid/therapeutic assistance

- Legal aid
- Establishing support systems and monitoring cases of violence
- Child care (hostels, foster care, schooling, etc.)

(c) *Focussing on the Community/State*
- Raising community/neighbourhood opinion against domestic violence.
- Initiating collective community action against domestic violence by mobilising men and women from other mass based groups, trade unions, etc.
- Garnering community support for the survivors.
- Bringing community pressure on the perpetrator of violence to change their behaviour pattern and ensure the safety of the women in their marital home.
- Educating violent men to refrain from violence.
- Collaborating with the state agencies to provide adequate services to the victims.
- Training medical/legal and other personnel to respond to the victims' needs/rights.
- Educating the police to develop new attitudes skills in dealing with gender violence.
- Pressurising the police to enforce the law, follow suitable legal procedures and prosecute the perpetrators of domestic violence.
- Set up an accountability mechanism and monitoring police handling of violence cases and police behaviour
- Using litigations and test cases to improve the performance of the courts
- Challenge and confront the courts to comply with the laws.
- Network and advocacy towards effecting policy change and evolving support systems.

The organisations who were part of this study have used these strategies to a lesser or greater extent. The strategies adopted by the different organisations are determined by their ideological framework, goals and organisational structures. By and large, these organisations have sought to prevent/root out domestic violence through various socio-economic and awareness programmes for women and pressurise the state to bring about socially sensitive legislations. Further, in order to empower women, many organisations have experimented with innovative preventive and conciliatory measures. They, like the Mahila Samakya Programme in Raichur, the Ahmedabad Women's Action Group (AWAG) in Ahmedabad, Astitva Mahila Utkarsha Sanstha (ASTITVA) in Valsad, the Women's Liberation and Rehabilitation Society (WLARS) in Tumkur, the People's Movement for Self Reliance (PMSR) in Kollegal, Janodya Public Trust in Bangalore and the Sumangali Seva Ashram (SSA) in Bangalore have experimented in forming local women's collectives. These collectives ensure that the agenda for action is locally determined. Further, through effective networking between collectives, the individual local collective are not isolated; they are confident of support from the collectives of the neighbouring villages.

Innovative Strategies

Given the paucity of funds and infrastructure, organisations have devised many innovative strategies, which are cost effective. They have used the local village community councils to effect conciliation. Furthermore, to circumvent the costly and lengthy legal procedure, organisations work towards out of court settlements, which are often recorded to maintain the appearance of legality on stamp papers. The main clause included in such agreements is that the man or his family members will not use violence on his wife. The innovative strategies highlighted here are broadly classified as preventive, conciliatory and punitive measures. These measures are further classified as efforts by the government and those of the non-government organisations.

State Initiatives

The government remedial measures comprise the vigilance, investigative and punitive measures as well as the various state mechanisms for effecting conciliation. Its preventive measures include the various government development programmes targeting women. Here the focus is on the following government initiatives: (1) the All Women Police Stations (AWPSs) and the *Mahila Suraxa Samiti* (MSS), a statutory vigilance body in Gujarat as examples of the vigilance, investigative and punitive state action; (2) the *Parivarik Mahila Lok Adalats* (i.e., the family courts) conducted by the National Commission for Women (NCW) in collaboration with the voluntary organisations and the Family Counselling Centres (FCC) initiated by the Central Social Welfare Board (CSWB) as examples of conciliation processes; and *Mahila Samakya* (MS) programme as an example of preventive measures.

The Vigilance, Investigative and Punitive Measures

Established in the 1980s in response to the demands made by the women's movement, the AWPS and the MSS indicate that the effectiveness of these measures is dependent on political will. The AWPSs were established to make the right of police protection accessible to women and children; it was premised on the recognition that women hesitate to approach a predominantly male police force even in life threatening situations. The current limitations of the AWPS in Bangalore and Ahmedabad should be contextualised within the overall deficiencies of the police force, which continues to function within the matrix of its colonial antecedents. The modern police force in the country was introduced during the British period as an instrument of repression. It continues to function within this framework because of political interference and the lack of political will to reform the system. Further, due to the poor service conditions, long hours of work and occupational stress, the police force is demoralised, particularly when it is confronted by the ineffectiveness of the criminal justice system. These overall problems are exacerbated for policewomen primarily because of the prevailing gender bias within the system, which sees them as peripheral. In addition, the predominantly male-centric ethos neither takes into account the multiple roles of policewomen nor the special needs of the complainants. There are no proper referral services to provide immediate medical or legal assistance nor are the policewomen trained to handle such personal issues with sensitivity.

Similarly, indicating the need for political will to effect innovative strategies the MSS was formed in Gujarat. Although envisaged in 1987, it was only implemented in 1991. The committee (comprising women members of the Legislative Assembly, social workers, activists and researchers in Gujarat) was able to enforce meticulous police investigation in cases of atrocities against women as they had the backing of the state Chief Minister, its Chairperson, and the Chief Police Officer, CID (Crime Branch) its member secretary. Through liaison with the police and a network of sub-units in the various districts and *talukas* (administrative sub-divisions in districts) the MSS was able to maintain vigilance against gender crimes and call to question criminal investigation procedures in such cases. It also sensitised the police regarding such crimes. With the change of government, this highly effective programme was allowed to fizzle out due to the lack of political support. Undoubtedly, because of the demand from women's groups it has since been revived, but with reduced powers; its local units are now under the jurisdiction of district collectors rather than the police.

State Initiative at Conciliation

The NCW is a statutory body established under the National Commission Act, 1990 to safeguard women's rights by reviewing legislations, intervening in specific complaints of atrocities and to undertake remedial actions. It has launched the *Parivarik Mahila Lok Adalats* (family courts conducted by women) to ensure speedy justice for women. These *adalats* (courts) are organised even in remote areas with the help of the state legal aid and advisory bodies, state/district judicial machineries and the women's groups. According to its 1996–97 annual report, the NCW has sponsored 68 such courts all over the country to which nearly 35,000 cases were referred and justice delivered to women in 7,000 cases.

A point made evident in this study is that it is often difficult in India to differentiate between government and non-government efforts. This interfacing of the two efforts becomes apparent while examining the FCCs established across the country by the CSWB. Constituted in 1953 by a parliamentary resolution, the CSWB is a semi-autonomous body, comprising predominantly social workers with knowledge of the prevailing social reality.

Its mandate is to provide technical and financial assistance to the voluntary organisations. Since 1984, attributing the escalating violence against women directly to maladjusted families, the CSWB, through the State Social Welfare Advisory Boards (SSWABs), established 22 FCCs Karnataka and 34 in Gujarat FCCs attached to voluntary organisations. The venture was expanded in the 1990s to the establishment of FCCs attached to select police stations. Despite limitations of staff and infrastructure, the FCCs provide preventive, referral and rehabilitative services to women and children, survivors of violence. Managed by trained social workers, some of the FCCs have effectively utilised the police to ensure that members of the complainant's marital family come for counselling. The FCCs attached to police stations, in particular, have been able to use police services effectively. Nonetheless, they have a conservative mandate to maintain the family unit in the interest of the children. This raises an important question: would the counselling process inadvertently silence women from an anxiety to maintain the family?

Preventive Measures of the State

The MS programme, initiated by the Department of Education, Ministry of Human Resource Development, Government of India, with funds from the Dutch Government, may be categorised as an attempt to prevent violence through the empowerment of women. It was born out of the stated goals of the New Education Policy (1986) that education must play a positive, interventionist role to bring about women's equality. This idea took shape in 1989 with the establishment of the MS programme in 10 districts of Gujarat, Karnataka and Uttar Pradesh and subsequently expanded to other areas. The programme is committed to ensuring that poor women have a say in development programmes. Seeking to reverse the prevailing 'top down' approach to development it establishes village level self-help groups. It aims at enabling the rural poor women to acquire the necessary knowledge and self-confidence to effect a change in their lives as women and as part of the rural community. It is through these collectives (which provide women with the necessary space to discuss and reflect) that women have tackled domestic violence and other social evils of child marriage, dowry and the devadasi system.

Non-Government Initiatives

Like the government initiatives, these may be classified as remedial and preventive. The differences in the approach of the various non-government organisations may be broadly attributed to the construction they impute for the existence of domestic violence. To elaborate, an organisation like the Pragna Counselling Cell (PCC) in Mangalore, views domestic violence within the prism of social work praxis. Therefore its approach would include: psychological, vocational, and family counselling services along with the medical treatment of the alcoholic at their de-addiction centre. The feminist organisations like (1) Astitva Mahila Utkarsha Sanstha (AMUS), Valsad, South Gujarat; (2) Ahmedabad Women's Action Group (AWAG), Ahmedabad; (3) Jagrut Mahila Sanghatan (JMS), Anand, Central Gujarat; and (4) Women's Liberation and Rehabilitation Society (WLARS), Madhugiri, Tumkur, follow women-centred approach. Their approach is summarised as follows: (1) to provide support, guidance and advice to women; (2) to provide survivors with shelter and enable them to become economically independent; (3) to rehabilitate survivors of violence; and (4) to support women in their struggle for justice. The strategies that have evolved through their struggles are extremely cost effective; they aim at collectivising women and to find solutions to their own problems through their collective strength. In contrast, community based organisations (i.e., organisations like the Janodaya Public Trust, Bangalore and the People's Movement for Self Reliance, Kollegal, Mysore district) focus on the overall upliftment of the community. In dealing with domestic violence, these organisations seek to save the family and therefore attempt to bring about a compromise.

As mentioned earlier, due to the paucity of funds and inability to provide the kind of referral services that are needed, these NGOs have devised a few innovative strategies that are described here. These include:

The Kayami Samadhan Panch (Permanent Conciliation Committee) conducted by the Kutch Mahila Vikas Sanghathan (Bhuj)

The aim is to provide counselling, legal aid and support to women in violent homes. The KMVS uses the services of lawyers, retired judges, village elders and social activists in order to resolve family conflicts. Seeking to bring about an amicable settlement, the committee calls both the parties for discussions.

Intervention by the Caste/Community and the Village Panchayats

This would imply the use of the existing community power structures in the conciliation process. This would mean that the voluntary organisations bring pressure on the woman's husband's family to stop harassing her. The system has proved useful in bringing succour to the woman, but there are instances when the process has led to the silencing of the woman. Therefore, the use of such power structures need to be judiciously used as they might strengthen the prevailing conservative values in society which will not allow for a long term social change.

Counselling

It is possible to discern different kinds of counselling practices based on the ideological moorings of organisations. The more conservative organisations emphasise the welfare of the family (often to the detriment of women's interests), while the feminist organisations have developed what they term as 'woman-centred' counselling practices. As explained by AWAG, the idea behind this approach is that the woman should be empowered to know what she wants, with the assurance that the organisation will support her in her decision. WLARS, for instance, has organised rural women into neighbourhood vigilance committees to prevent domestic violence. If the committee comes to know that a woman in their lane is beaten, they approach the woman (even if she is not a member of the organisation) with an offer of help. But unless the woman herself expresses a wish that the organisation should interfere, they do not do so.

Preventive Measures

Apart from counselling, legal aid and shelter, the NGOs also undertake various campaigns focussing on specific cases of violence against women and network with other organisations within the state and outside. WLARS on the other hand, caters to a rural community; it seeks to provide counselling not through professional social workers, but by the women in the community who discuss the woman's problems and devise political action. If the woman requires temporary shelter, these women take her into their homes and subsequently, if required, help her to set up a separate residence.

Socio-Economic Empowerment of Women

An important preventive measure adopted by the NGOs is through vocational training and income generation programmes for rural women and teenage girls from the weaker sections of the population. This focus on teenage girls especially has long-term implications, for it empowers them with the knowledge of their rights and also provides them with the economic means of being able to opt out of violent homes. As one of the young girls in a particular village said, "Many years ago my mother wanted to withdraw me from school. The members of the organisation advised her against it. They supported me through my school education and enabled me to become self-employed. The confidence that I have gained because of my association with them would enable me to resist any form of oppression or violence in the future."

Apart from focussing on such preventive strategies, these organisations have also sought to counter violence against women by organising women into collectives. It is through these collectives that women are empowered to counter all forms of oppression including the caste/community oppression and domestic violence. The women's *sanghas* (collectives) have devised innovative strategies to deal with domestic violence and the overall exploitation of women through interest aggregation. The many incidents narrated in the organisational case study indicates the sensitivity and commitment of the organisers to the social upliftment of dalits and women; nevertheless, based on our understanding of the ways in which women's rights seem to invariably conflict with that of a patriarchal community, one wonders how the organisation will tackle the issue of domestic violence when confronted with the choice of upholding the cohesion of the community when it conflicts with the rights of the woman.

This brief survey of some of the responses (with special focus on strategies used in Karnataka and Gujarat) makes it apparent that organisations have developed multiple strategies to counter domestic violence. More importantly, they have been able to develop many innovative mechanisms to provide cost effective solutions to domestic violence. This is not to imply that there are no shortfalls in the facilities offered by both the voluntary and the Government organisations. The shortfalls are primarily due to the paucity of funds and lack of infrastructure (such as telephones, help lines, etc.) as well as support/referral services (such as shelter and child care facilities). There are also no crisis centres that offer protection for women and children (particularly in the night) against domestic violence. Studies have indicated that women often remain in violent relationships because of the lack of support services. They are unable to access state-run shelter homes without following lengthy procedures. These shelter homes are spartan and unwelcoming. They do not have medical aid or other facilities to make women and children feel cared for and protected. Many women cannot avail of the facilities, however minimal, because of the outdated rules. These shelter homes, for instance, do not take in women with children over a certain age limit; nor do they take in women with severe psychological problems, as they are ill equipped to deal with them.

These inadequacies are particularly apparent while examining the effectiveness of state initiatives such as the All Women Police Stations and the Family Counselling Cells (FCC, Police) in Ahmedabad and Bangalore. The cases, which they have to deal with, are often serious enough to warrant immediate medical aid and protection for the women and children to recover from the trauma of their experiences. These cells, however, do not have provisions for immediate medical aid or childcare and rest rooms. Despite these limitations, it is commendable that the counsellors of the FCCS like their counterparts in the FCCs attached to voluntary organisations work with sincerity and dedication. They have low salaries and lack job security. They are often burnt out because of the sheer volume of cases they are required to handle. The state must recognise the professional contributions of these social workers and counsellors and provide them suitable remuneration. Despite these limitations, the study also makes it apparent that these organisations have (against overwhelming odds) created networks, support systems and structures that are cost effective and efficient. These models need to be highlighted but unfortunately the rich experiences of the various organisations tend to be lost as there is very little documentation. This is primarily because these organisations are short-staffed and do not have the time to document and critically reflect upon their experiences.

End Note

* This article (seeking to highlight some of the innovative practices adopted by the state and NGOs in Gujarat and Karnataka) is based on a much larger research study entitled, *Responses to Domestic Violence in Karnataka and Gujarat,* that I had undertaken jointly with my colleague Dr Divya Pandey (Hon. Fellow, Research Centre for Women's Studies, SNDT Women's University) for the International Center for Research on Women, Washington DC. A brief version of this paper was also presented RC 32 of XV World Congress of Sociology, Brisbane, Australia, and July 7-13, 2002.

Works Cited

Karat, Brinda. "Domestic Violence Bill: Adding Insult to Injury." *Times of India.* 16 March 2002, p. 8.

Sharma, Kalpana "Women's Groups Oppose Domestic Violence Bill." *The Hindu.* 8 March 2002, p. 13.

5

One Hundred Years of Violence

JOSÉ SOL LUCIA

"We were born into a violent world. We have created a violent world. We leave a violent world behind us like a legacy for those that follow."

Why?

This question has haunted me for years. The answers to it, though they start off simply enough, do not really satisfy me and have, bit by bit, become more complex and even obscure. Today I, like many others, would place myself in the domain of ignorance. I don't know, I don't understand, I don't want to understand why the world is so violent. As John Keane says, "any attempt at theorising [on the subject of violence] may seem, at first sight, a means towards a self-complacent rhetoric" (Keane, 2000: 110).

The twentieth century has been the most violent century in the history of humanity. Never before did we use such devastating bombs as those that levelled Hiroshima and Nagasaki in August 1945. Never before have we had bombs as cruel as those 110 million impersonal mines which are still planted in 70 countries world wide, some of them camouflaged like stones or even multi-coloured like an innocent butterfly. These mines kill 27 people a day and mutilate another 40 people a day for life, and can explode decades after a war has finished, destroying the life of an innocent child who might have been playing football with his friends near the town. Never before has humanity seen such a well-organised and industrial approach to death, such as was carried out in the Nazi concentration camps. Never before have collective massacres reached the scale that we have seen in the last century in Cambodia, the Soviet Union and Rwanda.

Not only has the twentieth century seen a quantitative increase in violence, something which would seem logical considering the huge demographical growth the world has witnessed (the world population has quadrupled over the last one hundred years), as well as the improved technology used in weapon-making, but there have also been developments in the sophistication and types of violence used – from the psychological torture carried out in Latin American dictatorships, to the "scientific" experimentation carried out by Nazi doctors on prisoners in the German concentration camps. Not only that, violence has succeeded in invading all aspects of society, even entering into people's homes, whether it be in the form of men attacking women, or through televised entertainment which is deemed surprisingly appropriate for all the viewing public. What kind of future does this offer to a society which allows and even encourages its young people to view violence as entertainment?

We could naively believe that the world is divided into two parts: one part of humanity living in peace and the other living subject to violence and chaos. It's a long time ago now that this idea stopped being true. Violence lies in wait at the door of every citizen that belongs to a supposedly peaceful country. This is how Olof Palme (Swedish Prime Minister) died in 1986, and Ernest Lluch (Catalonian economist, and Spanish ex-Minister, assassinated by ETA in 2001) and the group of Deputies from the Swiss canton of Zug (27th September, 2001). The arms industry, the drugs trade and the constant movement of people from country to country mean that violence does not remain confined to one geographical locality, but instead is distributed – however unequally – around the whole planet.

The widespread executions which took place in the Nazi concentration camps coupled with a slow process of degradation and humiliation; the bombardment of cities during World War II, causing huge human and cultural losses; the Cambodian massacre led by Pol Pot (2 million dead); the military repressions, supported by North America, which took place in Latin America (200,000 dead in Guatemala, 75,000 in El Salvador), and Operation Condor led to thousands of missing or murdered people in Argentina and Chile, in which people like Henry Kissinger (winner of the Nobel Peace Prize)were directly implicated; the Algerian War; the Vietnam War; the extermination of Kurds in Turkey and Iraq; the murder of a third of the population of East Timor following the Indonesian invasion of 1975, with the full consent of Great Britain, the USA and Australia; the postcolonial killing among the Tsutsis and Hutus in the Great Lakes Region in 1994 that was settled with around a million deaths; the "ethnic cleansing" by the Serbs in Bosnia during the nineties; nationalist terrorists, religious fundamentalists (more than 100,000 civilians have been murdered in Algeria alone); or must we recall the armies of drug cartels, the mafia, and the endless 'uncivil' wars? I suppose not. We all know that "*this century has seen a scale of violence, whether planned or not, that has surpassed all that has gone before*" *(Keane, 2000: 13).*

Violence or 'Violences'? The Singular Nature of the Phenomenon

One logical question that one may like to ask and seek clarification for is why do we refer to violence when there is not one but myriads of its form. It would now be fitting for us to clarify what we already understand by the word 'violence' when we use it in the singular.

John Keane supports his traditional definition: "*The term (which comes from the Latin word* violentia) *presents us with obsolete connotations which go back to its first English* uses (at the end of the Middle Ages) to describe 'the use of physical force' against a person, who 'interrupts *or bothers',* '*disturbs with roughness and bad manners*' *or* '*defiles, dishonours or offends*'. ... *The term is understood* better when it is defined as the action which an individual or group takes against another's body, without their consent, *and whose consequences may be concussion, bruising or scratching, swelling* or *pain in the head, a broken bone, a heart attack, the loss of a limb or even death*" *(*Keane, 2000: 61–62).

Others, in contrast, like Johan Galtung or Ignacio Ellacuría would prefer not to reduce violence to a concrete physical attack or to a specific moment in time, but instead they would widen it to include all that which voluntarily attacks the physical or psychological integrity of a person, or that which attacks human life in general. This would be the case with, for example, an economic system that generates social pockets of economic poverty through the way it is structured. Ellacuría, when referring to structural violence (radical and latent), and revolutionary violence (obvious, and a consequence of the structural), wrote in 1973: "*We are talking about two types of violence: one which is radical, and superficially the least visible, and which can be understood within the context of injustice; and the other, which is fundamentally a reaction to violent situations, classed as such because they go against human dignity and oppress one's freedom*" (Ellacuria, 1973: 94).

Johan Galtung points to a widening of the concept of violence, which goes beyond a specific physical attack. According to the Norwegian professor, "*violence is here defined as the cause of the difference between the potential and the actual, between what could have been and what is*", in such a way that "*if a person died from tuberculosis in the eighteenth century, it would be hard* to conceive of this as violence since it might have been quite unavoidable, but if he dies from it today, despite all the medical *resources in the world, the violence is present according to our definition (...) In other words, when the potential is higher than the actual the difference is by* definition avoidable and when it is avoidable, the violence is present" (Galtung, 1975: 111).

We know that many deaths through illness and hunger could be prevented in today's world if economic resources were used, (this is what Galtung calls "the potential"): this does not happen though ("the actual"), in spite of our capabilities. This should also be considered as violence.

So, the viewpoint of Keane, like that of Galtung and Ellacuría, exposes the central features of violence. Violence is much more than a specific physical attack; it is any attack on human life or on one's physical integrity, carried out in either a concrete physical way, or through a socio-economic structure (Galtung, Ellacuría, Medellín). However, we are not going to excessively dilute the concept of violence in such a way that, by the end, the concrete act of physical violence is forgotten (Keane).

Why do we use the term 'violence', rather than 'acts of violence' or 'violences'? Why does our language tend towards the singular, when we are talking about a phenomenon of multifaceted diversity? It is at this point that we are going to examine the singular nature of the phenomenon of violence, that is, the fact that one person can be capable of attacking the life of another, in this way seriously damaging their 'otherness', an essential trait of the human being. Violence presents itself in a number of ways, but we perceive it in a unitary way. This perception brings us back time and again to the same question about violence: 'Why?' Violence is an expression of the difference between what man observes to be and what he feels should be; it is an expression of the existential frustration that can be felt at all human levels, from the individual to the political. Self-loathing arises out of the difference between what I observe myself to be and what I believe I could be, and this leads to a violent rejection of everything that has caused this difference or everything that reminds me of it. Violence and dissatisfaction go hand in hand. Violence is a way of expressing frustration and disappointment: I destroy because I feel destroyed. If I must fall, then let others fall along with me.

The Main Manifestations of Violence

As we said previously, throughout the twentieth century, violence has invaded every aspect of humanity and, under the guise of innocence, has even succeeded in becoming a perverse form of entertainment for children. There does not seem to be any aspect of humanity left which has not been stained by blood. It is true that violence has always existed, at least, as far back as our historical memory and anthropological intuition can take us. However, in these last hundred years, violence has increased and become more sophisticated, more 'effective' (involving a lesser degree of risk to the perpetrator, and with more people being killed). Paradoxically, it coexists quite happily alongside democracy and human rights, which now seem more and more like worthless bits of paper.

The Economic Structure that Kills Slowly

The greatest violence committed in the twentieth century has been that of socio-economic injustice. This form of violence is the slowest killer of all and has taken the greatest number of human lives, leaving no room for hope whatsoever since it is part of a social structure. Throughout the last century a worldwide system has been shaped, becoming more and more global, which has seen the minority of humanity getting progressively richer, while the majority sinks into to an ever-increasing poverty. The UNDP (United Nations Development Programme) shows in its *Human Development Report 2001* that, of the 6 billion people on Earth, 4.6 billion live in developing countries. Of these 4.6 billion people, 2.8 billion live on less than $2 a day, and of these, 1.2 billion live on less than $1 a day. 854 million are illiterate. 325 million children don't go to school at the primary and secondary levels. 968 million don't have access to improved water sources. 2,400 billion do not have access to the most basic sanitation, and many more do not have access to a higher quality of sanitation. Every year 11 million children under the age of 5 die from preventable causes, which is equivalent to more than 30,000 children a day (UNDP: *Human Development Report 2001*, Chapter 1). The UNDP had already pointed out in its *Human Development Report 1998* that from the beginning of the nineties, the inequality of income between populations of richer countries and those of poorer countries had gone from a ratio of 32 (times higher) to 70.

All of this represents a huge injustice, because in the majority of cases, poor and rich people are way through no merit of their own. They are born poor or they are born rich. Without a doubt, some can become rich over the years, but they would have already been born into a cultural, social and economic mould, which gave them the capacity to break free. The huge majority of poor people today would already have been born into a poor environment, and will never be able to use their hidden qualities, because the system doesn't give them the opportunity to do so. The millionaire footballers of humble origins, such as Maradona, are an exception to the rule, and their example can be used to pacify the collective conscience. The economic system imposed during the last century after the European and American powers decided to dominate the world in order to overcome their own crisis of economic growth, is like a gas that slowly kills those who don't have the money to buy the protective mask. Neither does it stop there, since economic injustice can cause other types of violence as we have already seen, such as when the struggle for survival results in serious acts of aggression.

Nationalism and Imperialism: The Lay Divinity that Justifies Everything

Somehow, the concept of nationalism has seen some of the worst violence committed in the last century. French Jesuit philosopher and theologian, Gaston Fessard, stated that there had been three great false divinities in the twentieth century: the divinity of Reason (Liberalism); the divinity of Class (Communism); and the divinity of the Nation (National Socialism or Fascism). Fessard felt that these concepts were hovering over us and directing our conflicts like the ancient gods. "The fact that these three views of the world are thus dominating the minds of our comtemporaries is a sociological and historical fact which characterises our era and which nobody can dare deny" (Fessard, 1960: 22). These three concepts have been classed as "divinities" through their double claim of being able to interpret the totality of human existence in a definitive way, and of not having been based on anything that had come before. They are false in their need to destroy anything that tries to expose the lies on which they are based.

The term 'nationalism' is ambiguous. Hitler and Franco were nationalists and so were the Catalonian cellist Pau Casals and the Indian pacifist Gandhi and yet these two sets of people have very little in common. On the one hand, 'nationalism' is a collective feeling linked to a cultural mould. It is the members of a certain society that share a specific common history and feel that they are 'a people', with set traditions, a common language, a particular collective mentality and symbolism, which may even include their own mythology. In this first understanding of the term then, there is a love of 'a people', 'a history', 'a land' and 'a culture'. Nothing objectionable there!

On the other hand, "nationalism" can also be the deification of a country, as Fessard says, and therefore anything that goes against it must be criticised, rejected and even eliminated for being insolent and irreverent. Nationalism then becomes like the ancient forms of religion, with a critical and almost non-existent spirit. Humanity is suddenly divided into three groups: (1) the members of the 'nation',

(2) the enemies of it, and (3) the members of other nations allied to it or irrelevant to it. You only have to have a drink in some nationalist areas in order to understand this paranoiac division of humanity. This form of nationalism uses and abuses myths. The more mythical its history, the more its nationalist spirit becomes inflamed because of its bigoted nature. On the other hand, the more realistic its history, the more disappointing it proves for its nationalist spirit, because the historical appears to be too concrete, particular and arguable. In fact, the nationalist mind tends to convert the historical into the mythical, and will resist, even forcefully, any historical revisions that question the established myth.

This last type of nationalism has time and again led to violence over the last century. On many occasions, it has been the type of violence that breaks out among groups that do not belong to the ruling party (the IRA in Northern Ireland, ETA in the Basque Country, the Independent Movement in Corsica, or the Zionist movement in Palestine before 1948). On other occasions it might be orchestrated by those in power (Francoism in Spain, Nazism in Germany, Fascism in Italy and Japan, Imperialism in the USA, Argentina during the Falklands War, and Israel since 1948). The path towards violence has gone through the following stages:

1. Faced with the complexity of their historical reality, a group (a large group) chooses to simplify it by reducing it to the terms of 'nation', 'country', 'people', 'land', 'culture', or 'race', interchangeable terms which can be used to create a simplified form of speech;
2. The historical reality is then read according to one of these categories (for example, 'nation'), in such a way that everything becomes dependent on and interpreted through that category;
3. Anything that refuses to be subject to this scheme of thought is seen as the enemy ('anti-Spanish', 'anti-Basque', 'anti-Catalonian', 'anti-American', ...); and
4. The enemy must disappear. This is where violence starts. It is justified as a necessary evil in the service of the divine 'nation'.

The worst type of enemy of this nationalism is not its opposing group (for example, Spanish nationalism against Catalonian nationalism, or Corsican against French nationalism), but rather the individual or group that tries to form bridges between the two extremes believing that a peaceful and dual coexistence is possible. The other extreme only serves to reaffirm the nationalist philosophy, since according to the dialectic, opposites are identical. The existence of one defines and confirms the existence of the other, while the bridge questions the whole philosophy of nationalism because it rejects its ideology.

Nationalism also has a serious problem of tending towards imperialism. In the first instance, nationalism is usually defensive and self-justifying, or centrifugal which seems to say, "We have the right to self-determination because we are a people". It is a legitimate right: a human collective with cultural and historical maturity has the right to govern itself. In a second instance, nationalism becomes offensive and imperialist. The nation is so great, or needs to be so great, that it must devour its surrounding territories to give it room to breathe. Nationalist expansion is not always territorial; sometimes it is simply social; it tends to sweep aside the social groups that don't agree with it, even within the confines of a democracy.

Is Diversity Impossible?

It seems that social and cultural diversity is not possible then. It seems that Muslims and Hindus, Jews and Palestinians, Basques and Spanish, Irish and British, Serbs and Croats, Kurds and Iraqis, Tsutsis and Hutus, Flemish and French-speaking, Russian and Lithuanian cannot live together in the same land. A nationalist friend of mine once said to me: "it is historically proven (!) that two different languages cannot coexist in the same society; as time passes, one will devour the other". Aside from the fact that this said friend had obviously travelled very little around the world, he suddenly came to an immediate conclusion to this false premise: "so if the other language does not devour ours, we should be one step ahead and attack it first". And my friend went on to do this as best he could.

Now, let's look at the opposite argument, that diversity is possible. All of human history has seen itself bathed in cultural and social diversity. This is not only due to its frequent migratory movements (have a quick glance at the geographical origins of your own four grandparents and that of your eight great-grandparents, and draw your own conclusions), but also because it would be absurd to speak of 'one culture'. The more you insist upon this, the more pathetic your discourse will sound. 'Culture' does exist as an aspect of humanity, but can we speak of 'one culture'? If we were to spend some time talking about people who supposedly belong to 'the same culture', we would be overwhelmed by the great cultural diversity among them, which is a great part of the human condition.

Social Exclusion: You're Not One of Us

The rejection of diversity has led to many forms of social exclusion. The historical examples are numerous. We are so used to it now, that it already seems normal to us. We see in our society various social groups that have few opportunities of advancing themselves in life, but we don't react: the Haitians in the Dominican Republic, the Koreans in Japan, the Bosnians in Spain, the Kurds in Germany, the Christians in Algeria, black people in the USA, Catholics in Northern Ireland, or those who have lost their caste in India. In all of these places there are clear 'social frontiers', physically invisible, but more real than a simple customs check at the airport. It is clear to me who 'my people' are, and I work with them. We support each other. If anyone who is not one of ours should ask for help, we answer them with the unspoken words or attitude that says: 'You're not one of us', and the communication ends there.

This has been one of the main causes of violence in the last century, that is, defence of the social frontier by those who are 'inside' the system, and the attack against this system by those who are on the 'outside'. Those who are inside live in certain comfort, luxury even. They are afraid to lose what they have, to lose what they are, as we already mentioned. It was fear that kept the whites together in South Africa during the decades of *apartheid*, and it is that same fear that Europeans are starting to feel now when faced with the arrival of immigrants. Violence is used to block their way through into the system, while those on the outside fear death by starvation and may resort to violence to bring down the social barrier once and for all, in this way gaining access to the comforts on the inside of the system.

"You are not one of us". How is it possible that a human being could say such a thing? How is it possible to use the word 'you' as a form of rejection, and 'us' as a form of exclusion? The word 'you' was originally used to reveal the openness of the human spirit, and to show that humanity cannot exist without love and that this love cannot exist without otherness. The word 'us' serves to unite this diversity into one whole, in such a way that no individual is excluded from it, but instead is made possible through it. It is sad when the words 'you' and 'us' are used to make shameful social barriers.

The Schizophrenic Nature of Democracy

It is thought that democracy is a form of protection against violence, usually against the arbitrary aggression of one group towards another. In the democratic system, every citizen is equal before the law and wrongful violence is punished with imprisonment. But democracy has a schizophrenic nature because, while it goes under the guise of pacifism, it wears the uniform of combat every day. Does anybody doubt that the USA is a democracy? Is anybody still unaware at this stage of the involvement of North-American governments in the upkeep of horrific dictatorships that lasted for decades throughout the world (Asia, South America, Israel against the Palestinians ...), or in the big business that is the arms industry, including the manufacture of landmines? Does anyone doubt that France is a democracy? And does anyone still not know about the role of French governments in the horror that transformed the face of the African continent?

Democracies have many sins to confess when it comes to violence. It is not true that violence was provoked by totalitarian regimes alone. Democracies have also participated in violence, they have shamelessly supported dictatorial regimes and made weapons deals with the most bloodthirsty governments. The respect of human rights is not a primary concern in democracies, but rather seen as beneficial to the enrichment of the country, or even of just one social sector of the country. We therefore live in schizophrenic democracies, which are like something out of horror films, humanist by day, bloodthirsty by night. We are all aware of it, we all see it, but only a few people speak out against it, in particular, some Western Christian groups and also several non-governmental organisations. If anyone dares to speak on this in the political forum, he is thrown aside with all the power and means of social communication, such as was the case with the Communist Julio Anguita, one of the few Spanish politicians of recent times who refused to let himself be devoured by the system.

The great danger of democracy is that which Fessard points out in relation to reason, class and nation: self-deification. Democracy sets itself up as the last step towards human progress. Any alternative to it is accused of being regressive and anti-democratic. This self-divinisation of the system allows it to carry out violence without leaving itself open to hardly any criticism at all. Following September 11th, President George W. Bush said with his usual simplicity: "In the war against 'international terrorism', anyone who is not with us, is against us". So, the USA and Great Britain can bomb any corner of the world and can even openly support terrible politicians like Ariel Sharon, and call it the 'democratic struggle against international terrorism'; in contrast, al Qaeda does the same and we simply call this 'terrorism'. What is the difference?

The Final Step: Genocide, The Total Elimination of the Other

Genocide is the ultimate degree of violence. It is the total elimination of the 'other'. It responds to the idea of "let's finish off everyone in this group" without exception (a race, a people, or a religion). In the domain of violence, the 'other' which must be destroyed could refer to a person or a group, in the same way that the destructive 'I' as well as being one person could also refer to a group. Genocide brings about the complete eradication of the 'other' as an individual: instead the individual 'other' melts into the collective 'other'. One no longer sees Isaac M., but instead one sees 'a Jew', and says, "Jews are all the same to me". I make the whole group guilty of a series of wrongs they are supposed to have committed against me. Every member of this group is guilty, whether potentially so or by their actions. Everyone must suffer the penalty that I have chosen for them. Neither does it matter if one of these individuals is not even aware of being a member of this collective: I know it, and that's all that matters.

Many Jews in Nazi Germany did not feel Jewish, just like many of those who were murdered in Stalin's USSR, or more recently in Algeria, or Latin America. They did not feel part of this group which was being condemned. Genocide is about 'finishing everybody off' and if this isn't practical, hurting them as much as possible so that the group will not be able to recover quickly. Particular cruelty is usually shown towards the weakest, because they are the ones who are capable of stirring the most sensitivity in the other side: women, even pregnant ones, children, babies, the elderly. There is a need to make people suffer, and not just kill them, such as was the case with the acts of sadism carried out by the Nazi, Serbian, and Latin American militaries.

Contrary to what one would expect, acts of genocide are rarely based on decisions made in the heat of the moment, as was the case with the killing of Sikhs by Hindus in India following the assassination of Indira Gandhi. On the contrary, they arise from coldly taken decisions, or important meetings where the only item on the agenda is exterminating the 'enemy'.

We usually see genocide as an attack against our very spirit and yet, it is no more than a logical consequence of thought patterns which we openly accept every day. In our daily behaviour we shamelessly divide the world into 'my people', 'my enemies', and 'those I'm not bothered about'. Once we accept this pattern of thought, as we have seen, the discourse which justifies the well being of 'my people' follows, as does that which justifies the opposite for my enemies.

In order to support this mentality, the American industry produces dozens of films each year that monotonously divide 'goodies' and 'baddies', films that are seen in all the continents of the world. In such films, violence committed by the bad people is shown to be unjustifiable, while violence committed by the good people is more than justified. This desire to make all the 'baddies' disappear is at the root of the paranoiac and genocidal mind which flourished in the likes of Hitler, Stalin, Pol Pot, Reagan, Milosevic, Karadzic and George W. Bush.

Conclusion: Today's Oversights, Tomorrow's Wars

The violence of the twentieth century has overtaken us in many ways and, at the same time, originated in our own hearts. It has 'overtaken' us because it has spilled out into the domain of 'high politics' in some cases, (such as in the post-colonial distribution of territories), in which we feel we have hardly any influence. It 'originated in our hearts' because politics often puts into practice what its citizens feel. Let's not deceive ourselves, if there is genocide in the world it's because we are 'anonymous genocidal people' on the inside. If not, why do we consume so many violent films and support so many warlike competitive sports? If not, why do we identify ourselves so often with a group and desire the weakening or disappearance of this group's supposed enemies?

Many of the violent phenomenon of the last one hundred years have been the consequence of previous forgotten incidents. When an obvious historical injustice is overlooked or forgotten, with the ridiculous excuse that time heals all wounds, what actually happens over time is that people attempt to avenge the injustice through violence. Who were those 'privileged minds' that drew up the post-colonial division between the Tsutsis and Hutus in the Great Lakes Region or who in Washington, London or Paris invented countries on a map? Whose brilliant mind decided that capital and capitalists from the North could travel all over the world, while the workers from the South would have to beg their way to Europe or the USA, and with no permission to enter when they got there either? Who decided that humanity should be classified into races based on skin colour? Who decided that people should be classified according to nationality? Perhaps it's more important to have a passport than to be a person.

Human history is a path full of forgotten things, oversights, and injustices that offer false promises of a better tomorrow. It is like a land that has been fertilised to produce acts of future violence through the compulsion to exact revenge. As I said at the beginning of this study, I am aware that I am both ignorant of and perplexed by the absurd nature of violence. However, I, like many others agree that the only way to avoid or to reduce violence in the future is by actively working for the social and economic well being of all those who are part of the current history of humanity, and by sowing the seeds for a culture of universal fraternity as a way of overcoming today's culture that divides humanity into opposing groups. I make a point of saying universal fraternity, and not uniformity. I am not attacking diversity, but rather giving my support to the peaceful and harmonious co-existence of diversity. It is true that I am not saying anything new here. In fact, man was created to live like this. At least, that is my belief and my faith.

Works Cited

Keane, J. *Reflexiones sobre la violencia.* Madrid: Alianza, 2000, 110. (Original: *Reflections on Violence*, 1996).

Ellacuría, I. *Teología Política.* El Salvador: Ediciones del Secretariado Social Interdiocesano, San Salvador, , 1973, 94

Fessard, G. *De l'actualité historique,* Vol. I, Desclée de Brouwer, 1960, 122.

Galtung, J. *Essays in Peace Research,* Vol. I, *Peace: Research, Education, Action,* Copenhagen: Christian Ejlers, 1975, 111.

UNDP *Human Development Report 2001*, Chapter 1.

6

Functions of Violence

A Study of Caste Violence in David Davidar's *The House of Blue Mangoes*

P.K. KALYANI

At the very outset of the article a proposition has to be registered: no society is free of all manifestations of violence. There would obviously be a consensus on this point. Violence is ubiquitous and its roots are penetrative as well as pervasive in a society. Therefore, it would be simplistic to believe that violence can be rooted out from a society. One cannot but agree with Ralph Dahrendorf who emphatically says, "Conflict can be temporarily suppressed, regulated, channeled and controlled but ... neither a philosopher-king nor a modern dictator can abolish it once and for all" (Dahrendorf, 1959: 159). This statement of Dahrendorf has been expounded by Francis Abraham in his book titled *Modern Sociological Theory: An Introduction*. He says, "Social conflicts are inherent in the very nature of social organisation; they cannot be eliminated altogether, only their expressions in specific contexts can be resolved ...." (Abraham, 1982: 112). Driven to this sort of a *cul de sac*, one can only try to find out the positive aspects of this inevitable social phenomenon. This does not mean that violence should be encouraged. It is only that one is trying to snatch a glimpse of the silver lining of the clouds looming large above the head.

Before proceeding any further, it becomes imperative to draw an operative definition for the term violence. There is no dearth of definitions for this term and it is this surfeit of meanings that precisely poses the problem in studying the concept of violence. From among the proliferation of literature on the subject, Mackenzie's definition would be kept in the focus of the present analysis. In his book titled *Power, Violence, Decision*, Mackenzie defines violence as " the exercise of physical force so as to inflict injury on, or cause damage to persons or property; action or conduct characterised by this; treatment or usage tending to cause bodily injury or forcibly interfering with personal freedom" (Mackenzie, 1975: 39). This definition is focused on the physical violence – that is, manifested violence, as the social critics would call the same. These critics also hasten to say that there is yet another type of violence namely, psychological violence, which is hard to be tested empirically and which is as harmful as physical violence, if not more. Further, psychological violence, though it has a separate plane of occurrence, also accompanies physical violence. In the present analysis of David Davidar's *The House of Blue Mangoes*, both these types of violence would be taken into consideration, though separate spaces have not been provided for each category.

Having formed the operational framework of the term 'violence' for the present study, the functions of violence have to be identified. There would, no doubt, be universal agreement on the point that violence is essentially destructive. However, social critics like Marx, Sorel, Frantz Fanon and others have identified violence as an important catalyst for desirable changes in society. As far back as the 1930s Lenin opined that the liberation of the oppressed class is impossible without a violent revolution because it requires the destruction of the apparatus of state power which has been created by the ruling class and which is the embodiment of the alienation of the working classes from the mainstream.

Violence also performs a cathartic function. Violence erupts when there is an oppression of the ruled by the ruling, the powerless by the powerful, whatever the context be. Any oppression/suppression mounts tension on both sides, which at one point of time would naturally find an outlet. Whether the oppressed take control or not, an outbreak would give the oppressed an occasion to purge their pent up emotions. This cathartic effect provided by violence is identified as yet another function of violence.

In this article, these two functions of the social phenomenon of violence are to be studied with reference to the caste violence as portrayed in *The House of Blue Mangoes*.

Davidar's *The House of Blue Mangoes* has been chosen for the analysis for varied reasons. First and foremost, it is a novel that depicts conflict and violence in various contexts as they occur in a society: at home, in politics and in the society. The canvas wherein violence has been painted is a large one. Even the nature that provides the backdrop for the narration bears the colours of violence. The blue mangoes that give an identity to the Dorais is a riot of colours – a mixture of brilliant blue and glossy green tinged with golden orange. The river that ran across the town is called Chevathar – red river. It symbolise the river of blood that was to run through the town soon. Even dawn, which is the most serene part of a day was not spared of the touch of violence. The novel opens with the following sentences: "Spring 1899. As the ordinary violence of dawn sweeps across the lower Coromandal coast, a sprawling village comes into view. The turbulent sky excepted, everything about it is calm" (3). The dawn that is described is a specific dawn in Chevathar, where a celebration was to take place later that day. Festival or not, the violence at dawn portended the heinous outburst that was to shock the people soon; and which, thereafter, would lead to a series of violent events. The apparent calm of the Chevathar community had been disturbed so vehemently and intensely that the ripples it created would continue for generations. The specific dawn is indicative of certain facts: violence is natural and could occur anytime, even during occasions of celebrations; violence is in the dawn, which is the harbinger of hope, future and happiness; it is between the extremes of violence and peace that the society finds its balance; and finally, it is through the violent dawn that the sprawling village is exposed.

Therefore, as mentioned above, in view of the large canvas the novel *The House of Blue Mangoes* provides for an elaborate discussion, the same has been chosen to prove that violence does have a positive facet, that is, it serves as catharsis and catalyst. Among the various types of violence portrayed in the novel, the one related to caste has been chosen for study, as it is the pivotal point of narration.

Chevathar was a small town located on the banks of the river Chevathar from which the town drew its name. Like any other town in India, Chevathar had various caste groups. The two dominant castes of Chevathar were the Andavar and the Vedhar, besides several other numerically thin castes like the Parayan. The Andavars and the Vedhars "had a history of strife". For about generations, the Dorai family, which belonged to the Andavar community, had kept caste violence out of the village.

The last strife that struck the town was the Breast War of 1859. The Breast War or the breast clothes controversy "marked the culmination of an especially vicious phase in the caste struggle in the deep South" (16). The epicentre of the controversy was Travancore and the ripples lashed the neighbouring towns of the Madras Presidency. In *The House of Blue Mangoes,* war has been framed within the fictitious towns of Kilanadu and Tinnevelly. At the time of the infamous war there were three major castes namely, "the brahmins, the non-brahmins and those beyond the pale" (17), in Chevathar. For quite sometime, the resistance of the brahmin caste by the non-brahmins like the Andavar and Nadar, had been brewing in Chevathar.

> One of the social customs to be challenged was the dress: hitherto tradition had ordained that the various members of the caste tree should bare their breasts as a sign of difference. Accordingly the untouchables went bare-breasted before the Pallans, the Pallans before the Nairs and so on until the Namboothiri Brahmins who deferred only to their deities. (17)

It was also a time when the Christian missionaries were promoting concepts like equality, which, in a way, awakened the sense of dignity in the non-brahmins, which they never had enjoyed till then, and also, kindled an urge in them to resist the oppressive forces. At the urge of the Christian missionaries the women of the lower castes began to cover their breasts. This led to an outbreak of violence when the men from the upper castes, unleashed torture and humiliation on the women of the depressed castes in public. An upper caste landlord "wrenched the blouse of a pretty Andavar woman who had recently converted to Christianity", declaring that "we have a divine right to gaze upon your filthy breasts and you should be flattered that we do so. They are ours to enjoy. Whatever benefits your new faith bestows upon you, this is not one of them" (17). Such outrageous acts of the men of the upper caste, gave rise to riots in the town. In Kilanadu, the Andavar women were disrobed by the men of the Vedhar community. "Retribution was swift. A band of Andavar toughs went on the rampage, looting and burning houses in the Vedhar quarter" (19). As if another link to this chain of violence, in the nearby town of Nagercoil, a mob of men armed with weapons attacked the Christian Andavars by "burning and looting and stripping the breast clothes and bodices of the women" and the Andavar men retaliated. After immeasurable humiliation and bloodshed in various quarters, the situation was brought under control by the British Governor, by prohibiting the stripping of women.

The Breast War provided an outlet for the affected communities like Andavar and Nadar, which were seething with anger at their humiliation. The violent infamous war had to be fought to thwart the custom that had taken a very deep root in the tradition. Since the evil seeped through the communal tiers of the society, and therefore, no community being fit to set the system right, the interference of the external agency became essential to control the situation and to put an end to the humiliating practice. In this context, one cannot but recall the words of Frantz Fanon: "individuals and peoples can become whole again by participating in violent politics". Violence, according to him, is "a cleansing force" (73).

After the Breast War, Chevathar enjoyed peace for some time. Nevertheless, the place was prone to caste violence. As Max Weber opines, "castes can best be understood as status groups. A status group is a collection of individuals who share a distinctive style of life and a certain consciousness of community ... [and who] are ranked on a scale of honour" (quoted in Beteille, 59). The honour of a status group can always be challenged and this would lead to clashes between groups. And a clash could be triggered off even by a small incident. Even an object of common good, namely, the government road had to be sanctioned to use only after a struggle of violence. Even as the proposal for the road was mooted, there was stiff opposition – even from *thalaivar* Solomon himself. He anticipated not only local problems involved in the usage of the road, but also the chance of misuse of it by outsiders. Even a few of the upper class Brahmins and Vedhars began to oppose the proposal on knowing that they would not be specially privileged with a piece of road at their door step. However, finally the Government plan prevailed. Thereafter, at least for sometime, the road had been the background of violence:

> Soon after it was finished ... a group of young girls had been molested by drunken youths who had crossed the bridge and wandered into the village .... Four months later, a Parayan had been beaten almost to death by some Vedhar men, for daring to stroll through their quarter blithely smoking a beedi ... . (23)

These problems were brought before the *thalaivar* Solomon, and though with reluctance, he decreed that "everyone could use the government road without hindrance, though the polluting classes would have to comply with the rules as far as possible" and "thereafter, the road was freely used" (20).

The incidents mentioned above, provided an outlet for both the suppressed anger and the disappointment of the various sections of the Chevathar community. The incidents provided the *thalaivar*, Andavars, Vedhars and other members of Chevathar, to feel the satisfaction of having predicted the consequence of the road. However, the matter was not allowed to slip out of the hands of the *thalaivar*, irrespective of his not favouring the road. Being the *thalaivar*, much against his wish, he had to give the fair judgement of permitting everyone to use the road.

The apparent calm in Chevathar, nevertheless, contained a lurking disquiet. There was a heaving enmity between the Andavars and the Vedhars, and the pressure of the same, for ever tried to find an outlet. This situation was exploited by Vakeel Perumal. The Vakeel had a couple of reasons to trigger off the clash. He had the vested interest to promote himself to a significant position in the village; and secondly, he wanted to avenge the Vedhars for humiliating the Andavar men who tried to enter the temple. Therefore, he hired a few men from the neighbouring village to create tension between the two communities on the Panguni Uthiram day, when the village celebrated the festival.

However, the plan misfireds, as it resulted in the molestation of Valli, a girl belonging to the Andavar community, and thereafter the situation went beyond his control. Also, the warning about the possibility of the recurrence of the Breast War humiliation did not carry the anticipated results, since both Solomon Dorai and Muthu Vedhar exercised great restraint:

> Vakeel Perumal had never meant to have Valli molested. It was a Vedhar woman the thugs had been hired to terrorise in retaliation for the attack on the Andavars at the temple. Once the deed was done, the lawyer was sure the tension between the two groups would run so high that it would be easy for a man of his genius to turn it to his advantage. But it hadn't worked. He might still have salvaged the situation but things had continued to go wrong. Nothing had come of his idea of painting the incendiary message on Anaikal. (47)

As a self-promoter when the attempt on the Panguni Uthiram day failed, Vakeel Perumal tried to instigate a clash based on religion. Before the Chitira Pournami, the next festival that was celebrated grandly in Chevathar, Vakeel Perumal converted to Christianity with a cunning plan. Also, with a heinous intention, he consecrated a small shrine of Christ opposite his house on the other side of the road. On the Chitira Pournami festival day he blocked the path of the procession by putting up a pandal across the road connecting the Christian shrine and his house. This led to the most violent outbreak in Chevathar after the Breast War. Though, even in this attempt he failed to achieve his motive of turning the outbreak to his advantage, it led to a major violent outbreak that destroyed Chevathar.

A fierce fight exploded involving Solomon Dorai, Muthu Vedhar and Vakeel Perumal, consequent to the blocking of the road by the latter. Solomon Dorai was avenged by Muthu Vedhar for the humiliation he suffered in the panchayat meeting because of Dorai. On the orders of Solomon Dorai, the *thalaivar*, Vakeel Perumal left Chevathar before sunset. The infamous Vakeel was thus eliminated from the village once and for all. However, Muthu Vedhar and Solomon Dorai continued to challenge and vowed to do away with each other shortly.

After simmering, when riots ravaged the nearby towns, tension escalated once again in Chevathar. Muthu Vedhar, through a messenger, gave an ultimatum to Solomon Dorai that he "should leave the village by sun down on 15 June or he would feel the wrath of the Vedhars"; and the same messenger returned with a similar ultimatum from Solomon: "... if Muthu was in Chevathar after 15 June he would regret it" (70). Thereafter, there was no turning back for either men.

For the last sixty-four years, a rivalry between the leading family – the Dorais – and the one that challenged it for supremacy, namely, the Vedhars, existed and as the Collector commented, "They lived together for generations, grumbling away like an old couple, and occasionally there'll be a little scuffle that allows both sides to let off steam" (79). Further, "Muthu is not the only problem. A general sorrow has come over the land. Drought, taxes, unrest. It seems as though the evening of the world is upon us ..." (89), As Solomon rightly concluded there were many other reasons for the prevailing tension. The people must purge themselves of all these pent up emotions. They were propelled towards a bloody fight in the pretext of the outward reasons. The long heaving animosity between the two individuals and their people, had reached maximum intensity, and must now explode and purge itself ramifying into a class war, through which either of them could freshly establish his supremacy.

Muthu Vedhar experienced a satisfaction even as the preparations were on for the ultimate fight, blinding him totally to the impending disaster not only for others but even for himself. His thirst for power and revenge was unquenchable so much so that he did not even think remotely of a possible defeat. He engaged the Marudhars of the nearby villages who were known for their blind ferocity – "fighters hungry for loot. Marudhars didn't fight for principle. All that fuelled them was greed" (97). For Solomon too, it was a matter of prestige. He had to retain the dignity and position handed down to him by his predecessors. Therefore, he also started his preparation. He got about forty men trained in *silambu attam*, the traditional stickfight. It is certain that tension built up in Solomon and it became evident in the way he kicked the servant, which he had never done before, and picked on Daniel, his son, for not fighting well in spite of Joshua's pleading that he would teach him: " The impending battle was getting on to him" (98).

The ulterior motive for the fight between Andavars and the Vedhars was political – a fight between two the individuals to capture power. In this fight, many innocent lives were lost; and neither side fought a fair battle, since the hired/trained fighters had no personal involvement in the fight. Worst of all, the personal fight between the two individuals finally developed into a caste war.

> With the exception of a couple of Marudhars, none of the men fought professionally or for gain and certainly not to death …. Peace had prevailed in Chevathar for two decades and most of the men were not prepared for war. Their brief training melted away and with an undisciplined desperation the men slashed at each other with aruvals and silambus, determined only to live at whatever cost. (105)

The Marudhar chief who fought on behalf of the Vedhar was trapped and vanquished by a clever strategy of Aron, Solomon's younger son. Though the Andavars trapped the enemy, in the fight, their *thalaivar* Solomon was killed. The ultimate result of the war was the disintegration of the Chevathar town. Vedhars and most of the Andavars left Chevathar. Instead of Aron or Daniel taking control over as the *thalaivar*, it was Abraham, the good-for-nothing brother of Solomon who became the occupant of Solomon's house and position. Under his stewardship Chevathar gradually lost its importance, which, after a decade Daniel restored with all dignity. However, this decade of deterioration seemed to be needed to make both Andavars and Vedhars to realise the importance of peace.

Lewis Coser in his book *The Functions of Social Conflict* discusses two types of conflicts, namely, realistic conflicts and non-realistic conflicts. To quote him:

> Conflicts which arise from frustration of specific demands within the relationship and from estimates of gains of the participants, and which are directed at the presumed frustrating object, can be called *realistic* conflicts, in so far as they are means towards a specific result. *Non-realistic* conflicts, on the other hand, although still involving interaction between two or more persons, are not

occasioned by the rival ends of the antagonists, but by the need for tension release of at least one of them. In this case the choice of antagonists depends on determinants not directly related to a continuous issue and is not oriented toward the attainment of specific results. (Coser, 1956: 49)

The caste violence unleashed on the Chitira Pournami day is both a realistic conflict as well as a non-realistic one. The violence was triggered of by Vakeel Perumal to let of the steam he had contained regarding the humiliation of some Andavar men in the Murugan temple. When the initial attempt failed Vakeel set out once again with more determination mixed with his thirst for recognition in the new place. As with Muthu Vedhar, he had to take the challenge thrown by Solomon Dorai; and as with Solomon Dorai, he had to guard the peace of the village, being the *thalaivar*. But for the Vakeel initiating or rather baiting them into the fight, both Muthu and Solomon would not have cared for a violent fight of the magnitude of the one fought. And also there was a general deterioration, a general frustration in Chevathar due to non-personal reasons. As Solomon rightly foresaw, the death of the girl, which happened at a sensitive time would bring trouble:

> Happening as it did, in an anxious time, in an idle time, before the fields could be prepared, in a desperate time when the entire land simmered with frustration and hate, her death transformed her from an insignificant girl without affiliation ... into a weapon that would deepen the division and rancour within the village. (42–43)

The caste war fought on 6 June 1899, gave a separate individual identity to Abraham, Charity, Aron and Daniel. Abraham is the younger brother of Solomon Dorai. He hardly finds a place in the history of Chevathar till the outbreak. In the caste violence, when Solomon was killed, Abraham took over as the *thalaivar*, since there was no one to take the responsibility. Aron disappeared from the scene for a while and Daniel was least lured by the beckoning of power. Also, Daniel had been sent away to Nagercoil by Solomon when the former declined to fight the war. Abraham as *thalaivar* was of no match to Solomon. Though the village was free from the tensions that prevailed at the time of Solomon, Abraham could not deliver the goods. The very house where he now lived and which was a symbol of pride was in "an advanced state of despair".

Charity, wife of Solomon was a mute participant in the caste violence. "Charity Dorai was a beautiful woman. Fair in a land where the paleness of a woman's complexion outweighed every other attribute, it was expected that she would make a good marriage and she did" (10). She was a good wife, who even mutely accepted the occasional beating by the husband and reared the children and tended the elders and guest. Her identity was thus a limited one. She had no role to play in the decision making in the family.

The caste violence brought drastic changes in Charity. She took control of the household matters including monetary affairs as well as the education of the children and their marriages. She metamorphosed into a rock on which her children could lean upon in times of despair. When Chevathar was redeemed by her son, she stood with him through thick and thin. She carved her own identity without basking in the glory of her son.

Aron, the second son of Solomon had already made his mark even during his father's time. He had been the symbol of hope for his father. When he jumped the big well as the only person to do so other than his uncle, he became the pride of the Dorais. He was very good in *silambu attam* and fought for his father, along with him and his uncle in the caste war of 1899. In fact, it was possible to overthrow the enemy because of a strategy well devised and executed by Aron and his friends. After the caste war was over, Aron's interests extended itself to national politics. Identifying his ability, ferocity and sincerity, freedom fighters like Iyyer came looking for him specifically, and to get him participate in the national war of independence; and as for Aron, "... he thrilled to the idea of fighting for a cause, no matter that he didn't understand" (132) He travelled wide and took up various activities towards the cause of the national independence. He "repeated a simple oath, affirming that his own life was a small price to pay to free Mother India" (155). It only seems fitting that the most promising of the Dorai family was sacrificed for freeing Mother India.

Daniel was the eldest son of Solomon. Muthu Vedhar had envied Solomon when this son was born to him, as he would become the *thalaivar* after Solomon, the third consecutive *thalaivar* in the Dorai family. But as the boy grew up Solomon felt ashamed of him: "As he glared at the youth standing before him, his eyes reflected his disappointment: those thin wrists, that narrow hairless chest, the stooped bearing, the large expressive eyes that wouldn't have looked out of place in a woman. Was this really his son?" (99). When Daniel declined to fight, Solomon sent him away to his grandfather's house along with his mother. And this, in a way, provided Daniel with the opportunity to establish his identity. He became a doctor as he wished to be and his fame travelled far and wide with his invention of Dr *Dorai' Moonwhite Thylam*. He became the pride of Charity, his mother. Chris Cooke, the Sub-Collector who knew Daniel as a small boy, on seeing the mark he had made as a young man makes a pertinent observation: "How the serious young boy he remembered had grown! His face and bearing had acquired gravity, his manner was confident. He looked every inch the wealthy upper class Indian gentleman that he was" (182).

Aron had been the hope of Solomon, but he did not live up to his father's expectations. On the other hand, it was Daniel, whom Solomon was ashamed of, who recovered the lost glory of Chevathar. The new Chevathar that Daniel built on the debris of the caste war was unique in many ways. Though Daniel had resurrected the village all by himself, and though he was the elder son, the natural inheritor of the position of *thalaivar*, he did not stake his claim to the position. Instead, he made the village elder, whom he appointed as thalaivar when he dismissed Abraham, continue in the position, and Ramdoss, the brother-in-law of Daniel, supported the elder man in all matters as an assistant. Further, "To run the settlement, Daniel constituted a committee of elders drawn from the twenty-three founding families" (214), with him as the chairman. The Committee framed the rules to run the settlement. He banned politics in Chevathar lest he lost more members of his family, like he lost Aron. This was a crucial decision in the wake of the intensifying independence struggle. However, he could not ban caste as he wished. When his proposition to drop caste suffix on all occasions except in the rituals of birth, marriage and death, was not received favourably, he did not thrust it on the people. Instead, he decided to do so with regard to the close members of his family. Daniel was democratic when he accepted the majority opinion. This evolution of democracy in the hitherto autocratic administration of Chevathar has to be commented.

The caste war brought the brothers closer. Indeed it was this war that dispersed the family. It took Solomon's life, estranged Solomon and Daniel, Daniel and Aron and exiled Charity with her daughters and Daniel from the village. Aron's contempt for Daniel and Daniel's estrangement from Aron was set right a few years after the war, when each had made his mark as an individual. When the brothers shared what each of them had gone through, on the eve of Aron's death in the prison, the differences melted away, giving way to a new strong bond between them, which helped Daniel to redeem Chevathar. It was Aron's last wish that Daniel went back to Chevathar: "You should go back, anna, take our family to where we belong" (198). Chevathar from where he was sent away by his father, was re-founded by Daniel: "'I will recover it for you, Aron' he vowed. 'I will recover it for all of us'" (199). Not only that he made it big in his ambition, but also re-established the name of the Dorais with more pomp and glory.

Georg Simmel, discussing conflict to group affiliation, lays emphasis on the positive role of conflict in enhancing better relationship. In fact, he points out that conflict itself is indicative of interactions, unifications and organisation. To quote Simmel:

> Conflict is admitted to cause or modify interest groups, unifications, organizations .... If every interaction among men is a sociation, conflict – after all one of the most vivid interactions, which, furthermore cannot possibly be carried on by one individual alone – must certainly be considered as sociation. And in fact, dissociating factors – hate, envy, need, desire – are the causes of the conflict; it breaks out because of them. Conflict is thus designed to resolve divergent dualisms; it is a way of achieving some kind of unity, even if it be through the annihilation of one of the conflicting parties .... Conflict itself resolves the tension between contrasts. The fact that it aims at peace is only one. An especially obvious, expression of its nature: the synthesis of elements that work both against and for one another. (Simmel, 1955: 13)

The Chevathar that Daniel had reconstructed was obviously the synthesis of divergent dualisms of the earlier town. It was re-built on the annihilation not only of one of the conflicting parties, but all the four parties involved in the violence – the one which set it alight namely, Vakeel Perumal, the two major parties who stood confronting each other namely, the Andavars and the Vedhars, and the one which was forced to conform to one side or the other like the Marudhars for material gains and Charity and Daniel because of emotional bond. In other words, out of the ashes of the old community of Chevathar a new one emerged with greater vitality. This new town survived for a couple of decades, and even before the simmering conflicts could explode as it happened in Solomon's town, Kannan, son of Daniel and the inheritor of the House of Blue Mangoes, took control of the town, by diplomatically negotiating with the dissociating factors.

From the foregoing discussion certain inferences could be made. The caste violence portrayed in *The House of Blue Mangoes* has performed both the cathartic function as well as the catalystic function. Whenever the society or the individual was heaving with suppressed emotion as it happened in the case of Vakeel, Solomon, Muthu and Aron, they had let their steam off through caste violence. It had been indeed an annihilating experience. Nevertheless, the emerging discontentment and frustration would have naturally found an outlet. The best that was achieved in such a situation in the novel was the resurrection of Chevathar with greater integration and internal solidarity.

The discussion may be wound up with a quotation from Abraham, "It does not make sense to ask if conflict is good or bad, rather we should ask which conflict, with what consequences, and for whom. Conflict can contribute as much to social integration and stability as to disintegration and change; it may disrupt or restore equilibrium" (Abraham, 1982: 112).

Works Cited

Abraham, Francis. *Modern Sociological Theory: An Introduction.* New Delhi: OUP, 1982.

Beteille, Andre. "Caste and Social Status." *Tribe, Caste and Religion in India.* Ed. Romesh Thapar. New Delhi: Macmillan, 1977.

Coser, Lewis. *The Functions of Sociological Conflicts*. New York: Free Press, 1956.

Dahrendrof, Ralph. *Class and Class Conflict in Industrial Society*. Stanford: Stanford University Press, 1959.

Davidar, David. *The House of Blue Mangoes*. New Delhi: Viking, 2002

Fanon, Frantz. *Wretched of the Earth*. London: MacGibbon 1965.

Mackenzie, W.J.M. *Power, Violence, Decision*. London: Penguin, 1975.

Simmel, Georg. *Conflict and the Web of Group Affiliations*. Glencoe: Free Press, 1955.

7

Terrorism and Violence
Chitra Banerjee Divakaruni's *Queen of Dreams* and Kiran Desai's *The Inheritance of Loss*

T.S. ANAND AND MANJINDER KAUR

It may sound trite to reiterate but it is an undeniable fact that violence is ubiquitous. It could be in any form of protest, retaliation, injustice or repression; as an instrument for the furtherance of a nation's hegemony or protection of its sovereignty; and for the assertion of state control or meeting insurgency related challenges. Violence can be engineered by state against its citizens and encouraged by religious denominations. Violence is also perpetuated by the ideologies of racism, sexism and classism. There is violence in media, art and literature, at work place, in schools and in hospitals. We see violence in interpersonal relationships at the domestic front, within families, against women, children and old persons and at larger arenas of interaction, occurring in all settings – urban and rural, modern or traditional, well-educated sections or illiterate, and in rich or poor. Manjit Singh and D.P Singh remark:

> Violence, in general, is about power to control, subjugate and dominate others. It is about the power that violates dignity, integrity and sovereignty of individuals and nations. It is the power that denies the right to individuals or groups to exist as they wish and to oppress them. The context can be that of gender

relations, intra-nation relations and international relation violence and collective violence. (Singh & Singh, 2008: 7)

One of the worst forms of violence that the world is encountering today is terrorist violence because it is damaging to the psyche of the society as a whole; it generates fear, and cripples the entire political system. Terrorism is executed through organised campaigns with the help of seductive, politically disenchanted and dissenting shades of opinion against the regimes. Sometimes it is due to clash of political ideologies, another time it is the volatile issue of religion or alleged persecution of the followers of a particular faith. The word 'terrorism' is politically and emotionally charged and this greatly compounds the difficulty of providing a precise definition. One 1988 study by the US Army found that over 100 definitions of the word terrorism have been used. The common definitions of terrorism refer only to those acts which are intended to create fear (terror), are perpetrated for an ideological goal, deliberately target (or disregard the safety of) non-combatants. Terrorism is neither new nor a recent phenomenon in the human society. It has existed in all ages. It has grown in form and size along with the evolution of society. But, the terrorism that we see today, abetted by technology, is heinous. The variant forms of terrorism can be classified broadly as religious terrorism, regional terrorism, political terrorism, ideological terrorism, urban terrorism and international terrorism. Religious terrorism emanates from some fanatic groups who take it upon themselves to pronounce the superiority of their religion over all the rest on the planet. This form of terrorism seeks to coerce followers of other religions into acceptance of supremacy of their religion. Regional terrorism emanates in a federal republic, where the central government serves as a nerve centre of the station, some regions or territorial entities generate a feeling of neglect and discrimination and start ventilating those feelings of neglect in the form of protest which ultimately takes the form of terrorism.

Our primary concern here is to focus on violence that emerges out of acts of terrorism at the international and national levels as it wreaks havoc on the innocent and the unarmed civilians who do not have even a remote connection with the paraphernalia of terrorism. Besides the violence generated by the acts of terrorism, other forms of violence as domestic and psychological violence as delineated in Chitra Divakaruni's *Queen of Dreams* and Kiran Desai's *The Inheritance of Loss*, are subjected to scrutiny.

Chitra Banerjee Divakaruni's *Queen of Dreams* came out in 2004 and Kiran Desai's *The Inheritance of Loss* in 2006. Both these young women writers of Indian origin settled in the USA, take up issues of violence generated by the terrorist activities in which innocent people suffer. While Desai concentrates on the Gorkha problem, Divakaruni exposes the aftermath of the 9/11 terrorist attack on World Trade Center. It is the innocent who suffer when frenzy grips the public psyche.

Divakaruni was writing the first chapter of her novel *Queen Of Dreams* when the terrorist struck the twin towers of World Trade Center on September 11, 2001. Unfortunately, this resulted in the kind of repercussions in which the hapless Indians were subjected to suspicion, distrust and hatred. In an interview to Nancy Beardsley, Divakaruni remarks:

> What made it additionally terrible was that there was a whole slew of hate crimes across the nation towards communities that looked 'like terrorists.' And the Indian American community also suffered from this. People were afraid to go out of their houses. And I wanted people to know how it felt. (December, 2004)

In the aftermath of 9/11 numerous incidents of harassment and hate crimes were reported against Middle Easterners and other "Middle Eastern-looking" people. Particularly vulnerable were the Sikhs because of their turban and beard which are stereotypically associated with Muslims in the United States. There were reports of verbal abuse, attacks on mosques and other religious buildings (including the firebombing of a Hindu temple) and assaults on people, including one murder. Balbir Singh Sodhi was fatally shot on September 15, 2001, mistaken for a Muslim. Within America and its allies, an "uninformed and unreasoning Islamophobia" began to be implanted in their national genetics.

Chitra Divakaruni's *Queen of Dreams* throws up certain issues which recur in a diasporic text. Since the primary purpose of this paper is to focus on the theme of violence, we have chosen to skirt those issues but focus only on the prevalence of violence in the novel, especially as a consequence of the storming of World Trade Centre in America which mirrored up for the entire world community the hideous contours of the global terrorism fostered by perverted religious zealots whose sole purpose is to register their nefarious presence that militates against the norms of universal humanism. In an atmosphere of confusion and uncertainty when momentary insanity blurs the distinction between the Americans of different hues, feelings of distrust and suspicion take precedence over humanitarian concerns and people begin to clutch at each other's throats like maniacs and conveniently forget that "Man liveth not by self alone, but in his brother's face." In the land of the founding fathers of America, the un-Christian practices become galore and people become dumb spectators to the gory drama enacted by their own kin. In an environment charged by mistrust and characterised by fake patriotism, inhabitants begin to question the notion of their own Americans. When one's humanity is undermined and identity is berated, one is face to face with the most eternal human dilemma – who am I?

Chitra Divakaruni felt jolted by the happenings in USA after 9/11. In an interview published in *The Sunday Statesman* on February 2, 2003, she was asked what she felt she was – an Indian, an American or an Indian living in the United States. She candidly confessed:

> I have to live with a hybrid identity. In many ways I'm an Indian, but living in America for nineteen years has taught me many things. It has helped me to look at both cultures more closely. It has taught me to observe, question and evaluate.

This is exactly the predicament of her protagonist, Rakhi in *Queen of Dreams* who too attempts to divine her identity, and like others in her inner circle of friends, has to deal with the horrifying complexities about their acculturation in the wake of September 11. The mental and physical violence that Rakhi and her inner circle encounter has been deftly delineated with objectivity and clarity of vision. Rakhi and her friends' notions of citizenship are rudely questioned by the white Americans because their only crime was the colour of their skin or the turban the men wore. Thus, under the hostile circumstances in the post-September 11 USA, Rakhi's quest for identity gains urgency. In an atmosphere surcharged with violence and precariousness, Chitra Divakaruni delves into the bonding of Rakhi and her friend Belle (Balwant Kaur) who were roommates during their freshman year at Berkeley:

> They've nursed each other through romantic troubles, failing grades, bouts of flu and the pressures that only Indian parents know to apply to their offspring. They've loaned each other money and underwear, courage and lipstick, and held each other's heads when they threw up after drinking too much at parties to which they shouldn't have gone. They've confessed to each other things that they've never dared to tell anyone before, and seen themselves newly through each other's eyes. They've stayed up nights talking about how Rakhi sometimes feels too American, how Belle would love to shed the last vestiges of her desi-ness. (*Queen of Dreams*, 15)

It is through this strong bonding that Rakhi was able to survive the trauma of divorce. In spite of Belle's wildness, Rakhi accepts her and places more trust in their friendship, though Belle is often restless, as though something is gnawing at her insides.

This attitude is closely related to the parental concern and anxiety to tie their children to their homeland and tradition on the one hand, and the children's antipathy to be tethered to the hoary tradition of their ancestors. Belle could never approve of a rustic match from their native land for her freewheeling Americanised self. The sentimental baggage which her parents carried to America, she would hate to trifle with. Probably, better educated parents of Rakhi did not burden their daughter with the sentimental crap which Belle's parents wanted to foist on her. The objective of Rakhi's parents was to fortify her mind against any gnawing sense of duality in terms of commitment to the country of her adoption. Nevertheless, Rakhi's identity is questioned in a violent manner that leaves invisible scars on her mind.

The indifference and coolness of either parents to their children or vice versa, is a muted form of violence that causes bruises, if not wounds. Belle, as outlined in the preceding lines, has severed herself from her ancestral traditions and mores of life, yet her parents in their typical simplicity keep straining to bind their daughter to their ancestral faith and way of life. This is what Belle tells her friend, Rakhi, "When I was little and didn't know any better my parents would give me an extra two dollars per week to go to the language class at the gurdwara" (82). Rakhi, on the contrary rues, "What cruel karma had placed me in the care of only two Indians who never mentioned their homeland if they could help it" (82). Belle had told Rakhi that her parents – and the parents of the other desis she knew – loved to go on and on about India, which in their opinion was as close to paradise as you could get. Mrs Gupta, Rakhi's mother, admits her fault in bringing her up the wrong way as her plans eventually boomeranged unexpectedly:

> I thought it would protect you if I didn't talk about the past. That way you wouldn't be constantly looking back, hankering, like so many immigrants do. I didn't want to be like those other mothers, splitting you between here and there, between your life right now and that which can never be. But by not telling you about India as it really was, I made it into something far bigger. It crowded other things out of your mind. It pressed upon your brain like a tumor. (89)

The contrasting attitudes of the parents of Belle and Rakhi provide a definite clue to their failure to fashion the lives of their wards. While Belle through her callousness and indifference to the sensitivities of her parents causes them distress, Rakhi does not forgive her parents for insulating her mind from her cultural inheritance.

Another potent image is Rakhi-Belle's *Kurma House*, an ethnic café which does brisk business as customers, all Indians of advanced age, converge on it as the café does something unique. The old customers are fond of Indian music and Indian songs and in moments of nostalgia they question their decisions to leave their homeland and regret all that they have had to give up "in order to survive in America" (196) For the old Indians, a visit to the *Kurma House* becomes an invigorating experience where they feel strongly a sense of euphoria. This place connects them to their ancestral roots in a strange land. But there is subtle reference to the violence in the air that is concealed yet could be felt. Another café, owned by an American woman just opposite *Kurma House* adopt shoddy and false stratagems to attract the regular customers from there. The manager of Java Coffee shop through her abrasive body language, breathes contempt for Rakhi and Belle. Maybe, in a unique manner, Chitra Divakaruni begins to prepare the readers for something amiss to happen, something saturated with violent happenings.

From the mental violence that the American lady contemplates against Rakhi and Belle, we now turn to the physical violence that is directed against the *Kurma House* and its owners. At last, the most unimaginable happens; World Trade Center is hit by the plane piloted by Muslim terrorists owing allegiance to Al-Quaida. The American nation which was reeling under the euphoria generated by the end of the Cold War was traumatised by the terrorists' strike at the twin towers symbolising the invincibility of America. There is disbelief and alarm everywhere. Rakhi's estranged husband Sonny phones her to close the Café lest it should send wrong signals to the hot-headed people in the hour of crisis. Rakhi argues, "That closing is the only way we can show we care? What about the fact that it might be good for the country to keep running as normally as possible, and not allowing everything to come to a standstill, which I think is exactly what the terrorists want" (257).

In the atmosphere surcharged with madness the voice of sanity never rules. The hoodlums, masquerading as zealots and patriots, could go berserk and lose their sense of reason. When the whole world was glued to the TV sets looking at the visuals of the air-strikes in New York, Rakhi, her father and daughter, Belle and Jespal were in the *Kurma House*. They debate over the idea of putting up American flag outside their café to proclaim their Americanness, and their oneness with their American brethren. Rakhi does not subscribe to the view that the solidarity with the Americans can be displayed only by putting American flag outside their shop. She argues "I don't have to put up a flag to prove that I'm American I'm American already. I love this country – hell, it's the only country I know. But I'm not going to be pressured into putting up a sign to announce that love to every passerby" (264).

Brought up in a multicultural set-up, Rakhi and Belle think that in spite of their Asian backdrop, they were American citizens who have managed diversity in the context of their native societies, and also promoted the values of multiculturalism which go haywire in the face of the fatal onslaughts launched by educated and motivated young Muslims, on the standing symbols of America's might and invincibility. For these two young ladies they are American in and out, though their credentials of Americanness are disputed and questioned by the angry American young men who bay for their blood because the terrorists who caused mayhem in their otherwise tranquil lives, were not Americans but mid-Easterns. As they are arguing over this, four young Americans enter their shop. One of them says, "We're not thieves, shitface. We're patriots ... We've been watching you and your terrorist pals ... Celebrating" (266–267). The turbaned Jespal intercedes, "We haven't done anything wrong ... We're Americans, just the way you are. We all feel terrible about what happened." They grab Jespal, one of the young men spits and yells at him, "Looked in a mirror lately? You ain't no American! It's fuckers like you who planned this attack on the innocent people of this country. Time someone taught you faggots a lesson" (267). One young American holds a switchblade while two of his companions drag Jespal outside. Sonny starts forward, but one of the men holds up his baseball bat with a grin. Jespal is doubled up on the pavement, his hands protecting his head. One of the men swings the chain and Rakhi hears the soft thwack of metal hitting flesh. Sonny, Rakhi's husband, charges at one of the men with a metal pipe. The attacker, who gets Rakhi in a choke hold, is hit by Sonny. Meanwhile, one of the men raises his knife as Jespal screams. The sirens are heard and attackers jump into an ordinary-looking car which had an American flag tied to the antenna. In this state of mind Rakhi ruminates, "Will I ever be able to look at a flag without remembering this moment that I can't believe is happening, this taste in my mouth like copper, which later I'll discover is blood?" (269).

The police car screeches up to the pavement, and the officer leans out of the window. "*Get inside and lock the door,*" he yells. Rakhi, her father, husband and daughter, Belle and Jespal are left on the empty street to take care of themselves. Belle tends to Jespal, who has a cut under his right eye. His other eye is swollen shut. One of his arms hangs at an unnatural angle – but overall he, too, is lucky. Rakhi's traumatised daughter and her shocked father, badly wounded Jespal and Sonny are taken care of by the two women.

Rakhi is so shaken that she cannot drive out of her system the words uttered by one of the American attackers: "*You ain't no American.*" She painfully wonders and asks herself, "But if I wasn't American, then what was I?" (271). Rakhi epitomises the hurt psyche of all the Indian-Americans who wonder if they are living in democratic America or in Nazi Germany. All sorts of craziness in the aftermath of terrorist strike, leaves psychic scars and Rakhi painfully infers: "There's nothing out there that's worse than human beings" (270). Rakhi's and her companions' close brush with young murderers triggers off a process of introspection, an eternal existential dilemma, and they question who they are, in spite of their American birth, American citizenship and American passport. It is not only Rakhi and her friends but many innocent people suffered huge losses during the frenzy; besides, there were hundreds of innocent people in the towers and in the airplanes who lost their lives. The grieving survivors who lost their loved ones; the leaders and decision makers who lost belief in their invincibility, all are sufferers. "And people like us, seeing ourselves darkly through the eye of strangers, who lost a sense of belonging" (272).

Apart from the physical violence that was directed against the Indian-Americans, some perverted persons unleashed mental violence against Indians through very subtle means. No doubt, the Indian-Americans received letters from strangers denouncing the violence directed against them, but a few anonymous notes spouted invectives, and one person sent a large manila envelope with a Ziploc bag filled with turds (275). The actions of the hotheads among Americans traumatise Rakhi and her friend Belle so much that their faces mirror their disbelief: "Is this California in year 2001 or is this Nazi Germany?" (264).

The after effects of 9/11 were quite pervasive; fear psychosis gripped Rakhi's neighbourhood where Pakistani women barely come out of their apartments. The Afghan men take turns rounding up the children of their community and driving them to neighbourhood school .... Sometimes they sit wordless in front of the late-night news and watch bombs being dropped on a country halfway around the world, the elegant plumes of smoke rising above the fires (276). In violence-saturated environment, the creative consciousness of Rakhi is deluged by the images of 9/11 and she paints them:

A Sikh man shot at a gas station because someone thought he was Middle Eastern; terrified women peering from behind curtains that look like burkhas; Jespal's turban unravelled like a river of blood .... When she stands back to look, the colors and shapes come together ... and she gives it the only name possible: *You Ain't American* (279)

The fear psychosis generated by racist violence and hatred against the immigrants is so pervasive that some of the e-mails advise Rakhi to "stock up on garlic and oil of oregano ... antidotes to anthrax" (286). When uncertainty and fear stalk, one is afraid to sleep because of dread that something may have happened by the time one opens one's eyes again. In such a despairing scenario in which one's identity is questioned, humanity undermined and dignity and honour violated, the America-born children of first generation immigrants have to divine their own synthesis of Americanness. Violence is a destructive problem in the contemporary world, which has different forms, the most destructive form being ethnic and racial violence. What agitates the mind is the question how to prevent the ethnocentric tendencies from inclining towards violence while accepting ethnic diversity and identity. Violence is noticeable at all levels. It is in the bilateral relations between nations in the form of wars, religious fundamentalism. Violence is witnessed at community level directed towards ethnic, minority and racial groups, sometimes involving issues of nationalism as evident in *Queen of Dreams* (D.P. Singh, xvi).

Maybe, Chitra Divakaruni obliquely suggests that the skill to survive amidst contraries lies in shrugging off history, immersing in the moment. Rakhi too immerses herself in dance and music to shed suspicion and the memory of pain, the "small chunks of fear break off her and float away" (306). At the end of the novel she finds unexpected blessings in the form of her reunion with her husband and understanding for her family.

While Chitra Divakaruni's *Queen of Dreams* portrays the sinister designs of the international terrorists and the sufferings of those who are not even remotely connected with the happenings, Kiran Desai's *The Inheritance of Loss* brings into sharp focus the various dimensions of violence generated by internal extremist elements. The novel is set in the mid-1980s in Kalimpong, high in the northeastern Himalayas and centres on three people and one dog living together in an ancient house named Cho Oyu. There is the embittered, reptilian judge, lost in his chessboard and in memories of his youth spent at Cambridge many decades earlier; his beloved dog Mutt; his seventeen year old granddaughter Sai, who was orphaned as a child and his servant totally devoted to him. As the story unfolds, insurgency is growing in the region; the Indian Nepalese want their own country or state, a Gorkhaland where they will not be treated as servants. Young boys trying to be men, roam the mountainside looting houses, collecting ammunition. The canvas of the novel is peopled by many other characters such as the wizened old cook, and his immigrant son Biju whom he sent to the US to pursue the American dream; the anglophile sisters Noni and Lola; a Swiss national called Father Booty; the drunk called uncle Potty and the young Nepali tutor turned into an activist named Gyan (also Sai's love interest).

Before venturing into the violent world as it prevails in the novel, it will be quite appropriate to consider the biographical data of Kiran Desai, the daughter of an illustrious mother, Anita Desai. Kiran was born in India in 1971 and educated in India, England and the United States. She was fifteen when she left India and has been staying in the West, primarily in the USA.

As the title suggests *The Inheritance of Loss* is about dislocation and the sense of loss but it is also a definitive statement on the types of violence which the agitation for the Gorkhaland unleashes on the inhabitants of Kalimpong. The extremists use terrorising tactics to scare away the people whom they consider 'outsiders' so that they leave the land to the natives.

From the international face of terrorism we now shift our attention to regional terrorism that is depicted in *The Inheritance of Loss*. The novel shows how terrorism creates differences among communities and other ethnic groups, brings them to war against each other on the basis of religion, caste and creed and other narrow considerations. Terrorism also perverts human psychology. Society remains under fear psychosis and hence it cannot flower, nor can it orient its thinking towards rationality and logic. Terrorism has far reaching effects on the political situation of a country. It has the potential of bringing political disorder and its associated effects in the country.

Violence is politically defined as a power enforced in unlawful ways. Biologists call it quarrelsome behaviour to survive and sociologists know it as a social action with which at least one of the sides is unhappy. Regional terrorism or violence can thrive when certain favourable conditions like political and regional frustrations, economic disparities and media exposure are prevalent and to meet their ends terrorists can adopt various methods like hijacking of planes, bombing, kidnapping, selective killing and armed robbery of money and arms. The agenda of the separatist groups/regional groups and outfits is to seek separation or political autonomy within the existing entity.

The Inheritance of Loss depicts in its many details the tragedies of a third world country just free from colonialism. Against the gigantic backdrop of the Himalayas, Kiran Desai has portrayed the human soul, bare and naked. Apart from presenting the existential dilemmas of Jemubhai, the narrative reveals the post colonial dilemmas of the country. The locale of the action is Kalimpong area, it becomes the hub of the activities of Nepalis who are striving for autonomy as a result of the age-old prejudices and biases against them. The Nepalese' struggle to get their own rights and land, creeps into the lives of the characters: the cook, the judge, Sai, Noni, Lola; and gnaws and questions their very being. The characters like Father Booty and Uncle Potty who have been living in the area for years and never bothered to ponder over their right to live in this land, are very much caught in the dark just like the middle-aged sisters Lola and Noni, who, polished with an education, books and English literature get a rude shock when the GNLF leader molests Lola with his vulgar words and mocks at her middle-agedness. The movement, though born out of legitimate political and regional aspirations of the people, goes out of hand, and the hot-headed elements and wayward youths do not even spare Biju, the cook's son in America who comes back only to be robbed.

One has to understand the psyche of the Nepalese in order to make an accurate assessment of their political struggle which like any politically motivated struggle, tends to be violent with serious repercussions. The Nepalese were in majority but intriguingly treated like minority. They felt that in a land which was theirs, they were ruled by outsiders who followed English ways of living and liked English custom and tastes. The readers are brought to experience, observes Binod Mishra, the hatred in the eyes of local boys once they enter the judge's house. Irked at the judge's kindness towards his dog, Mutt and his privileged lifestyle, these boys make the judge obey their instructions. They seem to derive a temporary satisfaction in making the judge pronounce "Jai Gorkha" like a docile lamb (165). Kiran Desai minces no words in delineating the predicament of the Nepalese, "They wanted their own country, or at least their own state, in which to manage their own affairs. Here, where India blurred into Bhutan and Sikkim, and the army did pull-ups and push-ups, maintaining their tanks with khaki paint in case the Chinese grew hungry for more territory than Tibet, it had always been messy map" (9).

When looting and theft take place, the sense of insecurity grips the inhabitants of Kalimpong, especially those who are regarded aliens by the volunteers of the GNLF. Lola shrieks when she hears the judge's guns had been stolen from Cho Oyu. Her fear is that if they come to her house, they will not find anything but they will kill for fifty rupees. So much so, her mistrust of her own watchman, Budhoo who is a Nepali, is so strong that she doubts the integrity of each watchman in whose area/surrounding the robbery takes place. She recalls Mrs Thondup whose house was wiped clean, and a sense of insecurity envelops her. She knows "Nepalis make good soldiers, coolies, but they are not so bright at their studies" (73), yet she opines, "I tell you, these Neps can't be trusted. And they don't just rob. They think absolutely nothing of murdering, as well" (45). So Lola and Noni harbour suspicion against their watchman, Budhoo as "the new posters in the market referring to old discontents, the slogan scratched and painted on the side of government offices and shops," declaring "we are stateless" (126). As the narrative unfolds:

> The insurgency worsens to an extent that Noni and Lola are coerced into harbouring terrorists in their house. The incidents of horror grew, through the changing of the seasons, through winter and a flowery spring, summer, then rain and winter again. Roads were closed, there was curfew every night, and Kalimpong was

trapped in its own madness. One could not leave the hillsides; nobody even left their houses if they could help it but stayed locked in and barricaded. (279)

The author affords us a glimpse of the destructive activities of the GNLF boys who burned down the government rest house by the river; it was a beautiful spot full of natural beauty; here Father Booty had photographed the polka-dotted butterfly. In fact, the forest inspection bungalows all over the district were burning, upon whose verandas generations of ICS men had stood and admired the serenity, the hovering, angelic peace of dawn and dusk in the mountains (280). The circuit house and the house of the chief minister's niece were also set ablaze. Detonators set off landslides as negotiations went nowhere. Kalimpong was transformed into a ghost town, the wind tumbling around the melancholy streets, garbage flying by unhindered. Whatever point the GNLF might have had, it was severely out of hand; even one man's anger, in those days, seemed enough to set the hillside afire.

In an atmosphere marked by uncertainty, suspicion, hate and insecurity, outsiders like the two sisters – Lola and Noni – had the worst of humiliation from little children as the two went to Tshering's shop: "Little children lined up in rows to spit at Lola and Noni as they walked by, and when Kesang, their maid, was bitten by one of the squatter's dogs, she screamed away, "Look your dog has bitten me, now you must put oil and turmeric on the wound so I don't die from an infection" (280) but the natives just laughed. 27th July, 1986 was the day of reckoning for the Gorkhas of Nepalese origin who were agitating and had assembled on the day to demonstrate their strength by waving *kukris,* the sickle blades high and flashing in the light, "Jai Gorkha," the men shouted. "Jai Gorkhaland! Gorkhaland for Gorkhas" (275). The battle cry sent shivers down the spine of non-Gorkhas like the cook who had gone to the post office to fetch his letters from his son, Biju, the illegal alien in America. A volley of rocks and stone came pelting down from behind the post office, injuring some people. The marchers interpreted it as the handiwork of the police and their informers which the latter denied. The bloody skirmish between the marchers and the police claimed the life of thirteen local boys, thus fuelling the cauldron of hatred and vengeance against the lawfully established authority of the state. The reign of terror spread among the public, police and protestors.

The interjection of Kiran Desai at the volatile situation in Kalimpong sums up the uprising in the following words, "This was how history moved, the slow build, the quick burn, and in an incoherence, the leaping both backward and forward, swallowing the young into old hate. The space between life and death, in the end, too small to measure". (276). The cook's notion of the civilised and safe place had taken a severe beating which had killed the spirit of belonging to the place as it had become hostile to the outsiders though they had been living in the place for decades: ... "this place where he had with utter safety genuinely lost his temper with the deaf tailors, the inept plumber, the tardy baker with the cream horns; this place where he had resided secure in the knowledge that this was basically a civilised place where there was room for them all; where he had existed in what seemed a sweetness of crabbiness – was showing him now that he had been wrong. He wasn't wanted in Kalimpong and he didn't belong" (278).

The episode of Father Booty deserves to be recalled to augment the view that when parochial regionalism takes hold of the mind of the people, the voice of sanity and reason is stifled. Overnight, friends become alien. Father Booty had been living in India for forty five years. "He knew he was a foreigner but had lost the notion that he was anything but an Indian foreigner" (220). He had been nabbed by the police as he was clicking the pictures of the butterfly, and across there was a bridge which was interpreted by the police as "threat to our national security" (221). Father Booty goes running to everyone he knew who might help him, the police chief and the SDO who made regular trips to the dairy for sweet curd, Major Aloo in the cantonment who enjoyed the chocolate cigars he made, the forest department officials who had given him oyster mushroom spawn so he might have mushrooms in his garden during fungus season. One year when the bamboo clump on his property bloomed and bees from the whole district descended buzzing upon the white flowers, the forest department had bought the seeds from him, because they were available – bamboo flowered only once in a hundred years. When the clump died after this extravagant effort, they gave him new bamboo to plant, young spears with their tips like braids. In the attenuating circumstances all his acquaintances had turned their back on him due to the disturbed conditions and the prevailing environment of hostility towards outsiders/foreigners, "But now, all those who in peaceful times had enjoyed his company and chatted about such things as curd, mushrooms, and bamboo were too busy or too scared to help" (221).

Sai, the teen-aged granddaughter of Justice Jemubhai feels revolted by the activities of the Nepalese, including her tutor, Gyan. She lost faith in him when she realised that the GNLF boys' forcible entry in their home was meticulously planned by Gyan. "This was Gyan's doing, she thought. This is what he had done and what people like him were doing in the name of decency and education, in the name of hospitals for Nepalis and management positions. In the end, Father Booty, lovable Father Booty who, frankly had done much more for development in the hills, than any of the locals, and without screaming or waving kukris, Father Booty was to be sacrificed" (223). When the votaries of crass regionalism try to promote their agenda, whatever goes against their interest must be obliterated either through coercion, intimidation, threats of liquidation and deportation. These are the old tricks which the perpetrators employ to milk those who swear by the milk of human kindness. Lola, Noni, Uncle Potty and Father Booty are sacrificed at the altar of spurious and sham patriotism.

The question of not belonging anywhere haunts Biju too. Biju is the son of the Judge's cook who lives in America as an illegal alien and is exploited and underpaid by Harsh-Harry, an Indian and owner of the restaurant where Biju and his ilk, work, sulk and slog. Biju's case is pathetic so to say because he and his father have a dream which is shattered first in America and then in his own land; he is a foreigner, an alien in both. Biju was five when he lost his mother, his father brought him up with a dream in his eyes to make him a rich man, the cook (his father) gets for him a visitor's visa for US. Biju overstayed to join the ranks of thousands who are euphemistically called "Columbus," because when Columbus came to America, he did not have any visa. The tribe of Columbus multiplied but the sense of nostalgia never deserted them in the land of riches. Biju manages to give a slip to the authorities along with other

Indians and Pakistanis like him. During hard days he wonders why he should have come to the rotten place where he had no identity at all. When he gets injured his employer shirks his responsibility of providing him medical treatment. Biju's realisation of his alienation year after year had coagulated and now he wants to come out of the cobweb. His self-consciousness and self-pity made him detest himself and he asks, "shouldn't he return to a life where he might slice his own importance, to where he might relinquish his overrated control over his own destiny and perhaps be subtracted from its determination altogether?" (268).

Leaving America to return to India turns out to be a devastating experience for Biju. Kalimpong is no home for him now. He realises it too late. Torn by strife and strikes, Kalimpong greets him with a deathly and deserted look. Those were hostile times when life had come to a standstill in and around Darjeeling due to sustained insurgency and violence by the agitators who were clamouring for Gorkhaland. The GNLF men misguide him as he takes a jeep to reach his destination, Kalimpong, to join his father. On the way, Biju is robbed of all his possessions: dollars, bags and suitcases, clothes and even the clothes he is wearing. The presents he had bought so endearingly from America; and in fact, everything that is on his person is snatched away. The harsh encounter with the bitter reality awakens him to a new level of human awareness as he is almost naked when he joins his father. The encounter disillusions him, and he wonders if he was not safer as an illegal alien in America, than a native of India who was dispossessed of everything on return to the motherland. The regional violence gets so strong that the perpetrators of violence through their nefarious acts blur the distinction between Indians and the outsiders.

Biju is exposed to the hideous face of violence but the only consolation is his union with his long-lost father. Thus, violence on the domestic front and at the regional level wreaks a lot of havoc in the personal lives of primary and secondary characters in *The Inheritance of Loss*, who become unwary victims of temperamental insensitivities and inhuman cruelties, and are adversely affected by the rise of regional and parochial political organisations which militate against the composite culture of Indian nation. Bela Patel, Biju, Lola, Noni, Uncle Potty, Sai, Father Booty, Jemubhai and his cook experience different forms of violence which compel them to refashion their notion of Indianness as some of them are regarded as outsiders. Like Albert Camus' Mersault they suffer from feelings of strangeness and alienation in their own motherland.

Works Cited

Beardsley, Nancy. *Voice of America*, December 7, 2004.

Desai, Kiran. *The Inheritance of Loss*. New Delhi: Penguin, 2006. Subsequent references are to this edition of the novel, and are incorporated in the text in parenthesis.

Divakaruni, Chitra. *Queen of Dreams*. rpt., Abacus, London: 2005. All references incorporated in the text, are to this edition.

J. Pais, Arthur. *Profile@chitradivakaruni.com* Feb., 1999.

Kar, P.K. *Indian Society*. New Delhi: Kalyani Publishers, 1998.

Mishra, Binod. "Kiran Desai's *The Inheritance of Loss*: A Narrative of Conflicting Loyalties," in *Kiran Desai: The Novelist*, ed. P.D. Nimasarkar. New Delhi: Creative Books, 2008.

Singh, Manjit and D.P. Singh. *Violence: Impact and Intervention*. New Delhi: Atlantic. 2008.

Softky, Elizabeth. "A Cross-cultural Understanding Spiced with the Indian Diaspora." @ *Back Issue The Sunday Statesman*, February 2, 2003.

Trowbridge, Serena. Review of *Queen of Dreams* in *Midwest Book Review*, 24 September, 2004.

Internet Sources

http:/en.wikipedia.org/wiki/violence
Wikipedia, the Free Encyclopaedia

8

Violence in Indian Literature

Some Thoughts on Domestic Violence in Kiran Desai's *The Inheritance of Loss*

SILKY ANAND KHULLAR

Indian English literature abounds in numerous instances of violence of various kinds: it may be against women and children, communal violence, violence against the subaltern or even violence generated by the high-handed approach of the state. In the words of Bhim S. Dahiya,

> "the most significant contemporary Indian writing in English has come out from the women writers who, rightly ignoring the bandwagons of postcolonial fictionalization of India, have narrated the stories of women in the real India as the women have known it the hard way and managed to cope with, raising pertinent questions about patriarchy and its revered customs and traditions, exposing the sham and shame of it all. The other significant writing in the recent times has been the one done by authors like Arundhati Roy and Amitav Kumar who have addressed the cancerous formations in our culture, formations which have seriously impaired the vital organs of our polity and culture, our national destiny and individual domesticity". (Dahiya, 2008: 25)

To this we can now add Arvind Adiga's *The White Tiger*.

Literary creations always respond to milieu, moment and map. Fiction writing in the Indian sub-continent has never been alienated from its social, political or religious temperament. The first half of the twentieth century in the Indian sub-continent has been marked by unprecedented violence and cruelty accompanied by communal genocides. The very expanse and enormity of violence that attended partition has tended to produce in fiction an overlay of savagery and violence – a routine description of the approaching murderous hordes, attacks and butchering, conversion, abduction and rape, raging fires and wagon loads of corpses – the endless inventory of ingenious bestiality. To move to the contested site at once, Madhusudan Prasad and Alok Kumar, refer to the opening section of the archetypal partition novel, *Train to Pakistan* (1956) by Khushwant Singh:

> The summer before (1946), communal riots precipitated by reports of the proposed division of the country into a Hindu India and a Muslim Pakistan had broken out in Calcutta, and within a few months the death toll had mounted to several thousand. Muslims said the Hindus had planned and started the killing. According to the Hindus, the Muslims were to blame. The fact is both sides killed. Both shot and stabbed and speared and clubbed. Both tortured. Both raped. (Prasad & Kumar, 2007: 9–10)

Chaman Nahal's *Azadi* (1977) provides a heartrending scene of Hindu women being paraded naked through the streets of Narowal (Sialkot),

> They were all stark naked. Their heads were completely shaven; so were their armpits. So were their pubic region. They were all crying, though their eyes shed no tears. Their faces were formed into grimaces and they were all sobbing. Their arms were free, but so badly had they been used, so wholly their spirits crushed, their morale shattered, none of them made any attempt to cover themselves with their hands. (Nahal, 1977: 296)

Bapsi Sidhwa's *Ice Candy Man* (1988) mirrors another ghastly scene, though the novel is written forty one years after partition, "A train from Gurdaspur has just come in. Everyone in it is dead. Butchered. They are all Muslims. There are no young women among the dead! Only two gunny bags full of women's breasts"

(Sidhwa, 1988: 149). The violence depicted in partition literature is simply unnerving. It seems as if this literature of violence is unable to shake off its fixation to violence. R.K. Singh in a perceptive essay, "Anger in Action: An Introductory," writes that everyone expresses some kind of anger pattern as a result of his or her experiences, ranging from shock, denial, guilt-feeling, rejection, fear, loneliness, self-consciousness, depression, and various manifestations of sustained anger as violence, physical distress, mania, disabling, apathy and aggressive emotions" (Singh, 1995: 11). Each writer tries to find ways to counter his or her emotional wounds, feeling frustrated, disheartened, hurt, attacked, oppressed, exploited, manipulated, cheated, ignored or let down, thinking his/her peace, welfare, health, or survival is threatened, his/her rights and values are abused or he/she feels helpless – at not being able to do something to contain the despairing experiences and cruel indifferences.

There are various other forms of violence that have not gone undetected. Let us take for example the scourge of dowry deaths. It prompted Dina Mehta to compose both short stories and plays. She gets inside the experience of 'bride burning' and voices her own feelings and attitude to the seriousness of the issue in her play, *Brides Are Not for Burning* (1979). She analyses this extreme form of violence against women, and women's plight from a woman's perspective in her stories. Shashi Deshpande in *That Long Silence* (1988) exposes the sufferings women undergo in the name of tradition, family values and customs. She not only shares her personal concerns but also seeks to awaken readers to the reality of marital life in Indian society today.

Indian writers in English have been alive to the pernicious evils that afflict our society, and do not shy away from portraying the seamy side of life in all its nakedness. K. Satchidanandan has aptly summarised the concerns which inform the works of Indian writers in English:

> Our finest writers, young and old alike, have no doubt been alive to the major social, cultural and spiritual issues ... the erosion of individual liberty, the loss of identity, the corruption in public life, the communal hysteria (resulting in extreme forms of violence against human beings), the diverse forms of structural oppression

based on caste, race, class and gender, the ecological havoc wrought by man's hubris and greed, the absurdity of war. The heteroglossia of post-modernism probably springs from its multi-dimensional engagement with a hydraheaded reality. (Satchidanadan, 1992: 5–6)

Violence – physical, mental or verbal – has been deftly treated in Indian English literature. It stems from the elemental feeling of rage, anger, vengeance and prejudice which are individual as well as cultural. The poets and novelists try to manage their as well as others' anger through such modes as irony and satire, rudeness of speech and bitterness in tone, sexual anxieties and obscenities. Their 'fight' response includes using verbal power of anger like ethnic, racial, caste or colour abuses, dirty language, sly 'digs' into a seemingly innocent conversation, malicious gossip, offensive provocation, sexist/racist jokes or comments, stigmatising social groups, using caustic wit or unfair jokes. It is facing the beast within oneself, exploring the darker side of one's self, or acting out the repressed aggression, possibly to alert us to the negatives of decay around or to arouse feelings of sympathy, resistance or protest which may not be overtly loud or to mitigate against which is not agreeable or acceptable in the social or personal system. A creative artist, argues R.K. Singh, expresses anger to get away from anger.

Contemporary Indian English poetry, especially post-independence poetry, originates out of the interaction of highly educated minds with bewildering and complex nature of not only Indian reality, full of paradoxes and challenges, but also with human predicament in general. As against this, Dalit poetry originates in the Dalit Movement launched by Dr B.R. Ambedkar and Jyotiba Phuley. It has its roots in the Dalit struggle for emancipation from the barbarities of the upper classes. Among both the groups we have poetry of protest born of anger. But the ills against which the protest is registered are different with each group, so is its poetic expression. Dalit poets hail from amongst the Dalits who have submitted to centuries of oppression, injustice, indignities, humiliations, and social ostracism. They have been passive victims of inhuman atrocities inflicted upon them by the upper classes. Meek suffering has been their lot. Hence, Dalit poets are born with the intolerable burden of this sorrow. These cumulative agonising experiences are deeply embedded in their psyche and integrated in their consciousness and inheritance. These experiences find a strident voice in their poetry, a voice of protest, a voice of revolt born of irrepressible burning anger.

The Indian English dramatists were not behind as far as angry expressions through violence in life, are concerned. A playwright like Asif Currimbhoy, who is articulate in presenting life as it is and boldly tells the truth that politicians try to evade, deals with a political and sexual biography of Gandhi in *An Experiment with Truth* (1972) and in the process ironically reveals political dishonesty and some hidden emotions that reveal certain aspects of human nature that only raw and naked words can express: "Patel: '... You came from Punjab, huh? Experience the horror of post-partition ... was your wife raped, Madanlal? Or perhaps it was your mother in front of your eyes ... Perhaps she was forcibly converted into Islam'" (28). Currimbhoy reveals Patel's pro-Hindu stances just as he points to the frustrating experiences of Gandhian secularism in India: "Ali: '(furious) You ... you swine! We're in a Gandhian secular state today, whether you like it or not. Question the Muslim loyalty in public, and I'll smash you (35)."

The playwright uses violence and abusive language to reveal the tense moral dilemma of the characters as that becomes his narrative strategy to convey his own perception of man's misery, poverty and suffering that affect human relationships. Girish Karnad deals with life and time of Sultan Muhammad bin Tughlaq, his complex and eccentric personality which imbibes the psychology of anger, the paradoxes and the contraries, the ideal and the real, and articulates anger and violence essentially as part of the protagonist's search for identity.

Thus, the Indian English playwrights are not significantly different from poets and novelists who write with a sense of analysis, interpretation and evaluation of the contemporary social, political and economic realities. It is not possible to deal with all the texts that present violence and reflect their responses to the flux of experiences, including violent ones. Through their creative outpourings, they unmask the contradictions and disruptions that afflict humankind and condemn those objectionable aspects of contemporary life that have resulted from a kind of psychological inanity or complacency. They articulate their artistic choices to debunk the myths in various sections that perpetuate exploitation and moral duplicity, they use devices and expressions that challenge common sense or social propriety vis-à-vis the stark reality of economic poverty, insensitivity, debasement, despair, desolation, loneliness, violence, especially domestic violence. They eschew discrimination, corruption and exploitation at any level and draw attention to the sorry plight of the larger population, socio-economic degeneration, political gimmicks, factionalisation, rising tide of fundamentalism and terrorism, environmental pollution, and the spectre of violence that threatens human beings in various forms.

Since literature and society are bound in an interminable relationship, it is but natural that the socio-politico-psychological forces that operate in a society, exert their pressure on the creative consciousness of the novelists, poets and dramatists. The journey of the exerted influences from the mind of the writer to the printed word, is a process which requires selection, pruning and presentation in various genres of literature. When human consciousness is assaulted by the acts of subversion and violence, the creative consciousness of the artists feels benumbed momentarily, then through their judicious process of objective creativity the writer/artist begins to perceive these dilemmas of human life at a scale which transcends time and space. Then topical human dilemmas become eternal human dilemmas. Violence/terrorist violence or domestic violence or their various manifestations engage the attention of the conscious creative artists as they strain to find way through plethora of contradictory options. One must never forget that it is love, and love alone, that can bind humanity in a single community.

According to WHO, there are three broad categories of violence: self-inflicted violence, interpersonal violence and collective violence. Self-inflicted violence represents self-destructive behaviour of an individual and includes suicidal behaviour and self abuse such as self-mutilation. Interpersonal violence is violent behaviour between individuals and can be classified by victim–offender relationship, either among acquaintances or among persons who are not acquainted. Interpersonal violence include child abuse, bullying, criminally-linked violence such as assault and homicide, youth violence, rape and sexual assault and violence in institutional settings, workplace. Collective violence is violent behaviour of social or political groups motivated by special political, economic or social objectives. Armed conflict and war are the most organised types of violence. It can be of various forms: armed conflict between and within states, genocide, repression and other human rights abuses, terrorism and organised violent crimes. Other examples include racial or religious conflicts occurring among groups and gang or mob violence. Violence and human destruction comprise all the noxious acts that have effect of damaging and destroying human life and property; as also the aggressive quality of impulses, passion and emotions and abnormal behaviour underlying it. Such noxious acts need not have any common cause because they are entirely different from one another in the type and magnitude of damage and destruction. But they have the same innate irrational cause resulting from biological, adaptive, psychologically motivated, evolutionarily developed impulse. Sadistic pleasure and satisfaction are manifested in killing and cruelly destroying human life. The recent increase in violence at national and international level is quite appalling.

Domestic violence is not a new phenomenon. It has persisted all through our history and it still persists despite various legislations and rules and regulations. In the opinion of P.K. Kar, "the typical Indian patriarchal society, which bears a unique socio-cultural tradition, has been an oppressive one with regard to the life and behaviour of the women" (Kar, 1998: 52). Domestic violence is an ongoing experience of physical, emotional and/or sexual abuse faced by women within the household. The abuser could be husband/and or other members from the family. Domestic violence cuts across the boundaries of class, caste, religion, race and education. It has a debilitating effect on women's physical as well as psychological health.

Kiran Desai's *The Inheritance of Loss* depicts violence as a stark but mindless reality of life. Here violence works at two levels – extremist violence in society and domestic violence perpetuated by Jemubhai, the judge. It is sad and disconcerting to read how Jemubhai, with a veneer of having had his education in England and the sheen of the elite service class treats his wife shabbily. Bela Patel was the most beautiful daughter of Bomanbhai Patel. She lived a traditional life in a household where girls are tied down to their mothers and sisters in strict purdah, and lead an idle indoor existence. Bela was married to Jemubhai at the age of fourteen. Her family was of a higher standing than Jemubhai's though their caste was not high. About Bela's beauty, the author comments, "You could tell from her features which were delicate, her toes, nose, ears, and fingers were all very fine and small, and she was very fair just like milk. Complexion-wise, they said, you could have mistaken her for a foreigner. Her family only married among fifteen families, but an exception was made for your grandfather because he was in the ICS" (88).

The bride Bela who was carefully "locked up behind the high walls of the haveli" (89) in her parental home, was handed over like a commodity from her patriarchal father's custody to that of Jemubhai's. Her name was changed and in a few hours, Bela became Nimi Patel who had just left one suffocating, male-dominated bastion to enter into another androcentric home for a loveless, unsuccessful marriage. When Jemubhai returned from England as a successful person, he was twenty-five and she was nineteen, they vaguely remembered each other. Things went wrong in the first meeting itself and to assert himself, the judge resorted to the oldest trick in the book – phallocentrism. Bela's tale of humiliation, injustice, abuses, violence, and battered life commenced within those four walls on the day of consummation of marriage. The judge resorted to cruelty in his bid to hide his own inexperience. Nimi also grew accustomed to his detached expression and silence. In Jemubhai's eyes, Bela was completely inadequate, fully inconsequential, and totally incompetent. The first encounter between Jemubhai and Bela is a classic instance of marital rape. Being educated and having returned from England after qualifying for the ICS, Jemubhai, fed on rumours and tales of sexual exploits, runs after Bela in a room which was already locked by one of the aunts:

> Ghoulishly sugared in sweet candy pigment, he clamped down on her, tussled her to the floor, and as more of that perfect rose complexion, blasted into a million motes, came filtering down, in a dense frustration of lust and fury – penis uncoiling, mottled purple-black as if with rage, blundering uncovering the chute he had heard rumor of – he stuffed his way ungracefully into her. (169)

Jemubhai was glad he could disguise his inexpertness, his crudity, with hatred and fury – this was a trick that would serve him well throughout his life in a variety of areas. Though the grotesqueness of it all shocked him, he repeated the gutter act again and again. This distaste and his persistence made him angrier than ever and any cruelty to her became irresistible. In an authorial intrusion, Kiran Desai writes, "He would teach her the same lessons of loneliness and shame he had learned himself. In public, he never spoke to or looked in her direction" (170).

Bela grew accustomed to Jemubhai's detached expression. He would not take her anywhere and squirmed when the wives of other officers asked about his wife. She was left to sit alone in Bonda; three weeks out of four. In brief, she was uncared for, her freedom useless, her husband disregarded his duty. She had fallen out of life altogether. Weeks went by and she spoke to nobody, the servants thumped their own leftovers on the table for her to eat. On his return from tours, he would feel offended by her expression.

Another instance of Jemubhai's insensitivity and inhumanity deserves to be discussed in detail. One day he found footprints on the toilet seat – she was squatting on it – he could barely contain his outrage, took her head and pushed it into the toilet bowl. By the year's end the dread they had for each other was so severe it was as if they were trapped into a limitless bitterness carrying them beyond the parameters of what any individual is normally capable of feeling. Her misery made Bela invalid; she grew very dull; she began to fall asleep in heliographic sunshine and wake in the middle of the night. She peered out at the world but could not focus on it, never went to the mirror, because she couldn't see herself in it, and anyway she couldn't bear to spend a moment in dressing and combing, activities that were only for the happy and the loved (173). As if all this torture was not enough, he commanded her, "Don't show your face outside. People might run from you, screaming" (173). Bela's sensitive nature, loneliness and lack of love became the bane and burden of her lacerated psyche. She had witnessed the hollowness and futility of life because she soon realised that whatever she did or didn't do, the outcome was much the same. "His hatred was its own creature; it rose and burned out, reappeared of its own accord, and in her he sought only its justification, its perfection. In its purest moments he could imagine himself killing her" (305). Jemubhai's cruelty towards his wife could be gauged from the fact that even in her pregnancy he did not desist from hurting and hitting her when Bela revealed this to him: "For the first time he hit her, although he had wanted to before and fought the urge for some time. He emptied his glass on her head, sent a jug of water swinging into the face he no longer found beautiful, filled her ears with leaping soda water. Then, when this wasn't enough to assuage his rage, he hammered down with his fists, raising his arms to bring them down on her again and again, rhythmically, until his own hands were exhausted and his shoulders next day were strained sore as if from chopping wood" (304).

One wonders if the brutal judge ever felt sorry for what he did to Bela for no fault of hers. Kiran Desai feels, he did regret it after many years. He had "stolen her dignity, shamed his family, shamed hers, turned her into an embodiment of their humiliation" (308). The venom of his own failures dehumanised his wife, threw her into the abyss of insanity which resulted in the birth of their daughter who was useless and absurd. Her daughter Sai – Jemubhai's granddaughter – also seems to be a borderline case. Jemubhai's example typically reveals how the effect of domestic violence trickles down from generation to generation.

It is an acknowledged fact that children living in the atmosphere of domestic violence suffer and develop lop-sided personality. We can draw umpteen examples from literature. Arundhati Roy's *The God of Small Things*; Shashi Deshpande's *Small Remedies,* and *A Matter of Time;* Anita Desai's *Fire on the Mountain* do not have domestic violence as the major theme but these works show the corroding effect of the home atmosphere on the children.

Works Cited

Bowser, Benjamin P. Ed., "Introduction." *Racism and Anti-Racism in World Perspective.* London: Sage, 1995, x.

Currimbhoy, Asif. *An Experiment with Truth,* rpt. Calcutta: Writers Workshop, 1993.

Dahiya, Bhim S. "Some Thoughts on the Spectrum of Contemporary Indian English Writing," in *Emerging Trends in Recent Literature*, ed. Kum Kum Bajaj. Patiala: Publication Bureau, Punjabi University, 2008.

Desai, Kiran. *The Inheritance of Loss*. New Delhi: Penguin, 2006

Kar, P.K. *Indian Society*. New Delhi: Kalyani Publishers, 1998.

Nahal, Chaman. *Azadi*. Delhi: Arnold Heinemann, 1975.

Prasad, Madhusudan and Alok Kumar, "Sanitized Silence: Towards A Theory of the Partition Novel in English," in *Perspectives on the Partition Fiction of the Indian Sub-continent*, ed. Tejinder Kaur, Kulbhushan Kushal N.K. Neb. Jalandhar: Nirman Publications, 2007, 20-21.

Satchidanandan, K. "Reflections" *Indian Literature*, Vol. XXXV, 4 (150), July-August, 1992.

Sidhwa, Bapsi. *Ice Candy Man*. Delhi: Penguin Books, 1989.

Singh, Khushwant. *Train to Pakistan*. Delhi: Orient Longman, 1956.

Singh, R.K. "Anger in Action: An Introductory." *Language Forum*, 21, No. 1-2, January-December 1995.

9

Nuances of Gendered Violence
Shashi Deshpande's *The Dark Holds No Terrors*

JYOTI K. SINGH

Violence as a force is exerted either to check evil or control the subordinates. Being multi-edged, it can operate psychologically, physically, verbally and emotionally on social, economic and political planes. In a patriarchal community it is exerted against women and most of them know the private experience of specific forms as well as threats of violence – rape, sexual abuse, *sati*, dowry, female foeticide, wife battering, bride burning etc. Being a subordinate group women suffer violence at the hands of men as well as other women, who being successfully conditioned according to the patriarchal norms, become acolytes of patriarchy.

Shashi Deshpande's *The Dark Holds No Terrors* brings forth the story of Saru, a successful doctor who suffers violence by virtue of being a woman. Her story vividly reflects her experience of growing up as a girl in a patriarchal set up. To lay the background for understanding how violence operates in the novel and examine its relationship to gender, we would first take a cursory glance at the Indian ethos where woman's position as a passive victim of violence is conditioned socially through the myths of *Sita, Gandhari* and *Sati*. The valorisation of such masochistic behaviour in women leads to their degradation and mute suffering.

Indian society is largely patriarchal and male members are valued more than their female counterparts. In such a society the dignity and destiny of a woman is seen in marriage. What Beauvoir says in this context can be relevant to quote. She states, "Marriage is a destiny traditionally offered to women by society" (1977: 444). In the Indian culture marriage is a sacred institution where the wife is considered a complement to man, *Ardhangini*, but ironically submits completely to the husband for he is *Patiparmeshwar*, an earthly substitute for God around whom her whole being revolves. Though Indian women have attained emancipation from the binding stereotypical roles to some extent, they still lead contradictory lives. What Manu, the Hindu lawgiver decreed still runs in the blood of Indians. According to him a woman must be kept in subordination. In her childhood she should be subjected to her father, in youth to her husband and when he is dead, to her son. He compares a "woman to a river and a husband to an ocean" where after reaching the latter, the former completely loses its identity (Indra, 1955: 32). A woman is expected to submerge her whole being completely in doing her duty to her husband irrespective of what he is. This often leads to tension in the lives of women. Some continue in the battering relationship and others rebel. Those who dare to rebel against the oppressive traditions of the community are ostracised, scoffed as misfits, unfeminine or branded 'femme fatales'.

Almost all women suffer violence in one way or the other because of their male counterparts, some are aware of their victimisation and voice their protest now and then but some resign themselves to their fate choosing to compromise. Usually women compromise, for, endurance is a virtue extolled by the community. Woman's adherence to the self-image based on the traditional feminine of 'goodness' rooted in self-abnegation and self-sacrifice is strictly demanded by the patriarchal community. This social role of deferring and attending to the emotional and physical needs of the others negating the needs of one's own self hinders an 'authentic selfhood'. Reconciliation with the traditional feminine becomes conflicting and problematic though most of the women follow the set social pattern of taking on responsibility to the exclusion of self and adopt the feminine convention of self-sacrifice and martyrdom. This is due to their ineptitude to handle patriarchal pressures.

Fearing ridicule and ostracisation they validate their claim "to social membership through the adoption of societal values" (Gilligan, 1982: 79) of caring and nurturing relationships at the cost of their selves. Here covert violence by the community operating through gender bias and biased treatment to women is subtly conspicuous. In the following discussion endeavour would be to trace how violence, in conjunction with the gender-based community, operates in the *The Dark Holds No Terrors*.

At the very onset of the novel, Saru's revelation that her mother's "memory was as violent as an assault" (Deshpande, 1990: 15) easily makes the reader sense the hiatus between the mother–daughter relationship. Her mother, Kamala's accusation that Saru killed her brother, when she was unable to save her younger brother from drowning, converts her childhood and later life into an experience of emotional injury. Her mother's unmindfully uttered words in a depressed state, "You killed him, Why didn't you die? Why are you alive when he's dead?" (191), are taken for true by the child Saru. The words saddled with hatred and verbal violence burdens Saru's future with a feeling of guilt and embitters the filial relationship. As a result she dissociates herself completely from her mother stating vehemently, "If you are a woman, I don't want to be one" (63). After her son Dhruva's death, Kamala becomes uninterested in the world around her and herself as well. According to Judith V. Jordan, a Stone Center psychologist, "Depression also impairs the capacity for mutuality, withdrawal into the self to repair and heal, as well as frequent feelings of helplessness, lead to a regressive wish for nurturance and ministration from others …. Depressed people suffer from a diminished interest in the inner world of the other and little ability to attend to, let alone minister to, the needs of the others" (1991: 91). Therefore, to brand Kamala as a rigidly unforgiving, unkind mother would be unjust. The tragedy of Dhruva's death shatters her. She does not hate Saru but loved her son more. She does not understand the damage done to Saru's psyche by her carelessly uttered curse in her own overwhelming state of sorrow. She has a soft corner for Saru too otherwise she would not have celebrated her fifteenth birthday or gifted her a pair of earrings. It is more a clash of egos. Probably she wanted Saru to come and apologise which Saru never did and

Saru's going against her wishes and marrying on her own aggravated the misunderstanding and put a seal on the relationship. The tug of war between mother and daughter continues unabated till both separate their ways professing to hate each other. Saru fails to find the moment in time when she turned antagonistic to her mother and the mother fails to realise the reason for Saru's seething anger. In fact, the mother is so conditioned by the patriarchal culture that she cannot reconcile with her daughter's psychological demands. The mother does her duty towards her daughter without a vestige of emotions; it is here that Saru feels hurt. For example her mother brings earrings for her as a birthday gift but the same evening when Saru is late in reaching home the mother, instead of taking it coolly, scolds her. When Saru resists silently, she feels enraged and asks:

> "Can't you talk? Am I so much below your notice? You can talk to your friends for hours, but you can't speak a sentence to your mother. What am I? An enemy?" (170)

Later, she presents Saru the pair of earrings and wants to know if she liked them. Her question "Do you like them?" goes unanswered for it is tagged with a statement, "you're a big girl now. Time you had something nice to wear in your ears. We must make you some gold bangles next year,"(171) leads to Saru`s tough reaction and disappointment. She misreads her mother's words and construes that her feelings were unimportant to her mother and the earrings were presented just as a ritual so that the growing up must be made to use them. She put the box aside and flung herself on the bed to convey the point that it was the mother who was behaving badly. Later, she wears them even after her marriage, which is indicative of a secret attachment with her mother. She only removes them when Prof. Kulkarni told her that her mother never wanted to meet her while on deathbed.

The love-hate relationship continues to trouble them intermittently. When Saru goes in for higher studies and bags a first class in her Intermediate examination, her mother cooks something "special for dinner, something fried, something sweet and I knew she was pleased." (141). This is a spontaneous, motherly act but the communication gap is so wide that such acts of affection and concern do not help in paving it. Saru projects her anger and bitterness by going against her mother. She joins the faculty of medicine to become a doctor much against the wishes of her mother. Kamla calling Saru a 'responsibility' to be married off, sparks off further hostility and in a fit of anger she bursts out, "I am not talking to you, I'm not asking you for anything, I know what your answer will be no, forever a "no" to anything I want. You don't want me to have anything; you don't want me to do anything. You don't even want me to live" (142). Immense hatred surges within her to make her utter words like "I hated her, I wanted to hurt her, wound her, make her suffer. But did not know how" (142). Saru fails to perceive the hidden concern of her mother who wants her to marry and settle happily. Her refusal to let Saru study further is based on her worry as to how her husband (Saru's father) would be able to support her studies with his meagre salary and meet the expenses of her marriage later on, rather than an antagonism towards her daughter. If we try to understand the mother's concerns from the social context, we find that her anxiety is not baseless and it is confirmed by Saru's father's statement, "Look, she knows how it is. I can pay either for her marriage or her studies. She chooses to be educated. Let her. It's her choice" (144). Kamla's uneasiness and care over, as to "who'll look after her in Bombay?" (142) goes unheeded. This seals effective communication between the mother and daughter.

The problem with Saru is that she sees every act and word of her mother through the haze of those thoughtless words uttered by her mother when she held her guilty of her brother's death. She fails to initiate conversation with her, nurturing her anger against her and the communication gap widens. Just to defy her mother she marries Manohar, a man much below her status and fiery personality and from another caste. The mother always refers to him as "that man as if his name would have soiled her lips" (30). Her derision and the prediction of troubles in love marriages carries her covert concern for her daughter. She states:

> I know all these love-marriages. It's love for a few days, then quarrels all the time. Don't come crying to us then. (69)

> You won't be happy with him. I know you won't. A man of a different caste, different community ... what will you two have in common? (98)

Kamala's statement reminds one of what Akka says in *Roots and Shadows* when Indu, the protagonist marries Jayant against Akka's wishes. She too like Kamala had warned her saying, "such marriages never work" (Deshpande, 1983: 74). Later in life, Saru holds her mother responsible for her marriage. What Nancy Friday states seems quite true in this case when she says that "blaming mother is just a negative way of clinging to her still" (1977: 84). Like Jaya in *That Long Silence,* who marries Mohan simply because her mother opposed it, Saru too admits that she married Manu just because her mother had opposed it. She says, "If you hadn't fought me so bitterly, if you hadn't been so against him, perhaps I would never have married him" (96).

Saru's mother Kamla must have, in a fit of sorrow unmindfully branded Saru as the murderer of Dhruva. Under the garb of apathetic indifference her love for her daughter does not go unfelt by the readers. Unfortunately, Saru could not sense its undercurrent. Saru's mother died of cancer without even once wanting to see her. Her adamant behaviour can be read as hurt, for her daughter had not even once cared to visit her or inquired about them after her marriage. This led to her jumping to the conclusion that Saru did not care for them. So, she had stifled her memories of Saru and destroyed her photographs. Her rude words that haunt and hurt Saru must have erupted from these feelings and impressions:

> What daughter? I have no daughter. (109)
>
> Daughter? I don't have any daughter. I had a son and he died. Now I am childless. (196)
>
> I will pray for her unhappiness. Let her know more sorrow than she had given me. (197)

Saru flinches at these remarks and admits later to her father that it is because of her curse that she is "unhappy, destroyed" (197) and her admittance of her wronging her mother make her express her repentance; "the more I suffer, the greater the chance perhaps of my expiating the wrong" (204). At times Saru craves for forgiveness and wonders, "What about me? Did she think of me at all? She died at peace with herself, you say. How could she after what she did to me? ... Don't you know how she cursed me?" (195), but to her "The idea of forgiveness" appeared "stupid" (28). After Dhruva's death Saru had culled out the crux that she "didn't exist for her. I died long before I left home" (32). Saru felt she did not matter to her mother and her mother felt she had no daughter for after her marriage she forgot them completely. Her hopeless struggle for forgiveness and her mother's disownment of her for being ungrateful fails to bridge the gap in their relationship, for due to lack of communication and initiation they fail to iron out their differences.

Mother's verbal violence hurts Saru again and again. She recalls what her mother had said about her appearance, "I was an ugly girl. At least, my mother told me so. I can remember her eyeing me dispassionately, saying .... You will never be good looking. You are too dark for that" (61). Here again Kamala, successfully conditioned by the patriarchal culture, voices the community's demand, especially Indian, for fair skin. She warns Saru, "Don't go out in the sun, you'll get dark ... (123); "Don't go out in the sun. You'll get even darker ... We have to get you married" (45). Such colour prejudice is not uncommon in reality too but is perpetuated and honed by the media like the ads of fairness lotions, creams, and soaps and also confirmed by the matrimonial advertisements in the newspapers seeking fair brides. Women chasing the beauty standards to meet the rigid standards of cultural attractiveness often result in conflict and depression.

In her essay, "The Roots of Anxiety in Modern Woman," Marya Mannes observes:

> What I call the destructive anxieties are not the growth of women's minds and powers but quite the contrary. The pressures of the society and the mass media make women conform to the classic and traditional image in men's eyes. They must be not only the perfect wife, mother and home-maker, but the ever young, ever slim, ever alluring object of their desires. Every woman is deluged daily with usages to attain this impossible state ... the real demon is success – the anxieties engendered by this quest are relentless, degrading, corroding. (1964: 412)

Verbal and psychological violence inflicted on Saru by Kamala is triggered by Dhruva's accidental death. A perpetrator of patriarchal notions, she wishes her daughter dead in her son's place. In the second place, she opposes Saru's choice to study further which is again culturally influenced. This violence is answered with equal force by Saru. To spite her mother she goes a step further by marrying Manohar from another community, much against her wishes and never visits her parents after marriage. This might be the probable reason as to why her mother never wanted to see Saru while on her deathbed, having felt grossly hurt by her acts.

II

Saru, the protagonist suffers violence not only at the hands of her mother but her husband as well. She is a victim of marital rape. But before we understand violence suffered by Saru, let us admit that men too are victims of gender bias. The cultural pressures of attaining the masculine dream of power and excellence especially above womenfolk inevitably spawn jealous feelings within Manu, Saru's husband. He is unable to reconcile to the fact that his wife is far above him professionally. His jealousy is triggered by a question put to him by a girl who had come to interview Saru. Her query, "How does it feel when your wife earns not only the butter but the bread as well?" (35–36), bolsters his ego and it was the day when he converts into a rapist. Next time it is his colleague's wife's statement, uttered in mirth that literally wounds him. On announcing that Manu and family were going on a short holiday to Ooty, Bangalore and Mysore she had said to her husband that if he had married a doctor he too would have gone to Ooty." Such teasing statements wound Manu and the professional incompatibility – he a lecturer and his wife a doctor – becomes a sore point in their marriage. The reprisal comes in form of marital rape for Saru. Marriage is supposed to be an "equal partnership" (137) but for Saru it becomes "hell of savagery and submission" and "the sword of domination become lethal" thus spoiling it. She loses the "pride in my (Saru's) professional status" (78) for it was the cause of her suffering:

> ... a kind of disease had attacked their marriage. A disease like syphilis or leprosy, something that could not be admitted to others. This very concealment – made it even more gruesomely disgusting, so that she was dirty and so was he and so was their marriage. She wanted no more of it, but there were children and

she was still hung on the past, enough to make the word divorce a frightening one. (70–79)

Though unable to "passively endure" Saru goes on suffering silently. Marital rape remains unvoiced in almost all cases for it is another duty of a wife to fulfil her husband's desires. Divorce too is a taboo and on the grounds of marital rape it can be embarrassing for the wife. Saru too hesitates:

> She had thought of saying it to a lawyer, any lawyer, chosen at random, when once, in a moment of desperation, she had walked up and down a road, reading names of lawyers on ancient boards. Nerving herself to enter, to say ... Can I divorce my husband?
>
> Any Reasons?
>
> He's cruel.
>
> How? Will you be specific, please give details ... Bed, the one she shared with her husband, was to her a intensely private place. She could not, would not, draw aside the curtain that hid from the world. (97)

Finding herself unable to "passively endure" she suggests leaving her job to Manu, thinking it would help (70). But Manu rejects the idea outrightly for it would mean lesser finances and low standard of living.

Undoubtedly, Manu is a sadist who indulges in a non-consensual sexual activity but a discernible reader can look beyond what meets the eye. His behaviour is paradoxical. He shows signs of a caring husband like when he tells Saru, "I'm glad we came here .... You look very tired and strained, you need to take things easy, relax. Look, I'll take the children off your hands'. And no more dark circles under your eyes, Okay?" (112). On another occasion he says, "poor girl, you really are tired, it seems. Come on, wash your hands and lets go to bed. Relax now. Why don't you take a day off tomorrow? Forget about the hospital, forget about your patients. Stay at home ... (81). This concern is rejected by Saru as a "sham, a farce, a ghastly pretence" (112). He seems to be totally unaware of his sadism inflicted on Saru. It seems he unconsciously does so which means he is sick and a fit case for pathology. The bruises he inflicts on Saru are tell–tale signs of his sadism, but when he notices these in the morning he is utterly surprised and says innocently:

> "God, Saru ! Have you hurt yourself?
> Look at that !" (203)

At this Saru admits that his concern was genuine.

Saru realises "he doesn't know it himself what he does to me at night. That's why he never speaks of it" and she considers it "black outs about certain actions" yet "pitying him too" (96).To fathom the problem faced by Manu one finds that Saru too is in a way unconsciously violent to Manu. She herself admits that she was "impatient with Manu and "ignored" him at times (92). Her relationship with Boozie, her boss, who goes to the extent of favouring her above everybody else is disliked by him. Saru's success in getting a loan from Boozie highlights Manu's failure in arranging the money. He is aware of people's curiosity in Saru's and Boozie's relationship:

> I (Saru) knew that there was plenty of talk about me and him. I know what they said about my rapid climb since the day I met him, I could feel, even here, inspite of the assumed well-bred airs, the sniggers, the ugly meaningful looks ... If Manu noticed the looks and smiles, he ignored them. (93)

Boozie's gesture of putting both his hands on Saru's shoulders and shaking them gently results in raised eyebrows but Manu appears calm which can be construed as his detachment or maybe estrangement or was it his public embarrassment. Saru does not resist Boozie's advances and liberties probably because she has confidence in herself or she knows well enough that his interest in her was a man's interest in a woman but to Manu it is suggestive of her rejection and abandonment of Manu. It is more a kind of emotional assault, a betrayal, an injustice. In such a state the reaction is helpless rage and despair answered by his sexual sadism.

All this brings a dangerous turning point in their marriage and their relationship undergoes a catastrophic change. Nobody comes forward to de-escalate their tension. Both feel lonely within themselves. Saru does not protest but feels "a silent mourning wail inside her" (124). The "comfort and security" she had looked for in a marriage is corroded. Both Manu and Saru become sufferers.

III

The subplot of the novel too contains myriad flashes of violence in the lives of minor women characters. Saru's friend Smita is a victim of economic violence perpetrated by the husband through his total and absolute control over the family finances and denial of pocked expenses to his wife. Ironically, women are not even aware that this is a form of violence. Smita, a housewife, "shame-facedly" asks Saru to lend her hundred rupees secretly for if her husband gets to know, "he'll be furious" and in a meek tone says, "you don't know how lucky you are not to ask anyone for money. If you knew my problems ..." (119).

At another place we see Madhav's father has his own way of punishing his wife. Madhav's brother runs away and the father puts the whole blame on the mother and refuses "to eat anything she cooks" (207). Madhav's mother, conditioned according to the traditional feminine, puts her husband above herself and accepts his behaviour as a punishment whereby she is "deprived of a chance to serve her husband" (207). Nearer home, Saru remembers her maternal grandfather who had abandoned her grandmother just after a few years of marriage. His act had left his wife psychologically scarred and financially crippled, burdened with two daughters to look after and fend for herself. Saru too unconsciously hurts her children by depriving them of motherly care. She in order to escape torture at the hands of her husband heads for her father's house, fully aware that her children would miss her.

Masochism too is a form of violence. Women turn masochists chasing the self image based in traditional goodness of self-sacrifice; putting their selves into the service of others they indulge in nihilism. Reflecting the condition of women Saru muses:

> The myriad complaints, the varying symptoms, due thought, if put together would provide a world of data for treatise on the condition of women. Backache, headache, leucorrhoea ... all the indignities of a woman's life become silently ... stupid, silly martyrs. She thought: idiotic heroines. Going on with their tasks and destroying themselves in their bargain, for nothing but a meaningful modesty. Their unconscious, unmeaning heroism, born out of the myth of the self-sacrificing martyred woman .... (107)

Such sacrificing attitude and negation of self germinates from the patriarchal ideology and is its essence though it is tragically unfair.

Another example of verbal and psychological violence is reflected in Boozie's admonishment of Saru. The choice of his words used to taunt and insult Saru when she rushes with the lumber puncture, aptly points to the obvious sexist bias in the treatment of women. Boozie's words do undermine her self-confidence. In a cynical tone he says, "I don't want incompetent, clumsy, uninterested females cluttering up this place. Go home play with your rolling pins and knitting needles" (89).

Disgusting rituals in community like dowry ignite deep psychological and often physical violence. Why does Saru's mother thinks of her in terms of a "responsibility"? Just because the mother has Saru's marriage in mind and she knows how hard it is to arrange for a dowry. She also opposes Saru's desire to study further thinking that it would leave them with hardly any money to spend on her dowry. Padmakar Rao is forced into a marriage with a girl hardly of his choice, who brings in handsome dowry to save his parents from the trouble to arrange for his sister's dowry. Rituals like these cause a lot of mental and physical agony to the bride and her family.

Reading *The Dark Holds No Terrors* one sees that specific forms of gendered violence are those which germinate from the community itself. As both men and women are the products of their culture and they find it difficult to step out of the prescribed roles/norms. Saru's husband Manohar (Manu) is so conditioned by the societal code of conduct where men have to excel and attain the masculine dream of being superior that he becomes irrational and jealous of his wife. Thus, to prove his dominance, he resorts to non-consensual sexual activity. Economic violence on the part of Smita's husband; emotional violence that Madhav's father exerts on his mother, psychological violence through demand for dowry and a fair-skinned daughter-in-law all show that the relationship between violence, gender and community is circular. Men as well as women submit to the tradition which keeps women in subordination which is ultimately violent in order to validate their claim to societal membership. Concomitantly, this subservient relation of a female generates more violence and a vicious circle is formed. Probably an egalitarian relationship might check the outbreak of this epidemic of violence.

Works Cited

Beauvoir, Simon de. *The Second Sex*. Great Britain: Vintage, 1977.
Deshpande, Shashi. *The Dark Holds No Terrors*. New Delhi: Penguin, 1980.
—. *Roots and Shadows*, Orient Longman: Hyderabad, 1983.
—. *That Long Silence*. Penguin: New Delhi, 1988.
Friday, Nancy. *My Mother My Self*. USA: Delacarte Press, 1977.
Gilligan, Carol. *In a Different Voice*. USA: Harvard University Press, 1982.
Indra. *The Status of Women in Ancient India*. Banaras: Oriental Publishers, Second Revised Edition,1955.
Jordan, Judith V. "The Meaning of Mutualit'y in Women's Growth in Connection: Writing from the Stone Center in USA." The Guilford Press, 1991.
Mannes, Marya. "The Roots of Anxiety in Modern Woman". *Journal of Neuropsychiatry*, 5: 412, 1964.

10

Partition Violence in Jyotirmoyee Devi's *The River Churning*

A Gendered Perspective

SEEMA MALIK

The partition of India etched indelible scars in the collective memory that impacted the people's consciousness tremendously. It unleashed the cultural process of destruction and irrevocably tore apart individuals, families, homes, villages and communities forging new borders, new identities, new histories and new loyalties. Partition culminated in the violent fratricidal mania involving the three communities – Hindus, Sikhs and Muslims – both as perpetrators as well as victims. Though violence was the prominent constituent of the partition holocaust, nationalist historiography has "made an all too facile separation between 'partition' and 'violence'" (Pandey, 7). The historical imperative to deny the reality of communalism subsequently led to regarding the violence of 1947 as "someone else's history – or even, not history at all" (Pandey, 6). Gyanendra Pandey in *Remembering Partition* suggests that the historian's history works simultaneously to reveal and conceal the truth of the traumatic, genocidal violence of partition. Disciplinary history takes cognisance of the massivity of the partition violence but is reluctant to accept its reality and projects it as an aberration, something deviant as opposed to the norm of mutual understanding and harmony among the various communities.

However, violence inevitably engages the aesthetic sensibility of the partition writers. In their novels, they try to understand the nature of violence while representing partition, the politics behind it and its ramifications on the society and the individuals. Their approach is ineluctably 'tentative' and 'atemporal', creating secondary illusions through fictional narrative accounts. It does not generate a mere factual, unidirectional account of history. The essentially illusory and realistic nature of a fictional narrative liberates the analytical exercise by offering a multidimensional, open-ended discourse for further exploration. Thus, the creative responses to partition, explore the issue from the humane aspect at the core of which lie the wrongdoings and sufferings of the individual.

The history of partition, instead of formulating ideas, de-politicises and de-historicises the agency of women, as historical accounts are documented and analysed usually from a nationalist perspective and remain predominantly power-centred. Women have been considered as insignificant, non-actors who are generally at the receiving end. "They are presumed to be outside history because they are outside the public and the political, where history is made. Consequently, they have no part in it ... generally they are the flotsam and jetsam of historical events – present perhaps, but of no great significance" (Menon and Bhasin, 3). Though women were very much a part of the millions who witnessed and experienced partition, they seldom figure as the 'subject' in the master/male narratives. Accounts of women as agencies do occur but are projected only as supplementary to the male action. Women are also mentioned as 'victims' but no specific attention is given to their traumatic experiences. Women writers specifically address the representational deficiency of the large-scale gendered violence in the socio-cultural partition historiography. They furnish a more textured understanding of partition violence and focus not just on the visible and physical aspect of violence but also on the psychological impact of partition violence that scarred the mind of the victims forever. This article seeks to foreground this aspect of partition violence in Jyotirmoyee Devi's novel *The River Churning* after explicating briefly the multiple levels of gendered violence that women experienced during partition.

There is no doubt that the partition trauma left the general masses aghast but the tragic part of the story was that women were the worst sufferers. Partition was a pathogeny of the male lust for power. It was a typical male construct where women were made the site of macabre enactment. Driven by religious hatred, it was women who were singled out for humiliation and annihilation. The history of partition was a history of deep violation – physical and psychological – for women who experienced it. History of women may not necessarily be the same as that of men. The impact of this cataclysmic event on women was much different, more traumatic and enduring than on men. They were impacted by partition in many particular ways and undeniably experienced its fallout. The word 'partition' is inadequate to encompass the myriad meanings this event had for women or to even approximate the many levels of experiences they lived through.

As a result of the discourse of honour that gradually evolved under the matrix of macro-sociological dynamics, sexual purity of women had been endowed with the status of "the transcendental signifier" of male/community/national honour. It was not woman as an entity or as a being, rather it was her chaste body that had become a synonym, an icon of the honour of the nation, the religious community and the family. And perhaps this explains why women's sexuality occupied a special place in the enactment of violence that took place during partition. In this hyper masculine revenge drama of mutual humiliation, women's bodies were the 'territories' that were violated, mutilated and tattooed with the symbols of the other religion. During partition, rape and molestation of Hindu, Sikh and Muslim women became an overt way of asserting the identity of one community over the other. "Perhaps men on both sides thought this to be the best way to punish and humiliate – like Draupadi" (Devi, 90). Violation of a woman's body became an expression of triumph and intimidation of one community over the other. The notion of honour governed specifically by patriarchal values made women the symbols of the male honour: "Women's sexuality symbolises manhood; its desecration is a matter of such shame that it has to be avenged" (Menon and Bhasin, 43). Thus, ironically it was women who were ultimately subjected to systematic humiliation as their body became the sign through which "the dialogue between men was conducted" (Das, 186). It is equally ironic that despite the general prevalence of the patriarchal notion that women do not have any religion which is "in line with the misogynist north Indian proverb *'beeron ki kai jaat'* ('what caste {or nationality} can a woman have?'), during partition "they came for a moment to stand for nothing else" (Pandey, 165).

The notion that the honour of the community lay in protecting its women from the male aggression of the other community was so strongly embedded in the minds of the men that they resorted to another kind of violence against their own women. The fear, that the males of the other community might establish their territoriality over the bodies of their women, made the men of one community propel their women towards annihilation either willingly or forcibly. Thus women were hardly left with any option – it was either sexual appropriation by the other community or death at the hands of their own men and in between lay the option of suicide that was given the garb of martyrdom. In *Remembering Partition* Gyanendra Pandey points out that certain acts of violence during partition have been canonised/glorified and the bravery and suffering of women have been translated into "hallowed martyrdom" whereas the accounts of the survivors show that the line between choice and coercion was very thin. Moreover, women were intimidated by the impending fate and acquiesced due to 'shame-fear-dishonour-rejection' syndrome. Their conditioning was such that they were made to believe that actual death was preferable to death in life in the form of rape, abduction, conversion and forced marriage. During partition women had fallen prey to the patriarchal consensus (about killing their women) that prevailed among men not only as victims but also as agents because the elderly women, in line with their men's thoughts, also forced the younger women to die. Thus women not only faced violence from the men of other community but their own community/men/families were also perpetrators of violence against them.

Besides the pain and humiliation that the experience of partition brought for women, another trauma awaited them in the form of 'Recovery Operation'. This programme began not so much as a concern for the abducted women but mainly because of its political and symbolic significance – the abduction of women had directly hit the national honour. The state that had initially failed to prevent the abduction, physical transgression and displacement of women now wanted to play the role of the welfarist/responsible patriarch and rectify the past. It had become a prestige issue. Women, on whom the operation was to be implemented, were nothing more than insignificant sites, mere pawns with no choice in the matter. Once recovered, they were in a state of helplessness and dependency. Those very relatives who had raised a hue and cry for their recovery, had by now either settled with new companions and were therefore, unwilling to accept them or were reluctant to accept as their women were 'soiled'. Thus, they were not received back into their fold and had to lead a life at the margins of the society. The greatest jolt that these women received after recovery was the demand to part with their children born of mixed union as they were permanent reminders of their violation. The same was true of the pregnant women who were coerced into 'being cleansed' and terminate their pregnancy:

> Abducted as Hindus, converted and married as Muslims, recovered as Hindus but required to relinquish their children because they were born of Muslim fathers, and disowned as 'impure' and ineligible for membership within their erstwhile family and community, their identities were in a continual state of construction and reconstruction. (Menon and Bhasin, 98)

In the whole process of recovery, women were central, significant, yet no attempts were made to understand their feelings, their agonies and their pains. Instead the violence inherent in the recovery mission was 'normalised' as benevolence and magnanimity. Thus women on both sides witnessed the incomprehensible birth of two nation states by paying for the crimes of which they were the chief victims, thereby establishing their solidarity in the process of nation building.

Women, on both sides, were at the receiving end of violence as its victims – it was they who were raped, it was they who were widowed, it was they who were treated as outcasts and untouchables and finally, it was they who were left to pick up the scattered threads and begin anew the process of rehabilitation and resettlement of their families. And yet, hardly any master/male narrative on partition places women at the centre. Thus to get a wholesome view and to read partition as a gendered narrative of displacement and dispossession, we have to turn to women writers who speak for themselves. They articulate the voice of the 'fragments' which compels a different reading of partition. Women writers like Krishna Sobti, Qurratulain Hyder, Ismat Chugtai, Attia Hosain, Anita Kumar, Shauna Singh Baldwin, Bapsi Sidhwa and Amrita Pritam adopt a perspective that locates women at the centre rather than at the periphery. In her novel *Pinjar (Skeleton)*, Amrita Pritam criticises the nexus of religion, community and nation, exposes patriarchal hypocrisy and challenges the national obsession with borders. She portrays the gendered experience of partition with a felt poignancy, in her poems, short stories and novels. She empathises with young girls whose dreams were shattered, whose youthful bodies bore the scars of lust and whose psychological health was permanently damaged. Addressing Waris Shah, Amrita Pritam writes:

> From the depths of your grave, Waris Shah,
> Add a new page to your saga of love
> Once when a daughter of Punjab wept
> Your pen unleashed a million cries,
> A million daughters weep today, their eyes turned
> To you, Waris Shah.

This experience was not confined only to Punjab; women in Bengal also underwent similar trauma which has been portrayed variedly in Bengali fiction. And one of the most powerful of such 'fragmentary voices' is that of Jyotirmoyee Devi who highlights the hitherto marginalised situation of women within the socio-political space of the partition 'process'. Jyotirmoyee Devi's *Epar Ganga Opar Ganga* (*The River Churning*) was originally published in 1967 as *Itihasey Streeparva* (The Woman Chapter in History). Since time immemorial woman and her body is being hegemonised and colonised by men. Jyotirmoyee Devi's *The River Churning*, a partition novel, is a vehement voice to expose and counter these tendencies and is a powerful denunciation of hypocritical obsession of the patriarchy with women's sexual purity. In her Author's Note, Jyotirmoyee Devi clarifies and states her theoretical position by referring to the chapter *Stree Parva* in the *Mahabharata* and points out that the chapter hardly deserves the name:

> ... Even Vedavyasa could not bear to write the real Stree Parva .... Cowards do not write history. There are no great poets among women, and even if there were, they could not have written about the violation of their own dignity. Hence there is no recorded history of the real Stree Parva .... The Stree Parva of humiliation by men? ... The chapter that remains in the control of husband, son, father and one's own community – there is no history of that silent humiliation, that final pain .... The Stree Parva has not yet ended, that last word is not yet spoken. (Devi, xxviii)

Jyotirmoyee Devi makes a searing commentary on partition and on the erasure of women from the annals of history. This is analogous to Partha Chatterjee's point of view towards the 'fragments' or 'fragmentary voices' and their role in the entire process of nation building. "A woman's body is a pawn even in the game of nation building" (Devi, xxvii). History will continue to be 'his story' till the fragmentary voices like that of Jyotirmoyee Devi are heard and taken into consideration.

The narrative of the novel, hailed as "cerebral" by Mahasweta Devi throws the consciousness of the reader in the flashback amidst the sudden blaze of communal frenzy, which destroyed the 'peace' of a village on a certain night in 1946 in the erstwhile East Bengal. Harmony, peace and amity are trampled over and within a few hours, there is complete havoc in the Hindu households. A young adolescent girl Sutara is the only survivor in her family. Her father has been killed, her mother drowns herself and her elder sister ... who knows what happened to her? And Sutara? "She wanted to reach mother and began to run, but stumbled and fell. Then everything went blank" (Devi, 8). She is shattered physically and psychologically and her Muslim neighbours rescue her and give her refuge.

But the trials of fear and pain do not end with the molestation of the physical. The endless trials of 'assault' on Sutara had just begun. Tamijuddin, her father's friend, whose family takes her in and nurtures her, faces threat from his own 'community.'

Tamijuddin's wife's down to earth understanding of the social dynamics is proven right when Sutara's brother, on hearing about the news of her survival, responds in a meek lukewarm manner. Ultimately, Tamijuddin and his eldest son safely escort her to Calcutta, where she moves in as a guest of her brother's father-in-law.

The protagonist, Sutara is thrust into the whirlpool of torment unaware after sexual appropriation by the men of one community. Initially, partly because of her innocence and partly because of her unconscious state at the time of the assault, she is unable to understand the reluctance and indifference of her brother to take her back to Calcutta. But realisation gradually dawns upon her when she is forced to go through the process of exclusion in the household of her brother's father-in-law in whose home the family takes temporary refuge. Acceptance becomes a remote possibility. Instead, she becomes an object of curiosity and becomes the 'topic' of discussion either loudly through innuendoes or in whispers. She is considered as impure, an outcast, an untouchable:

> Six months in Muslim household – what caste purity could such a girl be left with !All right, you have brought her here, but at least let her remain in a corner like *hadis* and *bagdis*! (Devi, 36)

> ... we Hindus have some code of daily rituals. It does not allow such girls to be accepted back into the family. They have to be kept apart. She has eaten with Muslims, lived with them – how can she be accepted in the community? The pots and pans in the kitchen must not be touched by her. We have to respect the deity, the Brahmins and the codes of social conduct. (Devi, 42)

The problem of Sutara becomes an inextricable web which is difficult to untangle. Sutara's brother and his father-in-law see through the entire process of exclusion but succumb to the pressures of the other family members and the rigid stand of the community at large. Sutara's victimisation is covered under the garb of the will of God and conveniently left to the Karma of her previous birth because "individuals do not really count before groups" (Devi, 48).

Just by her presence Sutara, a refugee from partition, creates complications. She is marginalised and excluded from the ritually pure domains of hearth, drinking water and marriage. It is ironical that immediately after the assault, her marriage becomes an improbable necessity in the eyes of the community. Yet it is feared that she might jeopardise the marriage prospects of her niece and is unwanted at the weddings – at Subha's wedding she is discriminated against, promptly fed and dispatched.

A sophisticated way to keep her at a distance is carved out by sending her off to a hostel run by the Christian missionaries. The 'patriarchs' of the family unburden the sense of guilt by saying:

> This has been going on since the time of Amba of the *Mahabharata* and Sita of the *Ramayana*. (Devi, 47)

Thus, she becomes the exiled Sita and part of the history of women of all time – "Satya, Treta, Dwapar and Kali Yuga, ... she represented all women who have been insulted, tortured, neglected, deserted, through history. She tried to determine the actual age of her body in her conscious, subconscious and unconscious minds" (Devi, 69). At the crossroads of her life, Sutara is totally at a loss with a sense of unbelongingness and bewilderment. She experiences that state of liminality where she could not belong to Tamijuddin's family without severing her roots as she was a high caste Hindu; she was not accepted by her own family because she had lost her caste, her honour and consequently, defiled communal honour. And then, in the new environment of the hostel, with European teachers and among girls who had forgotten which tradition they belonged to, Sutara was once again an outsider.

Mother Earth emerged from beneath and took Sita with her in the *Ramayana*. But Sutara cannot and does not die like Sita. She leads a most precarious existence on the margins of the society – she is neither a widow nor married. The vicissitudes of her life make her realise that she will never have a home. While working in Yajnaseni College, she finds a place to stay but it is neither a home nor a household and least of all a nest created by a woman's love and care:

> Did that make it a home? She knew, only too well, the bitter truth that she would never have a home. But at least her brothers would no longer have to finance her. She would be a burden no more. Did that mean she was now independent? Do women ever become independent? Does anyone worry about her? If they did

what would they have done? Sutara felt the weight of age and the experience of centuries added to her body, flowing in her veins. (Devi, 69)

Thus, with one stroke she is doomed to the community of the destitutes. Suddenly, her entire world recedes, fades like a shadow. She is marked for life and pays for the crime of others of which she is the prime victim. The invisible fire engulfs every thing – her ancestral home, family, honour, happiness and hope. Sutara, who had everything once, now has nothing. The damage is beyond repair. She is in a peculiar situation where she is treated by her own as a distant stranger. She is exiled forever.

Facing rejection and alienation, her lonely soul accepts life as it is. But has she really? No. Sutara could hardly get her memories out of her system. Sakina's marriage proposal of her brother Aziz for Sutara, brings back all the horrors of the nightmare. She says, "How can I forget the fate of my sister, my parents?" (Devi, 93) and when Promode comes into her life as a silver lining, her heart is very heavy with conflicting emotions – "hope, despair, fear, fatigue had left her as burdened as the earth. And her mind? It had been reduced to pulp by the combined neglect and revulsion of society. There was nothing left of it" (Devi, 131).

Thus, through Sutara's predicament, Jyotirmoyee Devi foregrounds the perpetual, subtle psychological violence that women endured throughout their life after being physically transgressed during the partition. For them, the partition was not merely an 'event' of 'rupture' which moved on a path of "a continuum from pain to healing" (Francisco, 227) and where repair was through the "healing power of memory" (Francisco, 239) but was/has been a 'process' of continual trauma, marginalisation and exclusion where memory has served only to deepen the eternal raw wound rather than heal it.

The novel offers a critique of the nationalist patriarchal versions of history by opening them up at their critical erasures and exclusions. In the beginning of the narrative, while trying to tackle the inquisitive queries of young girls, Sutara says:

> History is a vast subject, it is not possible for one person to cover all of it. You can study in depth and write the history of your own

nation. You can do it, can't you'? And, remember, history is not confined to the pages of a book ... the victor is always prejudiced about the history of the vanquished, he keeps things from coming to light, he prefers to conceal. Does history tell you about the weak and the poor? No. (Devi, 3)

Thus, Sutara's situation asserts and substantiates what is termed by the author as the unfinished agenda of the yet to be completed *Stree Parva*. Such narratives explore the interstices of history, expose the inadequacy of the numerous narratives on the partition and compel a different reading. They add a new dimension to the partition as a process and emphatically point out that during the partition, it was the women, and not the vandals, who had to endure the crime forever because physical violence not only crushed their spirit but also alienated them from the society.

Works Cited

Chatterjee, Partha. *The Nation and Its Fragments*. Delhi: Oxford University Press, 1995.

Das, Veena. *Critical Events: An Anthropological Perspective on Contemporary India*. Delhi: OUP, 1995.

Devi, Jyotirmoyee. *The River Churning*. Trans. Enakshi Chatterjee. New Delhi: Kali for Women, 1995.

Francisco, Jason. "In the Heat of Fratricide: The Literature of India's Partition Burning Freshly." *The Annual of Urdu Studies*, no. 2, 1996.

Menon, Ritu and Kamla Bhasin. *Borders and Boundaries: Women in India's Partition*. New Delhi: Kali for Women, 1998.

Pandey, Gyanendra. *Remembering Partition: Violence, Nationalism and History in India*. Cambridge: Cambridge University Press, 2001.

11

Violent Women in Fiction by Women Writers

USHA BANDE

The cherished belief that aggression and violence are male precincts while submission and vulnerability are traditionally female receives a jolt when women protagonists turn violent in fiction by women writers. Particularly disconcerting are murders committed by women. Woman as killer is just unacceptable to our notion of femininity; the act of killing the spouse, or committing suicide is not only horrendous, it is bewildering also and calls for a psychological exploration to understand the psychodynamics of their violent behaviour. Of late, women writers are exploring various issues of female vulnerability including female agency and female anger. When male attitude becomes unbearable and threatens the self with annihilation, women retaliate. How they strike back depends on the situation and individual psyche – it may be through an act of unprecedented vengeance to shame the victimiser or through murderous rage. The question central to this enactment of violence is: what are the social and psychological compulsions and provocations that lead them to homicide?

In this article I propose to study two novels: Anita Desai's *Cry, the Peacock* and Bharati Mukherjee's *Wife*, and two short stories:

"The Inner Rooms" by Shashi Deshpande and "Dropdi" by Mahashweta Devi. I shall also refer briefly to Ann Petry and Gloria Naylor, two African American writers to substantiate my thesis. In *Cry, the Peacock* and *Wife* gruesome murders take place and raise many questions regarding the sanity of the murderous protagonists and the world of fantasy they create to justify violence. In "The Inner Rooms" the stigma of abduction and rejection traumatises Amba; the intensification of feeling of worthlessness and helplessness threaten her 'self'; her anger remains latent and is carried from this life to life hereafter; ultimately it spurts out in the form of fatal vengeance which destroys both, the victim and the victimiser. Mahashweta Devi's "Dropdi" does not kill but her response is violent enough to slaughter the manhood of her molester. The argument here is that if women, who are supposed to have internalised the virtue of silence, passivity and endurance, react violently, it could certainly have deeper psychological and social reasons than meet the eye.

Shashi Deshpande's short story "The Inner Rooms" deserves first mention as it shows the terrible volcanic force of repressed hostility and anger which seeps into the psyche and corrodes the personality unendingly. It retells the tragic story of Amba who, rejected, humiliated and frustrated at the hands of male chauvinists suffers a lonely and meaningless existence; ultimately, she finds peace only when she has wreaked vengeance on her abductor, Bhishma. Based on the *Mahabharata* episode it recounts the story of Amba, Ambalika and Ambika from a modern feminist angle. According to the *Mahabharata* tale, the three princesses of Kashi are carried away by Bhishma to be given in marriage to his brother Vichtravirya. While the two sisters accept their lot, Amba does not. She rejects Vichtravirya in the open assembly and professes her love for Salva, the king of Sauba. That a woman should take the reigns of her life in her hands is laudable and speaks of her agency. But that victory is short lived. When Amba goes to Salva, her heart full of love, he refuses to marry her on the plea that since he has been defeated at the hands of Bhishma, he has forfeited his claim on her. She returns to Vichtravirya fuming with rage who rejects her too on the grounds that he cannot marry a woman who has bequeathed her heart to another man. It is not "honourable", contends Vichtravirya to marry her. She then challenges Bhishma, "you marry me, then. It's you who have done this to me. You must make amends now" (Deshpande, 1993: 99). But Bhishma is under an oath of celibacy. Breaking it would be "dishonourable" he argues. Rejected and frustrated, Amba suffers untold miseries; she loiters in the wilderness, undertakes penance and ultimately enters fire to be reborn as Shikhandi to take her revenge. It is because of and through her/him (Shikhandi is neither man nor a woman) that Bhishma is killed.

In Amba, Shashi Deshpande recreates the representative of all women who suffer oppression and humiliation at the hands of the society governed by male set of laws. Amba revolts but her voice is stifled and becomes meaningless; she loses all relationships that would have given meaning to her life. Her softer feelings give way to "pride, anger, hatred and revenge" and reduce her to a pathetic figure, "neither a daughter, nor a wife, nor a mother" (100). Thus disinherited, Amba becomes a terribly lonely woman whose only wish now is to kill her tormentor. She does not mind if she has to wait for lives to come to take her revenge. She is almost like Sylvia Plath's terrifying woman uttering a warning to the male:

> Beware
> Beware
> Out of the ash
> I rise with my red hair
> And I eat men like air. (Plath, 1965: 5)

This is Plath's 'new woman' who has "the great and terrible gift of being reborn," as a critic puts it (Rosenthal, 1971: 70). In Amba, too, we see the reincarnation of the terrible woman. She seems to say, "the world has lost its soul, and I my sex." When the voice of protest is stifled, it exacerbates rage and makes an attempt to find "the public redemption for private pain." Psychoanalyst Karen Horney opines that vindictiveness is "retribution for injury done" (Horney, 1950: 201). Marcia Westkott furthers Horney's findings and asserts that vindictiveness is closely linked with feeling abused and it requires that "injuries received, whether ancient or recent," be treasured and kept alive. "Vindictiveness is revenge against individuals from the past but it is expressed toward others in the present" (Westkott, 1986: 172).

The pent up anger of Amba, it may be concluded, finds expression through violence of the worst kind that smoulders in her, distorts her femininity and culminates in revenge. The rationale for Amba's revengeful rage, the transformation of her personality and the final act of vengeance cannot be explicated as subversive behaviour and the only viable solution to an intractable problem. Her murderous feelings cannot be addressed at the level of self-defense or depression, nor can they be located 'outside' the self as 'madness.' Her rage is the consequence of the paralysing effect of systemic and mortifying humiliation, of a social set-up that reduces women to portable property. Her disempowerment is, thus, the function of the culturally embedded belief in women's subjectivity; at its basis is the rhetoric of disobedience and punishment embedded in the socio-cultural discourse. Her anger is the psychological consequence of repeated abuse.

The resonance of the above story is found in another form in Mahashweta Devi's short story "Dropdi." Again, the story is based on the *Mahabharata* episode of Draupadi's disrobing in the Kaurava court. Mahashweta Devi rewrites the *Mahabharata* episode within the present day context. This is the story of Dropdi Mehjen, a Naxalite Santhal tribal woman classified as "most notorious female" listed as "long wanted" in many police dossiers. The story, first published in *Agnigarbha* in 1978, has political overtones; but when Dropdi dares Senanayak by retaliating in the most unusual manner the political perspective acquires feminist overtones. The two issues are: first, the efficacy of the use of physical language as response to sexual violence, and second, the relocation of the representation of victimisation, humiliation and punishment; these can be read from a feminist perspective. Mahashweta points out in her introduction to the collection (*Agnigarbha*), "Life is not mathematics and the human being is not made for the sake of politics. I want a change in the present social system and do not believe in mere party politics" (qtd. by Spivak, 1981: 381–402).

Dropdi is a Santhal tribal, a wanted Naxalite activist in hiding. She and her husband go underground but are intercepted; the husband is killed in an encounter and Dropdi is captured and gang-raped at the behest of Senanayak. Next morning when she is summoned before Senanayak, she strips herself and encounters him with unprecedented force. Senanayak is terrified by this act:

What is this?

He is about to cry but stops. Dropdi stands before him naked. Thigh and pubic hair matted with dry blood. Two breasts, two wounds.

What is this?

He is about to bark.

Dropdi comes close. Stands with her hands on her hip, laughs and says, the object of your search Dropdi Mejhen. You asked them to make me up, don't you want to see how they made me up?

Where are her clothes?

Won't put them on, sir. Tearing them.

Dropdi's black body comes even closer.

Dropdi shakes with an indomitable laughter that Senanayak simply cannot understand. Her ravaged lips bleed as she begins laughing. Dropdi wipes the blood on her palm and says in a voice that is as terrifying, sky splitting as her ululation, What's the use of clothes? You can strip me, but how can you clothe me again? Are you a man? (Spivak, 1981: 402).

Dropdi rejects male supremacy; she challenges the tradition; she rejects Senanayka's values and attacks him by her rebellious words "Are you a Man?" Dropdi is not the victim but a victor in that she puts the victimiser to shame. It is Senanayak who is now afraid to stand before an unarmed target. Dropdi pushes Senanayak with her two mangled breasts, and for the first time Senanayak is afraid before an unarmed target, terribly afraid (Spivak, 402). Dropdi refuses to be shamed and in her defiance Senanayak sees violence of the most terrible kind. Her attack is not physical; it is verbal/moral. Her response to male violence and violation of her 'self' threatens to annihilate her victimiser's sense of manhood.

Unprovoked murders are committed by Anita Desai's Maya and Bharati Mukherjee's Dimple in *Cry, the Peacock* and *Wife*, respectively. Maya pushes her husband Gautama, off the terrace because he comes between her and her worshipped moon; Dimple stabs Amit because she wants to savour a kind of Americanisation of herself by acting out like "a character in a T.V. series" (Mukherjee, 1976: 195). Both Maya and Dimple are declared 'mad' or 'neurotic' by critics who have their sympathies with Gautama and Amit; on the contrary, those who feel for the two protagonists try to understand them as human beings placed in tight situations, struggling to get what they want. As a scholar points out, Amit is the victim and his "murder signifies how an innocent, duty-conscious husband falls a prey to the neurotic madness of his wife" (Inamdar, 1991: 195). Others trying to explore the immigrant psyche view pre-history as a conditioning factor colliding with the unknown forces of the new experience creating a threatening situation to which the female protagonists act with ferocity. As regards Maya, Gautama's inability to understand her desires is held at fault by some while Maya's exaggerated claims for attention comes under the scanner of others. Here, we do not wish to fix responsibility. Our question is not *who* is at fault, but *why* do the women writers depict violence so nonchalantly. Why do they seem to accept the actions of their creations? We, as readers, do not condone murders, but we wish to probe the reasons behind the inordinate anger. It does not suffice to contend that the heroines are 'mad' or that they are representatives of feminist anger and rebellion. They have other compulsions which need be raked from under the debris of their psychotic rage.

Depiction of violence is not new either to Desai or to Mukherjee. In *Jasmine*, for example, the heroine murders her rapist and escapes undetected. There is no scar on her psyche, no burden on her conscience. After being defiled she contemplates suicide, but instead, she decides to slit the throat of the Half-Face, her rapist. After the act she goes on with the business of living, managing to adjust to America, without valid immigration papers. An immigrant in her situation, with illegal documents, is always on the run but she draws strength from the cultural icons – Kali and Durga – and makes life possible.

In Anita Desai's *Voices in the City*, Monisha commits suicide unable to face the realities of a protean existence. In *Baumgartner's Bombay*, Hugo Baumgartner is murdered in coldblood by his compatriot for a handful of silver. It appears antithetical that Anita Desai, whose Sita in *Where Shall We Go This Summer?*, is upset by minor incidents like children fighting, Ayahs brawling or crows pecking at a wounded eaglet which she terms unbearable violence, should allow chilling murders/suicide in her fiction.

That Maya kills her husband in a fit of neurosis is an obvious fact. But what is the cause of her neurosis? Maya is typically feminine – weak, submissive, vulnerable and hyper-sensitive. In Horneyan terms, she is a "morbidly dependent" person. Horney clarifies that for a morbidly dependent person – man or woman – love is "the ticket to paradise, where all woe ends; no more loneliness; no more feeling lost, guilty and unworthy; no more responsibility for self; no more struggle with a harsh world for which he feels hopelessly unequipped. Instead love seems to promise protection, support, affection, encouragement, sympathy, understanding" (Horney, 1950: 201). Maya's idea of merger with Gautama is of this sort. Her urge for sexual union is perceptible in her exultation on seeing male and female papaya trees in the garden:

> ... I contemplated that, smiling with pleasure at the thought of those long streamers of bridal flowers that flow out of the core of the female papaya tree and twine about her slim trunk, and the firm, wax-petalled blossoms that leap directly out of the solid trunk of the male .... Besides, if I could pleasure in contemplation of the male papaya, how much more food for delight in this male companion, surely. (Desai, 1963: 92)

Her longing to drown herself in love remains unfulfilled as in Gautama's taciturn world there are other far more important things to attend to than dancing attention on his so-called child-bride.

Gautama cannot understand Maya's self-effacing drives. His outlook has been formed by the "self-sacrificing years of study and hard work, his refusal to concede, to compromise ..." (93), whereas Maya is fed on fairy stories where there are no realities, only an elusive ability to ward off sorrows and live happily. The events of Gautama's early life – his freedom-fighter father always on the move, mother left to manage things – give him a sense of responsibility which Maya lacks. He is resigned and reserved in nature; she is clinging and demanding. He shrinks from emotions and in order to hide his fear of too much contact, he becomes passive and disinterested. He tries to take shelter in the philosophy of the *Gita* and feeds Maya on it. This could have been a healthy move but, Gautama fails in fusing his "ought" and "is" that is, he wants to change his wife as he thinks she "ought" to be, instead of understanding as she "is."

Maya reacts sharply when Gautama fails to respond to her love. She feels rejected and in order to attract him, she projects herself as a helpless, suffering martyr; a childless woman, lonely and discarded. Her pet's death makes her conscious of the reality of death. The Albino priest's prediction surfaces and exacerbates her fears; and she is gripped by phobia. All these are allied factors which hasten her de-personalisation process. Estranged from herself she externalises her troubles to ward off her self-hate and save her "idealised self." The self-hate is then projected on Gautama. Since her primary instinct is self-preservation, she convinces herself that Gautama does not love life, hence he can lose it; she values life, so she must save herself. The Albino priest's prediction that in the fourth year of their marriage one of them would die comes true. But at what price!

In analysing *Wife,* critics chiefly base their explorations on the expatriate experience, feminist revolt of Dimple, and her neurosis. While those with the feminist stance choose to elevate Dimple to the level of an angry female hero, others with sympathy for the male character (Amit) dub her as mad. The reason, they feel, is the expatriate situation which leaves a new comer utterly lonely and fear-ridden. I have, of course, nothing against these interpretations, but my contention is that Dimple Basu is a morbid person like Maya, though her case is not identical. Dimple is not a copy of Maya; she is an individual in her own right and her inter-personal and intra-psychic demands are peculiar to her psyche and socio-cultural-familial situations. She is not a feminist as her rage is not born out of any understanding of her 'female self.'

The novel is set mainly in the USA and only partly in India but India remains a palpable presence all through. The beginning of the novel serves to prepare the reader and the protagonist for an American encounter. The newly wed couple has moved to the USA and encounters the usual expatriate problems of adjustment, culture shock and wonder. In an interview, Bharati Mukherjee maintains:

We immigrants have fascinating tales to relate. Many of us have lived in newly independent or emerging countries which are placed by civil and religious conflicts .... When we uproot ourselves from those countries and come here either by choice or out of necessity, we suddenly must absorb 200 years of American history and learn to adapt to American society .... I attempt to illustrate this in my novels and short stories. (Mukherjee, 1989: 1)

Wife shows how Indians face the question of adjustment and how they have to encounter innumerable and unimaginable problems in seeking jobs, finding apartments and settling in a new society. This is what Amit and Dimple have to undergo. While Amit struggles with the outside world, Dimple fills in the vacuum by trying to be Americanised yet remain Indian. The conflict between internalised image of wifehood and the lure of freedom creates anxiety and the concomitant alienation.

Dimple's problem can well be summed up in Jasbir Jain's observation: "It is difficult to treat the novel as a study of cultural shock for even while in Calcutta, Dimple is an escapist and lost in her private world of fantasy" (Jain, 1989:15). As the novel opens we see Dimple eager to get married. "Marriage means freedom, cocktail parties on carpeted lawns, fund-raising dinners" and of course "love". Very soon, in fact, a few paragraphs later we perceive that she is in an inordinate hurry to get married to her dream prince, that she lacks grace and self-possession and has superficial attitude to life. She has created a world of fantasy for herself and has given it the semblance of reality. But reality is prosaic: after her marriage she has to live with her husband's mother in a small apartment, attend to the occasional visitor from her in-laws family, greet a fatigued husband back home after a day's work and take up the responsibility of household chores. She feels frustrated because she was not prepared for ordinariness of life.

Inner demands and outer realities, as well as responsibilities of married life create a conflicting situation. To give her life some meaning and save herself from debacle, she takes recourse to escape: sitting idle endlessly, never getting involved in living, dreaming of America. On reaching the USA, however, things do not change for her. She escapes again, sometimes physically and mostly mentally. Her excessive addiction to TV is her mental escape; her trips with Ina Mallik or Milt Gassier are her physical attempts to run away from the realities that bog her down.

Dimple never asks the question whether what she is doing is good or bad; whether she is being instinctive or impulsive. But Mukherjee seals her heroine's fate when she paints Dimple as given to melancholy. Contrary to the exuberance of *Jasmine*, the present novel *(Wife)* has melancholy and despair hanging heavy in the general air. Dimple's natural inclinations forebode dangers – her rejection of what she cannot reject in reality, her instinctive repugnance for all reality and inclination towards fantasy, her instinctive 'desire' to get what is not possible.

Dimple does not belong anywhere – neither to Calcutta nor to the USA, neither to the Basus nor to the Dasguptas (her parents). She loses her sense of belonging and sense of security which results in fear-neurosis. To maintain her identity in Calcutta, she tried to see herself as somebody 'different' than the Basu-woman; in America, in order to look different, she clings to her Indianness compulsiveness. Undoubtedly, it is good to maintain one's national identity, but when the move is compulsive, it becomes a dissociated effort.

In fear, Dimple clings to Amit for security. He, on the other hand, is so preoccupied with his search for job and settling in it, that he cannot relate to Dimple's fears, nor can he understand her demands. To be fair to Amit, let us admit that he is not callous. He cares for her and worries over her welfare, particularly on the day when he brings her back from the Park frozen. Dimple, it is clear is given to self-torture. This is the strategy a self-alienated person adopts to punish others, to make the partner feel guilty for having neglected him/her.

Dimple loses her hold on her real centre of being. There is a strange turmoil within and without. She tries to reiterate her Indianness by clinging to her Indian style but she becomes Americanised in imagination. This conflict generates fear because failure lurks on either side – if she clings to her Indian self she would fail Amit who encourages her to be like other Indian-immigrant women who have adopted American ways; but if she becomes Americanised, she would lose her identity. Failure means defeat and its outcome is anger of the frustrated. Venturing out and moving around the larger outside world is a kind of freedom but this freedom has another connotation for her; it means dissociating herself from her old self and becoming new. And to become a new person entails giving up or losing something you already had. When one is constantly pouring energy into the question of security and propriety and protection, where is the possibility of self-determination?

For Dimple, the safest way out of the trap is withdrawal. She shuts herself in herself, avoids all contacts, neglects her home and Amit and shirks all responsibility for the self. She blames others for her failures – the Indian friends, Milt, Amit, in fact everybody. Her despair and melancholy is the melancholy of those who see themselves as helpless, weak, powerless and dependent; they lack spontaneity. Disintegrating forces are let loose and she loses contact with the real self. Dimple's disorienting process is clear from her dreams – like the dream in which she saw her head slit open or in which she was murdered. She gets self-destructive impulses and wants to commit suicide. But instead, she resorts to sudden, stark violence:

> She sneaked up on him and chose a spot, her favourite spot just under the hairline, where the mole was getting larger ... she brought her right hand up and with the knife stabbed the magical circle once, twice, seven times. (p. 213)

Even after this horrendous moment, she fantasises – characters in TV serials escape the law after a murder. Probably she, too, would! She fails to grasp the enormity of her crime and the reality of her situation. Both Gautama and Amit pay the price for not understanding the demands and desires of their wives. Their taciturn attitude may be appreciable philosophically, but it is of no value when dealing with the human problems of loneliness.

In the first two cases, that of Amba (Shashi Deshpande) and Dropdi (Mahasweta Devi) there has been pain inflicted upon the women, the pain of rejection and of violation, respectively but in the latter two, Maya and Dimple, there is no obvious reason for turning against their husbands and resorting to murder. Whether these cases go to court and what legal defense is taken against Maya and Dimple cannot be known as the novels are open ended and provide no clue. But one thing is debatable, should we pathologise their responses and argue that the two women lost self control? Why do Maya and Dimple feel threatened when there is no obvious cause? It is difficult to blame the men – Gautama and Amit – for their attitudes. Their only trouble is that they are steeped in masculine culture and are unaware of their wives' psychological demands. As per the male view, it is enough for a wife to have the security of a home and a husband. That women need their own space, and also need to express and fulfill their desires is not the part of male purview. For this not the individual man but the socio-cultural fabric is at fault. Both Maya and Dimple are childless women; they are lonely and they crave their husbands' company. Their demand is understandable but their act is not condonable. It cannot be pardoned as the pathological motivation to kill.

Both Maya and Dimple seem to be struggling with the question of survival – physically as well as psychically. In Maya's case it was the deep seated fear of physical death in the fourth year of marriage as per the prediction as well as the apprehension of a breakdown because of her dwindling mental health. As for Dimple, the dread of physical death was due to the insecurity she felt in an alien land and of a breakdown due to the destructive power of her self-loathing. Psychologists aver that such persons transfer their projective identification, at an unconscious level, on to the other person, locate all bad in him/her and hope for relief from feelings of rejection and self-hate by annihilating the 'other'. When Maya says Gautama must die because he does not love life and when Dimple defends her act on the plea that such things are common in the USA, they are both building a temporary defense mechanism to save themselves from a psychic debacle generated by fear, self-hate and guilt. In fact, the most distressing consequence of violence is that the killer cannot differentiate between fantasy and reality. This is exactly what happens to Maya and Dimple. One appears unaware of the enormity of her act, the other sits relaxed fantasising.

So far we have tried to work out a strong defense for all the four – Gautama and Amit on one side and Maya and Dimple on the other. Violence is a destructive and distressing phenomenon and cannot be ignored as an act of 'madness'. Nor can we rationalise violence by condoning it as an act of bad/mad women. The process is complex and requires a probe into the social dynamics and personal relationships. To view woman as 'mad' or a passive victim is not only to deny her female agency but also to ignore the social psyche that creates conflicting situations by keeping the choices limited. Living in a restrictive and constrictive social order takes its toll. It may be argued that Maya and Dimple have no social or familial restrictions; they are living in a new society where they have the choice to go out. And, both Amit and Gautama, tell their wives to carve a career or a vocation for themselves. But the conditioning does not allow them to be adventurous.

The trend of depicting violent women and women's murderous rage is also present in African American fiction. In Ann Petry's *The Street* and Gloria Naylor's *The Women of Brewster Place* gruesome murder scenes are enacted at the end. In the former, Lutie Johnson kills Boots Smith to defend herself from rape; in the latter, Lorraine kills Ben after a gang rape. Both the incidents graphically present the harshness of life which leads to violence of the worst kind. The pent up rage of the two protagonists bursts out with volcanic force. Each takes her revenge on society at large and in each case one man becomes victim as a representative of the society and has to pay for its ills. But, while Smith is a party to the agency of oppression, Ben is not. He is innocent yet he is made to pay the price for being a 'father'. The murder scenes in both the novels are powerfully constructed to illustrate the strong reaction of women to the existing social order that denies them recognition as human beings. The difference is only in the manner of presentation – Petry uses external details to justify and magnify Lutie's anger, Naylor achieves it with minimum use of words.

In all these cases, the authors seem to suggest that violence may not be an answer to human problems but violence *per se* poses questions whether women can maintain their humanity in an oppressive and hostile environment. The epigraph to Naylor's novel suggests that when dreams are deferred, they explode. Accumulated hurts and betrayals give vent to violence which erupts on displaced targets.

When physical and psychological violence by men hurts the 'self' of the women, they are driven to take revenge. In *Jane Eyre*, Charlotte Bronte lets her mad Mrs Rochester burn down Thornfield, rendering Mr Rochester blind and maimed. In Jean

Rhy's *Wide Sargasso Sea*, Antoinette sets fire to the attic and in Anita Desai's *Fire on the Mountain* Raka, the girl child, sets the mountainside to fire. Susan Glaspell's play 'Trifles' is a superb exploration of the protagonist's anger and female bonding to defend another woman. Minnie Wright has been charged of murdering her husband by strangling him. While the men are busy finding the motive for murder as evidence against Minnie, the women – Mrs Hale and Mrs Peters stumble upon a concrete piece of evidence – a canary with its neck wrung. The women understand Minnie's psychological compulsion and successfully hide the dead canary. Their sympathy for the woman who has suffered at her husband's hand overcomes their sense of ethics and moral duty to the law.

Violence and aggression in women's writing reveals the variety of subtle forms of violence against women and their reaction to it. It also suggests options for dealing with that violence. Although it is not easy to unlearn the lessons of a culture and shake off the conditioning which requires women to be passive victims and men to be victimisers, the process of unlearning is taking place. As Jasbir Jain points out women's writing cannot be treated as a monolithic structure. Their works reflect their preoccupation with social and political issues, with moves outside cultural boundaries and with theoretical perspectives.

> The act of writing has enabled them to move outside the narrow role of man's helpmate, outside the role of the seductress, the angel or the witch. It helps problematize the areas of conflict and facilitates a search for alternative models. Women as they deconstruct literary forms and politico-social constructs continue to struggle with the ghosts of their fathers and the inheritance of their mothers. And they invite the reader to do the same. (Jain, 1996: 9)

Women's silence and passivity have broken at long last. No doubt, the angry woman, the killer, can be seen as setting right the wrongs of centuries and rejecting victimisation. But is being reactive a solution to social violence? By killing, are women not doing what their oppressors are doing? Are they not endorsing violence and walking on the same path as their oppressors do?

Works Cited

Desai, Anita. *Cry, the Peacock*. New Delhi: Hind Pocket Books, 1963.

Deshpande, Shashi, "The Inner Rooms." *Intrusion and Other Stories*. New Delhi: Penguin, 1993.

Devi, Mahasweta. "Dropdi." *Critical Enquiry*, Winter 1981. Vol. 8. No 2, pp. 381–402.

Horney, Karen. *Neurosis and Human Growth*. New York: W.W. Norton, 1950

Inamdar, F. A, "Immigrant Lives: Protagonists in Bharati Mukherjee's *The Tiger's Daughter* and *Wife*." *Indian Women Novelists*. Vol. 5. Ed. R.K.Dhawan. New Delhi: Prestige, 1991.

Jain, Jasbir, "Foreignness of Spirit: The World of Bharati Mukherjee's Novel." *The J & E.*, Vol 13, No 2. July 1989.

Jain, Jasbir. *Women Writing: Text and Context*. Jaipur: Rawat Publications, 1996.

Mukherjee, Bharati. *Wife*. Delhi: Sterling, 1976.

Mukherjee, Bharati. Qtd in *Sunday Review, The Times of India,* October 1, 1989.

Naylor, Gloria. *The Women of Brewster Place*. London: Sphere Books, 1980.

Plath, Sylvia. *Ariel*. New York: Harper and Row, 1965.

Petry, Anne. *The Street*. Boston: Houghton Mifflin, 1946.

Rosenthal, M.L. "Sylvia Plath and Confessional Poetry." *The Art of Sylvia Plath: A Symposium*. Ed. Charles Newman. Bloomington: Indian Univ. Press, 1971.

Westkott, Marcia. *The Feminist Legacy of Karen Horney*. New Haven: Yale Univ. Press, 1986

12

Victims of Violence

A Study of Three Stories from Tribal and Dalit Writing

USHA BANDE

Gayatri Spivak's well-known and oft-repeated question, "Can a subaltern speak?" if reworded as "What, when a subaltern speaks?" has the potential to lead us to a plethora of questions and a mind-boggling number of diverse answers. That Spivak's question is in itself a powerful statement of the hard realities of marginalised existence and contains a subtle streak of resistance is an unquestionable fact. The subalterns' will to resist the existing patriarchal power structure and the validity of their struggle, counter the notions of the marginalised as stereotypes of passivity and submissiveness. There is no denying that the voiceless – women, children, tribals and other disadvantaged sections – have been given voice, howsoever muffled; but 'voice' and 'visibility' carry within themselves the seeds of dissent and the consequent possibilities of retaliation from the powerful and this retaliation can be in the form of violence. In the field of literature, the postmodern trend of double writing has provided a potent tool to the writer to deconstruct the "hidden ideologies"[1] of the social order. By re-writing the versions of time-honoured mythologies, culture, history and tradition, the authors are trying to subvert the settled notions of representation to show the responsibility that comes with voice and visibility.

My aim in this article is to analyse three short stories coming from cross-sections of writers from three different parts of the country: "Satyakaam and Jaabaali" by Amitabh, a Dalit writer from Maharashtra; "Thaurani Devi" by E. Somnamani Singh from Manipur; and "Phoolkunwar" by Ajit Singh Jogi (ex-Chief Minister) from Chhattisgarh.[2] The stories were written/published at the end of the twentieth century and the beginning of the twenty-first – 1999, 1997 and 2003, respectively and give us glimpses of the lives of the doubly marginalised – incidentally, the backdrop is tribal/Dalit and the protagonists are women – living in the new India which we often like to gloss over as "Shining India," "Incredible India," or "Mahan Bharat."

The question I would like to raise and answer is: what happens when a subaltern speaks? The stories themselves represent precariously simple moments of collision with patriarchal power structures and bear testimony to the dynamic of powerlessness despite the assigned voice, and conversely, the vigorous self-assertion despite the obvious powerlessness. The women protagonists, who have the courage to stand on their own, are severely crushed but the rhetoric of the narratives deploy an alternative to the model of periphery against centre by making available a discursive territory highly suggestive of individual triumphs.

II

Amitabh's short story "Satyakaam and Jaabaali" published in Sahitya Akademi's *Indian Literature* is a re-written version of the Upanishadic story of Jabala and her son Satyakam. The mythological story runs thus: Jabala, a public woman, has a son for whose future she nurtures great dreams and when he is of age, she sends him to Sage Gautama to be inducted as his pupil. But the sage sends him back with a query about his father's name and the family gotra. The child comes back home and asks his mother; thereupon the mother broods that she has had relations with so many men that she could not tell him whose seed it was. She tells him without qualms, "Go and tell the revered Sage that you do not know who your father is, but you are Jabala's son and hence you are Jabala Satyakam." This frank assertion does not put off the Guru; instead Gautama accepts Satyakam and initiates him into higher knowledge. With time, the child attains self-realisation and becomes a known sage himself.

Amitabh's story is not so simple, though. It is set in a Harijan Basti, meaningfully called Bheempura, a filthy, crime-infested settlement packed with all possible perversions – rape, domestic/psychological/sexual violence, cunning, cheating, fraud, depravity and the pain and anguish of existence. The story at once becomes a tirade against the lop-sided development of modern India, of a woman's vulnerability and her final self-assertion. It subverts the old Upanishadic story and on its model it builds a more authentic tale of our times.

"Jaabaali was widow," the author puts it simply. "Within two years of her marriage, she had been widowed. So, everybody scoffed at her calling her husband-gobbler" (46). Jaabaali lived in Bheempura with her in-laws. They were old and feeble but strong enough to make her life difficult by their constant nagging. She was, however, the only earning hand and they could ill-afford to throw her out. She got a job in the mill after a long struggle with utter poverty. But life had more in store for her. She was gang-raped while on her way from the mill. Her in-laws died of shock. Jaabaali lost all interest in life. Her in-laws, though troublesome, provided her support and security. Lonely and desperate now, Jaabaali became a prey of the lecherous men of the Basti.

A son was born to her, whom she named Satyakaam. Life seemed to have a purpose now and she started dreaming of a great future for him. When he became of school-going age, she took him to the school. But a big question loomed before her – his father's name? It was then that she took a strange decision. She trained him thus, like the Jabala of yore:

"What name will you tell him, if asked?" she asked her son.

"Satyakam," he answered as taught.

"And the father's name?"

"Eh... the father's...?"

"Forgotten so soon, have you?"

Which father? – Jaabaali reflected – God knows how many have slept with me … how can I tell him whose seed he belongs to? (Italics mine, added for emphasis)

"I haven't forgotten … the father's name is Jaabaali," said her son.

"And your mother's?"

"The mother's is also Jaabaali."

She picked him up and kissed him again and again, holding him close.

"He'll ask why do you want to study … what'll you tell?"

"I'll say, I want to study and become as great as the revered Babasaheb," he answered, as always. (50)

The story is thickly textured and within its six printed pages it contains many layers. At one level, it could be read as a feminist text which rejects the father's claim to one's identity; at another level, it is the story of the suffering of a woman pitted against an unsympathetic society; and at yet another level, it interrogates the efficacy of using Ambedkar's name when his own people are not following his ideology.

Ironically, the story begins with the description of Bheempura and ends with Satyakaam asserting (via his mother) that he wants to be great as the "revered Babasahib." But the space in-between belies all these tall claims precisely because there are external pitfalls and internal aberrations. Externally, Bheempura is filthy – home to stray dogs, pigs, open drains, children defecating everywhere, crows circling over rotten flesh, garbage dumps and stink and stench suspended in the air. The scenes of abuses, quarrels, wife-battering and sometimes even the wife whacking the husband are routine. Knives and daggers are drawn at the slightest pretext which shows the criminal tendency and intolerance of the residents. Jaabaali is the inmate of this world where humans are like "insects and worms" and her son growing up in this atmosphere is likely to imbibe the culture.

It goes to the credit of the writer's art that without indicting the system or political apathy towards the Dalits openly, as is the current trend, he has tried to look at the problem from within. He resists the complacency of the Basti people who "use" their leader's name and expect it to work magic, without any contribution on their part to bring in changes. Probably, they are doing great disservice to the leader who visualised a bright future for them. There is no qualitative difference in their social structure, no improvement or no transformation. The threat is, therefore, from within as they have failed to view social change as a process and instead have taken it as an ideology.

It is from within its own folds that Jaabaali is exploited. Basically, it is the story of Jaabaali set against the backdrop of Bheempura, but the backdrop is so compelling that it needs to be taken into consideration if one wants to understand Jaabaali's problem. Martya Pehalwan and his party of loafers, along with a few older men who like to sit on the wrestler's platform near Maruti (Hanuman) temple enjoy leering at women going to the mill. When Jaabaali resists Martya, first by daring him and later by slapping him, she is made to pay a heavy price for opening her mouth.

One day, Martya did call her:

"Hey ... look how her boobs are shaking ..."

"Why you ... don't you have women at home?"

"Yeah ... a basketful of them, but what I need is you ...". (47)

This conversation has its repercussions. In the male dominated system, the subaltern, a woman in this case, has no right to counter the man. Angered at her audacity, Martya tries to grab her arm and she "struck him across the face" (48). Three days later, Martya, along with Damya and Ramya, rape her inside the Maruti temple, scorching her with the burning wick from the sacred lamp. There is nothing holy for these ignoble men. No help comes to her and the Basti people connive to make the episode happen; even Fakra, a widower working with her in the mill and wanting to marry her, shuns her. Jaabaali accepts her fate stoically, "So, the people were talking – what if they were? Can their lips be sewn up? She who spawns, gets stretched – she reflected. Where were the people the other day? No mouth was opened, then. All just sat transfixed, watching the scene" (48). From thence on, Jaabaali lives life as it comes; gives birth to Satyakaam and diverts her energy towards making him as great as Babasahib.

Jaabaali's self-assertion, her rejection of the patriarchal system and her ability to stand on her own are appreciable but the open ending leaves several doubts: given the background of Satyakaam's birth and Joshi Master's own interest in Jaabaali, will he be as liberal as the Sage of yore? Will he be able to get over the class/caste barriers? After all, the present-day Jaabaali is raising an individual voice against injustice; will that be tolerated?

Discussing the mythological story of Jabala and Satyakam from a feminist angle, Vasanthi Sankaranarayanan observes that Jabala, the Matriarch, in asserting her son's identity through her own name, brushes "aside the need for a father to claim one's identity" ... and "also dismisses the idea of a two-parent family" (Sankaranarayanan, 1997: 11). Such subversions from our own literary traditions provide us "germs of feminist thought" that it is the mother who is the real identity-giver because she is the creator. "Shifting one's origin to the mother who carries the child in her womb and nourishes it through her own blood and with her own life from the formation stage onwards asserts the importance of the mother, her function as the creator of the human race, her womb being the chrysalis in which human beings are molded is a very positive example of female assertion" (Sankaranarayanan, 1997: 11).

III

The next story is from Manipur entitled "Thaurani Devi" giving a glimpse of the Maite clan of Manipur. The protagonist, Thaurani Devi, suffers because she has the courage to disregard patriarchal norms and stand on her own. Sensuous, coquettish and lively Thaurani was around thirty when she came back to her parents with her three children driven away by her tyrant husband. Life was happy for a few months as the brothers and their wives thought her sojourn to be temporary. But when there was no sign of her going or of her husband sending for her, they found her burdensome. The atmosphere changed and quarrels ensued. Thaurani, realising the importance of having a personal income, made efforts to eke out a living by taking up sundry jobs of which she tired soon. She opened a paan-shop which immediately became popular and Thaurani started earning well that changed her status in her own home. The paan-shop, however became a haunt of all kind of men and women and brought her a bad name. Her brothers dissuaded her from pursuing the business, her husband threatened her of dire consequences, and the elders of the village forbade their daughters from visiting the shop. These tactics could not deter Thaurani. Vexed by their hypocrisy she decided to expand her business to increase her earnings and so she stocked her shop to the brim. The next morning she learned to her horror that her shop was gutted in a fire. Thaurani ran to the spot wailing and after that there was no trace of Thaurani. The story ends with the author asking, "Where is Thaurani, Umesh? Have you seen her?" (87).

Here again, as in the previous story, it is one individual pitted against the society; the backdrop is of the Maite clan but the patriarchal structure is as oppressive and taboo-ridden as in any other part of the country. The story suggests that single women are particularly vulnerable – widows, divorcees, aged spinsters and separated women. Thaurani being separated, has no right to live her life on her terms. The authorial comments are sufficiently clear that Thaurani became the butt of ridicule of those very people who eyed her lecherously. A woman leaving her husband's house is suspect and is often under strict watch of the community even if she is the daughter of the house living under the protection of her parents (82).

What goes against Thaurani is her vivaciousness, restless energy and her intense love for the good things of life – cinema, shopping, dressing up and the like. But there is no hint in the story of her fall from morality. Those who spread rumours about her are the ones who enjoy flirting with her. All she does is exercise her choice and opt for freedom – freedom to earn a living by a means that is within her reach. She refuses to be the "Other" and live as a dependant, exposed to the taunts of her brothers' wives. The author here subverts the concept of goddess as he allows Thaurani her own recipe for success, "I must become a Devi – the new millennium's Devi – have my own income despite the difficulties …. Despite the wagging tongues and the society that scoffs at me, I must become a Devi. Let this body display its contour, let my lips be honeyed and my smile scintillating. I may even ogle at the well-heeled rakes. I want money because money makes the mare go, as they say! If money brings respect, love, friendship and happiness, let it be so!" (84, my translation). Such thoughts show a reckless temperament, not easy to tame.

Money comes to her and with it come small, harmless joys that bring happiness to her arid life – the cheer of getting her freedom to watch a movie in a theatre, to participate in some exhilarating festival like Yavsang Thabal, the festival of climbing up the mountain and so on. She chooses to be "fully human" as Simone de Beauvoir would put it. When de Beauvoir exhorts women to choose their freedom and not be a second sex, she means that women should not look to men to grant them their freedom. But what is theoretically feasible may not be so in reality. A woman always remains the 'other' and to be anything else beyond that, she has to pay a heavy price. Thaurani's refusal to let her husband's brutality destroy her, and her rebuttal to her brothers who reduce her to a thing in her parental family, and her resumption of her subjecthood demonstrate her strength both as a resistant individual and as a woman. She has carved for herself an identity as a courageous and resourceful person. The story examines the role of society in eliminating a woman of courage for man's honour and the honour of the community. Thaurani's final disappearance is not only foreboding it is also upsetting. How do we interpret it: her triumph or her defeat at the hands of patriarchy?

IV

Ajit Jogi's short story "Phoolkunwar" takes us to the Adivasi village in Chhattisgarh and shows the bizarre side of the tribal customs and beliefs. The ethos is not only oppressive but also male dominated. The story shatters the glossy concept of the 'noble savage' so lovingly perpetuated during the colonial era and lays bare the inhuman atrocities that shatter an individual. In telling the tale of Phoolkunwar, the author indirectly extols the indomitable spirit of the tribal woman.

Phoolkunwar was a tribal beauty from village Chukti Jhiria to whom almost all young men of the surrounding fourteen villages had lost their hearts. But the young belle, in the prime of her youth, with a voluptuous body and a dark complexion was enamoured of Bharatiya, the farm manager of Mukhiya. Dark, tall and sturdy

Bharatiya was a middle-aged widower with four children while Phoolkunwar was in her late teens. That however, did not deter her. She accepted his 'bangles' as per their custom and became his wife.

Life took a sudden turn for them when an epidemic broke out in the village. Bharatiya's four children died and soon it claimed Bharatiya too. The lonely and destitute Phoolkunwar was branded as a Tonhi, an evil woman who kills and eats human beings and the "Baiga" (village Panchayat) decided to rid her of the evil spirit lest she should bring misfortune to the village. According to the Gond custom, she was dragged before the "Baiga" and an exorcist tortured her to take out the evil spirit. She lost consciousness and was left there to herself to recover. On gaining consciousness Phoolkunwar found herself completely drained of strength but she was not a woman to be intimidated. She started her routine despite the agony. The men in the village derived a sadistic pleasure in seeing her beauty mutilated, but a young man Sudhin, genuinely moved by her distress suggested that they run away from the clutches of the her tormentors. Phoolkunwar rejected his plea. Next, the village school master sent a message that if she surrendered to him, he would put a stop to her misery, a proposal she rebuffed. More torture followed with redoubled intensity but when she did not surrender, it was surmised that her beauty had trapped the evil spirit and to rid her of it her body should be destroyed. At night they set her hut to fire to burn her alive. What horrified them was Phoolkunwar's tenacity to hold on. With her belongings tied in a bundle, she jumped across the flames and lay down in the open scorched and exhausted. In her semi-conscious state she re-lived her past and the options open before her. Decking herself in her bridal dress, she slept for ever, hoping to be reunited with her Bharatiya.

The story creates a powerful ambience and is an immediate expression of patriarchal power vis-à-vis the power of the female spirit. Phoolkunwar suffers because in the male imperial imagination, the voluptuousness of the female body and the invincibility of the female spirit epitomise evil. But more than that in the oppressive social structure, it is unimaginable that the 'other' should have a voice or even a choice to resist, and so it is punishable. Consequently, her inner strength invites more nuanced reaction from the dominant order because as the 'otherness' of Phoolkunwar

– both literally as woman and metaphorically as possessed – becomes a conceptual blockage, the oppressor is gripped by fear of its own weakening power.

The female body is, in fact, the site of power as well as that of evil. The male, unable to use it for themselves, create a bogey of her body and insult and mutilate it in a desperate bid to possess it. Their inability to subjugate Phoolkunwar is directly related to their anger, fear and the intensification of torture. That Phoolkunwar is not subdued by their breaking tactics but instead she shames them by her unbroken spirit, reduce much of the agony of her condition. Till the end, she keeps her choices open and in that she rejects her enslavement to the society and in her act of freedom she chooses to liberate herself. In a final act of defiance she decorates her body and beautifies it right in the face of her tormentors who had dubbed her body as the site of a malevolent spirit. Herein lies her assertion of her own authority over it. The power structures can neither annihilate her body nor kill her spirit. The ultimate choice is hers and instead of her oppressors getting rid of her, it is she who gets rid of oppression. She, thus, becomes the controller of her own self and in her quiet end is her triumph.

V

The three stories discussed here from gendered perspective show the exploitative nature of the patriarchal power structures. Within the dominant cultures of the three states – Maharashtra, Manipur and Chhatisgarh – the tribals/Dalits form the sub-culture and within these sub-cultures women are the gendered 'other' and hence doubly marginalised. Jaabaali, in the first story, is a Dalit; Thaurani belongs to the Maite clan; and Phoolkunwar is a Gond. It is worth noting that oppression, mutilation, torture and cruelty inflicted upon these women comes from within their folds and not from outsiders. The only upper class/caste men depicted in the stories are Joshi Master in Jaabaali's case and the Master Sahib in "Phoolkunwar." Though they express desire for these women, they are virtually ineffective and powerless. The villains are their own men. Reading these stories from a feminist perspective affords ample room and scope to address the question of the right or the wrong in respect of societal conduct.

Another significant issue is the implication of resistance. Though resistance is called "the weapon of the weak" by resistance scholar James Scott, it gives the silent but effect weapon to the powerless to exert power by penetrating the "ideology" of the dominant and thus "demystifying" it (Scott, 1985: 29). In their study of resistance in everyday social relations, Douglas Haynes and Gyan Prakash find that resistance is a subtle form of protest and can "tear through the fabric of hegemonic forms" (Haynes and Prakash, 1991: 1). Of the three women discussed here, Jaabaali resists the entire value-system whereby one's identity is formed by the father and asserts the matriarch's claim to the identity of her son; Thaurani Devi enters the male precinct when she opens the paan-shop, and counters her detractors boldly; Phoolkunwar undermines the attempts to subjugate her. The confrontations between the societal norms and individual will, though subtle, have formidable implications because besides resisting the hegemony, the women also speak – and speak with voice and with action. This brings us to our initial question, "what happens when a subaltern speaks?"

Jaabaali counter-questions the rogue Martya and has the 'audacity' to slap and bite him. Thaurani gets furious with her husband when he wants her to close her shop; she also flings the hard realities in the face of her brothers telling them that she has not crossed limits of decency and that without money she would have no place in their homes. Phoolkunwar rebuffs the Master Sahib and Sudhin with the fury of a tigress and repeatedly and deliberately counters her virulent opponents.

These female protagonists live without male support; they are iconoclasts and they display an independence of spirit. Each is a "female hero" in her own right, as feminist psychologist Marcia Westkott may put it, having self-esteem, individuality and the ability to take on her own responsibility. Westkott elaborates that the 'female hero' "shatters the internal form of her victimisation" and "conscious choice rather than fearful compliance informs her action" (Westcott, 1986: 214). Each of these protagonists conforms to the picture Westkott draws. Their fight is between what is 'possible' and what is 'permissible;' between socially acceptable norms/taboos and individual self-respect; and between the dilemmas of silence and voice. That they speak up, suffer and endure leads us to return to Spivak's question "Can a subaltern *really* speak?" Well suppose they can; then at what cost?

Violence perpetuated on these women – Jaabaali, Thaurani and Phoolkunwar – by the self-appointed custodians of morality is a denial of human rights. Thaurani Devi and Phoolkunwar lose their lives in a painful and undignified manner; Jaabaali has to compromise with her stigmatised existence and live pinning hope on her son and probably on the change of heart of the system. Writing in the context of fundamentalism, communalism and gender justice Vibhuti Patel discusses the fundamentalists' ire at female-headed household and points out, "Fundamentalists perceive female-headed households as an eyesore and make all efforts to persecute, stigmatise, isolate, marginalise and terrorise deserted, divorced, single and separated women leading an independent, economically self-sufficient life with dependent children or senior citizens. They do not accept women as heads of the household. Wherever the fundamentalist forces have become powerful, the female-headed households face persecution and witch hunting" (Patel, 2005: 199). In the stories studied here the forces are not fundamentalist but they certainly are patriarchal and social. The remnants of these savage, subversive forces remain with us as ever. And the tribal and Dalit women remain mired in poverty, social and political backwardness as the reactionary forces monopolise power, victimisation and violence.

Notes and References

1. The term has been used by Viney Kirpal in her "Introduction" to *The Postmodern Indian English Novel*. Kirpal opines that the "postmodern technique of double writing or 'de-doxification' – writing and re-writing received versions of tradition, culture, patriarchy, politics – has greatly freed Indian English novelist and armed her/him with a new technique." She further clarifies that this is a powerful tool to dismantle and subvert power structures and to turn traditionally-received myths upside down to re-define women's self-image. "Deconstructing the hidden ideologies of a patriarchal society that mould an Indian woman and shattering the long-revered traditional assumptions and stereotypes that contain her, is common to many women-centred

postmodern Indian English novels by women and about women engaged in breaking their silence" (p. 20). What Kirpal says about the novel can also be said of shorter fiction.
2. The three stories selected for this study are as follows:
"Satyakaam and Jaabaali," originally written in Marathi by Amitabh, translated into English by Vijay Diwan and published in *Indian Literature*, 194. Nov-Dec 1999. pp. 45-50. Amitabh is a Dalit Marathi writer and working as a senior Scientific Officer, Govt. of Maharashtra.

"Thaurani Devi," written by E. Sonamani Singh has been translated from Manipuri into Hindi by E. Vijay Laxmi. It was published in *Samkaleen Bharatiya Sahitya*. 72 July-Aug 1997. pp. 81-87. E. Sonamani Singh is a recipient of Manipur Sahitya Akademi awards.

"Phoolkunwar" by Ajit Jogi is the title story in an anthology entitled *Phoolkunwar* by Ajit and Renu Jogi. New Delhi: Rajkamal Publications, 2003. pp. 49-59. Shri Ajit Jogi is erstwhile Chief Minister of Chhattisgarh.

Works Cited

Amitabh, "Satyakaam and Jaabaali." Trans. Vijay Diwan. *Indian Literature*, 194. Nov-Dec 1999. pp. 45-50.

E. Sonamani Singh. "Thaurani Devi." Trans. E. VijayLaxmi. *Samkaleen Bharatiya Sahitya*. 72 July-August 1997. pp. 81-87.

Haynes, Douglas and Gyan Prakash. Eds. *Contesting Power: Resistance and Everyday Social Relations in South Asia*. Delhi: Oxford, 1991

Jogi, Ajit. "Phoolkunwar." *Phoolkunwar*. Ajit and Renu Jogi. New Delhi: Rajkamal Publications, 2003. pp. 49-59.

Kirpal, Viney. *The Postmodern Indian English Novel*. Bombay: Allied Publishers, 1996.

Patel, Vibhuti. "Fundamentalism, Communalism and Gender Justice." *Religion, Power and Violence*. Ed. Ram Puniani. Delhi: Sage Publication, 2005.

Sankaranarayanan, Vasanthi. *Manushi*, 103, November-December 1997. pp. 11-13.

Scott, James C. *Weapons of the Weak: Everyday Forms of Peasant Resistance*. New Havens: Yale University Press, 1985.

Westkott, Marcia. *The Feminist Legacy of Karen Horney*. New Haven: Yale University Press, 1986.

13

Power–Violence Nexus
Girish Karnad's *Tughlaq* and *Tale-Danda*

VINEETA KAUR SALUJA AND SHIBANI BASU DUBEY

Literature has always explored the meaning and relevance of human behavioural patterns and their execution in a world that is perpetually in transition and in which they constantly collide with each other. One aspect of human behaviour that seems to have continued through time is an unquenchable thirst for power. Psychologists believe that one of the most important social motives or needs is the power motivation which Donne Byrne defines as the desire to control others' actions and to determine their fate; it is man's prestige want and is universal and timeless (Byrne, 1956: 335–36). The desire for power and superiority is what man shares with the rest of the creation but whereas in animals it is limited to survival needs, in man it is unlimited to the extent that in pursuance of it he becomes almost irrational. The desire for power is generated by his need to assert his superiority over others of his kind but it also generates resistance in the other which consequently gives rise to anger and violence. Bertrand Russell puts it thus: "Between man and animals, there are various differences; some intellectual and some emotional. One of the chief emotional differences is that human desires, unlike those of animals, are essentially boundless and incapable of complete satisfaction" (Russell,

1957: 7). History is replete with examples of the power–violence interface and Girish Karnad makes use of those historical situations wherein power created a gap between those who had it and those who suffered it resulting in use of force and oppression on the one hand and protests and resistance on the other. That the well-intentioned moves of a ruler like Muhammad-bin-Tughlaq should misfire and end in transforming him into a tyrant; or that Bijjala's social zest to eradicate the caste divide should end in violence and death provide an eloquent commentary on the nature of power.

Girish Karnad's talent to universalise the individual urges and his social predicament is an acknowledged fact. His plays, though entrenched in Indian history and mythology are contemporary in the sense that they show the existential crisis of modern man, his insatiable desire for power and glory and his capacity to wrest it through violence, if need be. Karnad explores how the quest for power lands the individual in intense psychological and philosophical conflicts because of the intricacies and intrigues of power and how the megalomaniac stands powerless in the end.

This article proposes to study two of Girish Karnad's historical plays: *Tughlaq* and *Tale-Danda*, the former based on the medieval ruler Muhamad-bin-Tughlaq and the latter on the times of Basavanna, the social reformer and the regime of Bijjala, a 12th century king of Kalyan. The politics of power and the subsequent violence leave the kingdoms in a state of chaos and trauma. Power, says Foucault, is inseparably associated with resistance and resistance brings into conflict the 'new truths' and the 'dominant truths.' It is the dominant order that crushes all dissent and the regimes revert to the prevailing order.

Tughlaq, published in 1964 is Karnad's second play, the first being *Yayati*. Originally written in Kannada it was translated in English by the author in late 1970s. While *Yayati* is a self-consciously existential drama on the theme of responsibility, *Tughlaq* is the story of an alien ruler struggling to monopolise power for the good of the people, thus "subjecting the culture of people to colonial strains" (Dodiya, 2000: 32). The playwright opines that the play reflects the chaos, disillusionment, and prevailing corruption that followed the Nehru era:

What struck me absolutely about Tughlaq's history was that it was contemporary. The fact that here was the most idealistic, the most intelligent king ever on the throne of Delhi, and one of the greatest failures also. And within a span of twenty years this tremendous capable man had gone to pieces. This seemed to be both due to his idealism as well as the shortcomings within him such as his impatience, his cruelty, his feeling that he had the only correct answer. And I felt in the early sixties India has also come very far in the same direction – the twenty-year period seemed to me a striking parallel. (Dodiya, 2000: 49)

Historically, Muhammad-bin-Tughlaq is a known figure – known particularly for his irrational schemes, his mad resolve to pursue his ideas to the end and his total disregard for the sufferings of the people which his irrational ideas cause. Prince Juna Muhammad was the son of Ghiyas-ud-din Tughlaq Shah. He was in charge of the estate of Diplalpur. He got his father killed and became the Sultan in February 1325, just three days after his father's death. Forty days later he reached Delhi and ascended the throne without any opposition and ruled for twenty-six years with an iron hand, spelling death and destruction. He was, indeed, a mixture of opposites: he brought untold miseries to his people and yet he undertook many welfare measures like building hospitals and alms-houses, being impartial to both Hindus and Muslims and displaying generosity towards all. In short, he was the "humblest of men" and also an "intense egoist" – traits that Karnad makes use of to depict a period that was replete with treachery, fraud, cruelty and hypocrisy of the lowest order. Greed for power breeds distrust and leads to corruption, crime, cruelty, frenzy and violence. The canvas of the power–violence nexus is blood-stained and one reads the play not only as a historical document but also as a commentary on contemporary situation analysing the power conflicts within the personal, social and political spheres. Ironically, the man who eliminated all those who stood in his way should have the audacity to say, "I was too soft, I can see that now. They will only understand the whip", can be nothing short of being mad and blind.

The play opens with a third person account about the state of affairs in the country, on the pattern of the traditional classical Indian drama in which things are reported by the *Sutradhar*. Here, it is the common people who perform the task of the *Sutradhar*. Outside the court of justice, people are seen sitting in an open yard waiting for a judgement. The Sultan publicly praises the Kazi for his impartiality and tells the people how justice is administered in his kingdom. He then announces the shifting of the capital from Delhi to Daulatabad, a predominantly Hindu populated city which he thinks would be safer than Delhi. But the Sultan is held in distrust and fear because of his past deeds – he had got his father and brother killed in a so-called accident, which he himself had engineered. The first act presents the atmosphere of fear, uncertainty and distrust in the regime. In Act II Tughlaq'a discussions with his stepmother and later with his Vizier, Muhammad Najib and the historian Barani reveal some of his contradictory traits. He tells his stepmother that the whole day he thinks of a better future for his people and at night he makes great plans. The scene shows that he solves a difficult move in a game of chess but is unable to think of real life moves when Ain-ul-Mulk marches towards Delhi with thirty thousand soldiers. The news makes him uneasy because he does not even have six thousand to encounter Ain-ul-Mulk. This is an obvious indication of his inefficiency and mismanagement.

Soon we learn that Sheikh Imam-ud-Din is instigating the public against the Sultan; Najib is wary of the Sheikh's intentions and wants him eliminated because the Sheikh is not only a respected religious leader but also a manipulator, greedy for power. The Sultan, apparently unmoved by Najib's views and showing large-heartedness in praising the Sheikh as a saint, has nevertheless crooked plans to get the Sheikh killed without getting the blame on himself. For Najib, both Ain-ul-Mulk and Sheikh Imam-ud-Din are traitors and should be punished. He says, "a traitor is a traitor, friend or saint, and must be crushed" (Act II). But the Sultan knows how to eliminate him without suspicion and provoking public ire. He wins the Sheikh over by his tolerant approach, appoints him as an emissary of peace and when he marches towards Ain-ul-Mulk's camp all decked in royal robes like the Sultan, he is trapped. Tughlaq's army was lying in wait for the Sheikh's elephant to approach Ain-ul-Mulk and as soon as the Sheikh stands on his elephant to address Ain-ul-Mulk, a trumpet is sounded; Tughlaq's soldiers mount an attack; there is chaos, violence and killings. The armies clash, and in the bedlam that follows Sheikh Imam-ud-Din gets killed. Ain-ul-Mulk also falls and his army is scattered. The Sultan poses to be upset by the news of Sheikh's death, arranges a public meeting to commemorate him, makes an élan that he lay down his life repelling Ain-ul-Mulk's attack and thus deserves a martyrs status. The public believes him and the Sultan crushes the Sheikh's ever-increasing power without antagonising the public.

In the power-politics nothing is held sacred and morality and ethical values become the first casualty. No scruples, no ethical principles deter the power hungry. Ratan Singh is the Sultan's well-wisher and trusted man but he hatches a plot with Shihab-ud-Din to get the Sultan killed while at prayer because that is the time when everybody is without arms. After hatching the plot the same Ratan Singh turns an informer so as to gain the Sultan's trust and eliminate the Amirs. The unsuspecting Amirs and Shihab-ud-Din prepare to attack the Sultan as planned and are trapped. About twenty Hindu soldiers surround the Amirs and forestall the assault. The Sultan finishes his prayer unperturbed and while Shihab-ud-Din asks him how he could know about the plan, the sultan shows him the letter from Ratan Singh; stabs Shihab-ud-Din to death and orders Najib to see that all traitors are caught and killed. He then makes an announcement to the public that there was a rebellion in the palace in which the Sultan was attacked. In a bid to save the Sultan from the rebels Shihab-ud-Din lay down his life. Shihab-ud-Din was declared a martyr. It is here that Barani, an objective observer and a historian comments that the Sultan does not spare even the dead. "Oh God, aren't even the dead free from your politics" (Act V).

Race for power, the Machiavellian scheming and the resultant violence does not end here. Tughlaq's stepmother eliminates Najib and in turn Tughlaq orders his stepmother to be stoned to death. Karnad brings in two more characters Aziz and Aazam who act as foil to Tughlaq. They complete the picture with their several acts of cheating, fraud and devilry. Aziz kills Abbasid, the religious leader invited by the Sultan and then himself poses as Abbasid to dupe the Sultan. Corruption, decay, degradation of moral and ethical values that power brings with it become the order of the day. The Sultan is ultimately remorseful and undergoes spiritual crisis but the damage has been done and nothing can redeem his strife-torn self. In Act V when the stepmother reminds the Sultan of the futile deaths he has caused, he asserts, "No, they were not futile. They gave me what I wanted – power, strength to shape my thoughts, strength to act, strength to recognise myself" (Act V). The man who wanted to "spread his branches in the star" (Act IV) gets entangles in the cobweb of corruption, misplaced sentiments, violence and ultimate remorse. The play ends with the Sultan sleeping in the final Act, which is symbolic of his failure and frustration.

Unlike *Tughlaq*, in *Tale-Danda*, Karnad deals with a situation in a caste-class ridden society of 12th century Karnataka. Here is a group of people, the upper-caste Brahmins and the ruling class nobility which along with King Bijjala's son Sovideva play power-politics, first deftly and then ruthlessly, to suppress all opposition and finally to kill the rivals. There is a terrible blood-shed at the end of the play in Kalyan (where the play is set), drowning the whole city in blood, chaos and infernal fires. The Hindi translation of *Tale-Danda* is appropriately called Rakt Kalyan. The play seeks to shake the value-system which is just not acceptable to the society and the confrontation can only lead to disaster.

Basavanna, poet and social reformer, has agreed to be King Bijjala's treasurer because he is of the view that a king is only the keeper of public money. Basavanna is a revered figure whose ideals of forming a casteless and classless society have generated a movement and he has gathered around him a large number of believers – the Sharanas. Basvanna has the King's support because the King himself is a 'Kalchoori' – barber – by caste and it is only Basavanna who does not take that into consideration but accepts him what he is. In fact, King Bijjala has married into a Kshatriya Royal family of Hoysala and has tried to forget his low origin but he is conscious of his background. Since Basavanna does not question caste or class, the King feels safe in his protection.

In Act II Bijjala recounts his family history: "For ten generations my forefathers ravaged the land as robber barons. For another five they ruled as the trusted feudatories of the Emperor himself. They married into every royal family in sight. Bribed generations of Brahmins with millions of cows. All this so they could have the caste of Kshatriya branded on their foreheads" (Act II). This is how power politics is played to remain in power. Ironically, Bijjala's power-politics is inspired by Basvanna's ideals. In the same Act he says:

> Some fifteen years back I was a feudal lord in Manglalwad with Chalukyas. I thought being a feudal lord my life was blessed. Then I met Basavanna. He was hardly twenty then but his life-philosophy was ready – king is not by birth but by merit, by authority. Suddenly I thought this is absolutely right. I can rule a kingdom very ably. The fool that rules Kalyan, I can rule better than him. So I finished him off and became the king. Without Basavanna, would have never thought of such a thing. (Act II)

The kingdom he got by a violent act is snatched away from him by gruesome violence. It is his son Sovideva who engineers his assassination. Sovideva is particularly angry with his father, King Bijjala because he (Bijjala) did not name him heir apparent. Moreover, he hates Basavanna's idealism and his influence on his father. In addition to these personal grudges, there are other social reasons to spurt anger; it is the reformist zeal of Basavanna and his Sharanas who rejected idol worship, rituals, class–caste distinction and other obscurantist ideas that have long had socio-cultural sanction. With the help of Damodar Bhatt (Queen Rambhavati's priest), and Manchanna Kramita (Advisor to the King) Sovideva plans a rebellion, dethrones the King to grab power and in the chaos that follows Jagdeva kills the King mercilessly while he is in the Shiv temple. Sovideva persecutes the Sharanas violently and mercilessly. Since Basavanna is away, the Sharanas lose heart and scatter. This angers Jagdeva and the powerful Sharanas who resolve to take revenge on Sovideva. The city reels under all sorts of crime, rape, arson, killings and looting. When Sovideva learns of this he blames Damodar and when an argument ensues, Sovideva's guard kills Damodar. Sovideva orders his men to follow the Shravanas and eliminate them all:

> Pursue them. Don't let them escape. Men, women, children – cut them all down ... from this moment all sharanas, foreigners and free thinkers are expelled from this land on pain of death. Women and lower orders shall live within the norms prescribed by our ancient tradition, or else they will suffer like dogs. Each citizen shall consider himself a soldier ready to lay down his life for the king. For the king is God incarnate. (Act V)

This decree is not only heartless but frenzied. Sovideva's coronation ceremony is held in the palace while the city is ablaze; the cries of the victims rend the air amid the eulogies of the new king sung by the Brahmins.

Tale-Danda not only illustrates social deformity and the hold of tradition on the culture but also hunger for power that easily discards all ethical and moral principles in the bid to grab power. As the city of Kalyan is drenched in blood, we remember Basavanna's words, "Violence is wrong, whatever the provocation. To resort to it because someone else started it first is even worse. And to do so in the name of a structure of brick and mortar is a monument to stupidity" (Act III). The result of the entire situation is rather ironical as Girish Karnad avers, "You can perceive deep irony, because, after all the martyrdom of Sharanas, when they re-emerged after three centuries of underground survival as Lingayats, they were totally caste-ridden." The sub-plot of the play focuses on the issue of inter-caste marriage and Basvanna's reluctance to give it sanction despite his professed ideals to eradicate caste-class divide. As a leader given to the welfare of the people he feels that time is not yet ripe for such a revolutionary step and he is right in his assessment because the marriage of a Brahmin girl and a Dalit boy gives rise to social fury that leads to bloodshed. Commenting on its contemporary relevance Karnad opines that what happened in the 12th century is still happening today and observes, "It seems 800 years have solved no problems. We are back exactly where we started" (Dodiya, 105).

Works Cited

Byrne, Donne. *Essays on Freedom and Power*. London: Thomas and Hudson, 1956.

Dodiya, Jaydipsinh K. "Girish Karnad: The Man and the Writer." *Indian English Drama: Critical Perspective*. Ed. Jaydipsinh K. Dodiya and K.P. Surendran. New Delhi: Sarup and Sons, 2000.

Karnad, Girish. *Tughlaq*. New Delhi: Oxford Univ. Press, 1975

Karnad, Girish. *Tale-Danda*. New Delhi: Ravi Dayal, 1993.

Russell, Bertrand. *Power: A New Social Analysis*. London: George Allen and Unwin, 1957.

14

A Study of Chaplin's Film *The Great Dictator*

Violence as Irrational, Laughable and Avoidable

SHYAMALA VANARASE

Increasing violence in social and individual life is a matter of concern today. The twentieth century with its tremendous technological advancement and two world wars has offered a full-scale picture of the gains of violence. Value-free rationality and objectivity were on the pedestal. Religiosity, spirituality and sheer humanity were secondary to the calculation of gains of the advantaged. A ring of truth and inevitability ascribed to the destructive mentality generated an anxiety about the rise of tyrants and terrorists. Several artists in different media dealt with the degradation and inhumanity of it all, responding with depression to the whole scene.

Artists create images. These images remind us that reality could be otherwise. Are we, the ordinary people bound to lead lives of pawns in some tyrant's game? Here is Chaplin, saying, 'not necessarily'; we experience those images and assimilate them. A popular artist like Charlie Chaplin makes expressive images of the upheavals in life and society of his times through comedy. He has made several films on social issues of the early twentieth century, e.g., the nature of work, poverty and prosperity. Films like *The Gold Rush, The Kid* and *Modern Times* raise hearty laughs, which are almost therapeutic, but also stimulate examination of well established (and well worn out) conventions of belief and of conduct. *The Great Dictator* is absolutely hilarious, even though it is all about violence in dictatorship.

This article studies how *The Great Dictator* presents violence as a value entity, which is laughable, as also irrational. But it is not enough to reveal just that. In actual conduct, change is possible only when the individual owns responsibility for his/her behaviour and puts in efforts to work for change as per his/her wish. For that result, violence has to be seen not as an inevitable part of human nature, but as an avoidable one. Chaplin's vision in this film goes well beyond the mere comic. It probes the levels of irrationality in human affairs, which make life avoidably complicated, and needlessly unhappy.

The obvious comic level of *The Great Dictator* lampoons Adolf Hitler and the dictatorial regime in Nazi Germany. Thematically, the film reveals the inconsistencies generated by the dictatorial framework. The film places several scenes in two sharply contrasted locations, the dictator's palace and the Jewish ghetto. This device enables the director to show how the sharp binaries of dictatorship wipe out the possibility of existence of any human shades within a system. Human values would include a wide range of clusters of attitudes, of habits and of perceptions, as the struggle to survive within the rigid frame of dictatorial binaries continues. However, the characters, both in the palace and the ghetto manipulate others and use very similar stratagems in the incessant effort to prove their own claim to a sense of worth. Chaplin, of course, sides with the human victims with a sense of charity, even while he does not spare exposing their foibles. He argues that the misery of humans is of their own making, despite their innate capability for living together happily with sufficient room for everyone. The plot of the film shows the numerous devices through which we make ourselves unhappy, for example, the ways in which we stick to worn out beliefs, or how we constantly wish to fight and win the battles merely to prove that one is better than the other, or how we strive to reach that one higher step on the ladder of hierarchy without even realising that the ladder itself is of our own making. Complexity seems to interest human beings in a strange way. It makes them lose the sense of perspective on ends and means. In effect, *The Great Dictator* is a film about the sheer irony of how difficult it is to be simple.

There are three basic sources for the norms of living together, viz., the individual himself/herself, the community, and the state. The individual is imperfect, and therefore fallible. This itself creates a need for norms to be accommodating. He/she needs help which, of course, comes from the other individuals around. Thus individuals help each other and live together in harmony. We can love, we can belong, and we can share. The norms must apply uniformly to all individuals if society has to function in a smooth manner. However, if the norms were not uniform, there would always be some people in that society who suffer the stifling of expression of individual thought, through word and action. Where several groups exist, each with different norms, conflicts will occur when one group struggles to dominate another group. Supremacy, however temporary, would always seek legitimacy for itself. The rule by majority is one such method of making power legitimate. Chaplin takes the clear position that real power is vested in the people. Dictators usurp that power and enforce their rule by coercion. Brute force can easily nullify resistance by an individual. The lone person can be physically overcome, eliminated, or else manipulated into silence. Likewise, the power of state machinery can meet the resistance of groups by other similar strategies. Manipulative devices can divide people. Persons, who are, in fact, not much different from their fellowmen can be made to regard themselves higher to other persons on the ladder of hierarchy. A spurious belief structure can be generated and fixed psychologically to support this stratagem. Once this is done, the eventual conflict between the groups becomes inevitable. Chaplin sees the self-perpetuating dynamics of brutality of power relations inherent in any system of dictatorship.

Chaplin also knows that the mere individual pleading for amity in living together is no match for the gigantic machinery created by warmongers of the world. Hence, *The Great Dictator* uses the device of the chance factor: a common man reaches the top of the hierarchy by chance and it is he who makes the plea for peace, simplicity and love. Chaplin uses the device of making a common barber as the look alike of the great dictator. This device also expresses the essential sameness of all human beings, big or small, powerful or powerless, despite extreme contrast in their functional activity. A barber grooms anyone around while a dictator seeks to subjugate all those near him.

A major debate during early period of industrialisation was man vs. machine. Machine was considered superior to man on several counts. It was more work efficient and result oriented, which ensured profits. It was easier to control and to calibrate. Many artists have tried, sometimes in confused terms, to image the machine either as man's friend or foe. This plot of the film uses both kinds of machines, aggressive ones like guns and tanks, as also benign ones like cars and planes. The issue is: who takes the decision to use machines and for what purpose? Aggressive men and machines can be ruthless terminators. Chaplin takes the firm position that the inviolable right to choose is with the ordinary people. Violence and violent mentality are connected with the idea that possession of better machines and better weapons defines superiority of man over other men. The notion of competitive race emerges from this idea. People can choose to remain simple and not complicate life by developing complicated machines to do simple jobs. If the people retain this right, it would ensure happiness and amity.

Chaplin's hilarious treatment of oneupmanship brings out the sheer irrationality and childishness of such social behaviour. Oneupmanship is a futile device anyway, even though it gives a transitory sense of triumph in scoring a point. At the root of such behaviour is insecurity, an anxiety, and a desire to run away from facing one's own inadequacies. A wide range of such situations is shown in the film. For example, an individual could be seen maneuvering for a prominent position while the photograph is being organised, or, at another extreme, the dictator could be conceiving the grand idea of initiating a world war and dominating it. Scenes of oneupmanship in this film actually pose serious issues related to signs and symbols of power.

The plot of the film balances the hate and strife in the dictator's palace through the foil of human response and innocence of simple residents of the Jewish ghetto. The foibles of ordinary human beings are shown in the same detail as the chinks in the armour of the dictator. However, faults in the behaviour of simple people can be corrected if the system provides space to make the mistakes and correct them. But the suffocation caused by the impersonality of dictatorship leaves no chance for any human being to make the effort at self-actualisation. Under dictatorial oppression, the gentle and the tender could actually degenerate into boneless submission in such a manner that their lip service to sacrifice for valour would simply be a mask, the desire to save their own lives. Also, the victim could react in several ways. He could talk back, resist, be brave even though panic-stricken, hold on while planning to migrate, form a resistance group, or else be on his own and fend for himself. Chaplin reveals each one of these situations, but with great compassion. The expressive device of Chaplin's humour makes it all very enjoyable, even though, in effect, we are laughing at ourselves.

Thus, Chaplin's comic vision examines both aspects of violence, as its perpetrators generate it and as it affects the victims. We are made to see through the predicament and the pretense of it all, and laugh it off. But sure enough, this situation itself is no laughing matter. However, if human beings have ever to effect any change, we must first take the first steps towards awareness and acceptance of our shortcomings. *The Great Dictator* succeeds in doing precisely this. We are able to recognise all those painful situations in the screen events because Chaplin has made us laugh at ourselves.

Some Notes on the Design of the Film

One guiding principle of design of the film is the joke in the opening title: "Any resemblance between the dictator Hynkel and the Jewish barber is purely coincidental". It is precisely the look-alike coincidence, which enables the ordinary Jewish barber to replace the anti-Jewish dictator at the high victory podium and broadcast a message of peace and human amity. This itself is a laughable flop for the great dictator. Expressively, it is also a direct anti-dictator appeal. There is hope for each one of us everywhere when any dictator anywhere in the world flops. This hope constitutes the thematic foundation of the film.

Looking at serious matters through the lens of comedy, Chaplin flips up hope and holds. The dictator flops. The plot works as a design of flip flops, proposals and disposals, of happenings on both sides, that of perpetrators of violence as also of its victims. The design is built up by the consistent use of comic interpretations of inconsistencies that are built in the war machine and the tyrannical operations. The use of opposites, contrasts and inversions comes in as handy device to reveal the hollow pompousness, brutality or simple fallibility of the characters. For example, the constant interplay of scenes in the ghetto and the palace links the narrative through a large range of similarities and contrasts. For example, all human beings dream. The Tomanian dictator dreams of a world spinning around his little finger or of himself as a brunette emperor in a world of blue-eyed blondes. In contrast, the common people dream of simple lives. The pilot Schultz, even while his plane is crashing, dreams of an idyllic life in the countryside with his beloved Hilda. Dreams push the action forward, even while they flop. Grand or petite, humans shall dream. It is not a prerogative of a self-declared pack of chosen few.

Chaplin was a great star of the American silent comedy cinema. He uses in this sound film numerous devices of the silent era, most importantly, his own screen image, the face with the Hitler-like butterfly moustache, the hat, the cane and the shuffled walk of Charlie the Tramp. Thus, this sound film has prolonged scenes of silent comedy routines. Chaplin also makes abundant use of well known passages of Western classical music for sustaining the pace of comic events of misdirection, mismatch and confusion in this film.

In constructing this film, the balance of the oppressor and the oppressed, man and machine, ends and means is worked through similarities and contrasts not just for the sake of laughter, but also to suggest the role of reason in differentiating between real human strength and the façade of power. The barber would stake his life to deliver the final appeal for peace and amity and the dictator literally climbs up the wall draping rope at the thought of the grand position of absolute power. It makes the audience look at the options and realise the value of choice.

After all the laughter of hilarious medley of fun, the film takes an amazing turn around during the last scene of the speech after the invasion of Osterlich. The fictional pretense of the barber and the dictator seem to merge with the reality of the great humanitarian artist Charles Chaplin as he makes an impassioned appeal for sanity and peace from the film screens of the world. The year of the film was 1940, and the Second World War provoked by Germany's aggression was in full conflagration.

Outline of the Film

The plot of the film is a scarcely veiled caricature of events in Germany from its defeat in the First World War in 1918, through the twenty years of the rise of Hitler's party, up to 1938 with the invasion and annexation of Austria. Germany is Tomania, The Nazi Swastika is shaped and named Double Cross. Austria is Osterlich. Some characters in the story have rather suggestive names, and physical looks. Adolf Hitler is Adenoid Hynkel. The ministers: Goering is the rotund Herring, Goebbels is lean-and-mean Garbitsch, made to sound like garbage. The other dictator Mussolini of Italia is Napolini of Bacteria. Significantly, the Jewish barber has no name. He is just himself, a human being.

The story is told in three parts. Part 1: From the end of First World War to the rise of Hynkel's terror as dictator of Tomania. Part 2: A temporary suspension of persecution of the Jewish people, and then its furious resumption. Part 3: The turn around sequence at the invasion of Osterlich, when the dictator is mistaken for the look-alike barber and prevented from reaching the victory rally, while the barber gets to the high podium and broadcasts a stirring humanist anti-War speech. The viewer had been warned about the pure coincidence of look-alikeness of the dictator and the barber right at the opening of the film.

Part 1 contains the events on the very last day of the First World War. It introduces a reluctant soldier (later, the Jewish barber) as he saves the life of the pilot Schultz, (later a personal friend of Hynkel, but a reluctant officer of the dictatorial regime). Schultz would later reciprocate by saving the Jewish barber's life, and also lead him to make an anti-War speech at a War-victory rally.

The opening action is of fierce battle, with our man in the thick of it. He is no brave Tomanian soldier fighting for his country, but a simple confused human being. Here is War – the ultimate act of human violence. However, Chaplin composes it as a spoof. We see discipline flop through errors of defective machines, matched with human error. The orders are to fire the gun, the soldier pulls the trigger, and nothing happens. He pulls the trigger again, and the shell is fired, but lands a little distance away. The soldier turns and shrugs to the next soldier, who also turns and shrugs, passing it down the line. Everyone shrugs. No one accepts responsibility. Anyway, wireless orders come from some far-away higher-up to examine the defective shell, and are promptly passed down four levels of hierarchy. Hierarchy is, of course, always designed to ensure that the higher ranks are protected by the lower ranks. The lowest has to get into actual action since he cannot pass the order any lower down. The shell suddenly comes to life behaving as if to target our man, who, quite naturally, speeds away. But the shell has a will of its own, and stays right there to revolve and fizzle out like a firecracker. However, all the other soldiers in the hierarchy fall flat on the ground to save themselves from the explosion, which, of course, has not happened. This is when the enemy opens fire, and orders are radioed from somewhere above to fire the big anti-aircraft gun. Our man messes it up again. He overdoes the skyward pointing of the gun, which makes the gun reverse and point towards the ground. More orders ... more mess up. Ultimately the erring soldier is asked to report to the commander ....

We have laughed so far at the pompousness of hierarchy and the failure of machinery. Further scenes set up a series for laughs on errors of human beings. A hand grenade is to be thrown: the order is to pull the bolt and count up to ten before throwing it. The soldier wonders how fast he would take to count up to ten. The grenade slips out to slide down the sleeve. Frantic struggle lowers the grenade down his pants, and when he finally recovers and throws it, the soldier has fainted with fear. During a lineup, he thumps his rifle butt on the foot of next soldier. The forward march in poor visibility is sheer confusion. Eventually our man finds himself marching along enemy soldiers. A very human error, indeed. Our man escapes into an enemy bunker, only to receive the immediate charge of the gun post: the enemy is most willing to be relieved by anyone, friend or foe. Further mayhem, as our soldier faints due to shock of firing his machine gun. When revived, he hears a cry of help. A plane has been grounded. The fainting pilot persuades our soldier to help him take off, even though our man does not know the first thing about flying.

The flying sequence is hilarious. While instructing the innocent soldier to fly the plane, the pilot keeps on fainting in and out. Our man tries to do his best. In doing so, the plane turns upside down but keeps on flying, with our man dangling out holding on to the joystick. It is an upside down world on the screen. The sun shines upwards, a pocket watch defies gravity, and drinking water from the bottle flows upwards. The offer of a cigarette by the pilot has to be refused for obvious reasons. However, the plane is flying towards home territory. The fuel tank is empty, and Schultz, the pilot thinks these are his dying moments. He talks aloud about his lady love, Hilda, who is so kind that she would not even commit a violent act to any living plants by picking daffodils during the spring season in April. He is still talking of Hilda when they crash land safely in home territory. The War has ended. Tomania has lost. The documents being carried by Schultz are of no value now. He wails with disappointment.

One may note that comedy of the flying sequence is possible only in the film medium, which is based on images recorded by machines like the camera and the sound recorder. The spectator sees on the screen what the camera shows him, in this case the upside down plane with the water flowing upwards.

Post-War developments are now shown in a montage. Giant printing machines keep on reporting events, The Armistice, injured soldiers being treated, recovering in hospitals, and returning to civilian life. Headlines of civilian unrest in Tomania and the fast rise of Hynkel's party to political power are also flashed. Our man, the injured soldier has stayed in hospital all these twenty years. He has lost all past memory. Between the wars, ordinary people forget the woes very fast and the warmongers keep on getting more and more violent, developing better weapons for mass destruction. When he returns home to the Ghetto, he is totally unaware of the changes around him. And that is a potent source of comedy events.

Then one is introduced to Adenoid Hynkel, the dictator of Tomania. Appropriately, he coughs when any extra aspirated accents occur in his speech. Tomania seems to have a mania for marching under his dictatorship. The dictator is related to the vast multitude of a large rally by compositional devices of film. Hynkel is physically a small man, and the rally is mammoth, but film camera makes you see precisely the opposite relationship. One little man looms mighty high and large above the mass of thousands of men in the rally. Language and gestures are vastly exaggerated in the force of speech. Social responses are, as if, mechanically manipulated. For example, when the dictator pauses in his speech, the masses respond with thunderous applause. A flick of the dictator's hand produces instant silence. The inner hollowness of the situation is covered by the stranglehold of mechanical responses. It is a situation of terror for humanity, but Chaplin makes it all good material for our laughs.

The rally speech defines Hynkel's political objectives for the nation. Visuals in the first segment glorify the military might of Tomania, while the words denigrate the value of democracy. Next, he asks for the tightening of belts by the nation. The fat General Herring takes this order literally and finds it difficult to do so because of the girth of his tummy. Herring is war minister; Garbage (Garbitish) is minister for home and propaganda. Both have been Hynkel's friends during his long years of struggle. Next, Hynkel opens up with such furious anti-Jewish wrath that even the microphones bend and wilt. Then follows a dream, a dream of glorious motherhood for bearing children who will grow up to be Tomanian soldiers and would dominate the world. More marching as the rally ends, and Hynkel prepares to leave the rostrum. Visually the sequence is wrapped by very similar frames.

The humour in this sequence is based on exaggeration. A German-sounding gibberish is the language of the dictator's speech. A few identifiable words here and there (e.g., democraceey ssshhtunk) are designed to suggest what the verbal fury is about. Hynkel's expressive face and body language during the speech also say it all. The rough manner of speaking provokes bouts of cough, which need to be controlled by sipping water. Sheer slapstick works even with the drinking of water. Hynkel pours it in the ear and spits it out of the mouth.

The rally ends. At formal leave taking bows, the rotund Herring accidentally pushes the small-in-size Hynkel, who rolls down the stairs. Apologies are not acceptable, and the angry leader rips off half the medals from the general's glittering chest. Then, the situation is instantly back to normal. The waiting publicity photographers record formal greetings by the blonde mothers and blonde children. The Leader holds up a child. Driving away from the cheering crowds, they talk of the successful speech, though Garbitsch thinks that the anti-Jew harangues which may be resisted by some groups in Tomania.

The film has by now settled in its style. It can make the audience laugh over such a serious matter like war. The core of its comedy is hard hitting satire.

We now move to the Jewish ghetto. The amnesic barber returns to his shop and home, completely oblivious of the changes around, and of the constant threat of the marauding anti-Jewish storm troopers. He gets into scraps with them, demonstrating how the meek and innocent can rise to resist tyranny. Also living in the ghetto is Hannah, a young woman, an orphan who has nowhere else to go. She sustains herself by housework, under the protection of Jaeckel, the senior resident of the ghetto. Hannah and the barber are now set to make the ideal romantic couple.

Incidentally, in this film women are victims of the system, as also sources of tender dreams. The overdressed blondes, who greet the leader after the rally and those in the palace offices or in the evening ball, are women of little consequence. Hannah is different. She is full of vigour and with the will to fight back the arrogant soldiers for the rights of the common people. She would like to stay on in Tomania where she belongs, even though under stress she has no choice and ultimately crosses over into Osterlich with the Jaeckel family. It is interesting that the first mention of a woman in the film is by Schultz the crashing pilot during what he thinks are his dying moments. He starts talking of the loss of a future idyllic family life with Hilda, his gentle beloved. A continuation of that idyllic dream could well be the last segment on Hannah in the distant peaceful countryside as she listens over the radio to the words of hope from her lover. The very last visual image of the film is a radiant close-up face of Hannah, dreaming of future happiness.

Once we have the amnesic hero back in the Jewish ghetto, the time is ripe for fights with the arrogant soldiers for whom even simple enquiries from a Jew are affronts. A fight begins on a serious note, but Chaplin turns it into slapstick, with Hannah banging the soldiers merrily on the head with a heavy cooking pan on an upper window. For a change, once she hits the barber, who breaks into a reeling dance on the pavement in a musical variation of the bang-thud theme.

The barber now sets up shop. But soon enough there are more fights with the storm troopers. On one occasion, the soldiers catch him and are planning to hang him on the nearest street post, when Schultz, now a commander in Hynkel's setup, appears in the nick of time and orders the soldiers to let the barber go and always keep off him.

This ghetto sequence shows the lives of the ordinary people, through which Chaplin presents the argument for values of simple humanity. These people help each other. They have compassion for the amnesic and the orphan and they would let them be. They have a concern for dignity in life and would even fight against injustice. This is the kind of people who are the real source of power in society.

We now change the style of presentation of this essay. So far we have been talking of numerous details in the plot relating to the theme of violence. Now onwards plot details could be brief, even skipped. The focus will be on value aspects in relation to violence. We suggest that the readers make an effort to see the Chaplin film for relishing the real flavour of our analysis. VCD and DVD copies of *The Great Dictator* are now readily available in India.

Sequence from the Palace

This sequence examines the dictator as a figure of supreme authority and as a person. The dictator is now presented in the setting of his palace in the following terms: (i) Power: its signs and symbols and (ii) Self-image: internal and external.

Exaggeration is used as a device for filling the gap between real authority and its signs or symbols. For example, at the office, two artists working in adjacent room, making Hynkel's portrait and a bust, are given very brief sittings. For a leisure activity like playing the piano there is just a passing moment for Hynkel. He takes instant decisions for dismissing large number of people from jobs. There is no middle path. Everything is either at this extreme or that, yes or no and there are inevitable consequences of each.

Flops in the war machine are shown in terms of a bullet proof uniform and a portable parachute designed to be worn as a head dress. When demonstrated for Hynkel's approval, both fail.

Reverse Swing Technique

A hidden microphone produces very loud sound output. Man-woman relationship is completely devoid of any emotion, so that sex resembles violence. Hynkel is ready for instant turn around in policy towards Jews, while he is seeking loan from a Jewish financier.

Complete self-centeredness, complete neglect of needs of people, self-admiration in hidden multiple mirrors and contempt for any dissenting opinion are some of the personal characteristics of the dictator.

Part 2 is the flip and flop for the Jewish community. During this part of the plot there is a short period of good times for the ghetto. Hynkel needs money from a Jewish tycoon for financing the planned invasion of Oesterlich. Hence, he has to suspend the persecution of Jews. The character of the people in the ghetto is unfolded. The barber may even expand his business and set up a ladies' parlour. Hannah dreams of a life of social harmony. Others in the ghetto relax enjoying the persecution free days.

The Palace continues war preparations, with interesting acts of display of power. Hynkel has put a letter in an envelope. He summons an aide merely to lick the envelope before closing it. A letter is being dictated directly to a typist. A long, long spoken sentence results in a short typing action, a short monosyllable is typed at considerable length. A period is, of course, a period. When Hynkel has to sign, the pen gets stuck in the inkstand. He throws a tantrum, calling every one around stupid and sterile, which may well be a reference to an earlier scene of his virile action with a blonde typist. The fat general Herring reports on a new poison gas, only to be deflated verbally by Hynkel. When a factory strike is being discussed for orders to remove the troublesome leaders, an on-the-spot spy reports that the leaders have already been shot dead. Hynkel's self-centredness is stimulated into megalomania. Garbitsch suggests that everyone in the world could be looking up to Hynkel, as if he was like God. This idea actually scares Hynkel. However, the dream of world dominance is pleasant and Hynkel plays it out in dancing with a rubber globe balloon. The balloon at last bursts, and Hynkel is in despair. The mighty dictator too has chinks in his personality.

The next sequence in the ghetto emphasises togetherness, mutual help and happy gentle life. There is a funny bit in which as per instructions on the radio, some piece of work has its rhythm adjusted to the happy music from the radio. Older persons in the ghetto like Jaeckel are however uneasy about it all. They are so used to the bad times that they find it hard to believe in the good times. Neighbours are delighted when the barber and Hannah go out on a date for the evening dance.

Happiness in the ghetto is followed by bad news in the palace. Hynkel is refused any financial support for invasion of Oesterlich by the tycoon. This triggers off the dictator's wrath. The persecution of the Jews is to be resumed. When Commander Schultz tries to plead, he is promptly arrested, as if by a force of habit of Hynkel. However, as Schultz is being led away, he warns loud and clear to the dictator right on his face: "Stupid ruthlessness towards innocent people is bound to fail." Hynkel reveals a human strain when he actually grieves that a close friend like Schultz should abandon him. However, Hynkel gets ready for anti-Jew radio broadcast.

The crackdown broadcast catches the young couple unaware. There is a stiff resistance put up by the meek of the ghetto. The fights are composed in slapstick style. The barber and his girl have been identified as leaders. The barber's shop is burnt and the soldiers are determined to get them. However, the others help them hide on a safe roof. Schultz has also escaped captivity and is hiding in the ghetto.

While all this looting and burning is going on, Hynkel plays the piano. Is Chaplin quoting the Emperor Nero of Rome?

The next sequence shows the weakness of the ordinary people. Schultz is planning revenge. A Jew from the ghetto is to be chosen by lottery as the "lucky" person to assassinate the dictator. But no one is willing to vie for that honour. Schultz himself is above it all as a proud Aryan. A hilarious coin-in-the-pudding sequence presents this flop side of the character of the ordinary people as well. All this about country, honour and sacrifice is mere high talk.

The film continues in this style. The events are entirely serious, but the treatment entirely Chaplinesque slapstick. Both the barber and Schultz are eventually arrested from the ghetto, and sent to prison. Jaeckel, Hannah and the others in the ghetto cross over to the security of the countryside in Oesterlich. Eventually Schultz and the barber also escape from prison, and reach the victory stand in Oesterlich.

We need to laugh at diplomacy too. When a nation is ready for war, diplomacy must fail. Napolini, the dictator of neighbouring Bacteria too has his army ready, intent to invade Oesterlich, quite like Hynkel's, and this is good enough reason for Tomania to declare war on Bacteria. However, diplomatic negotiations persuade Napolini to make a state visit to Tomania to sort out matters between the two dictators. A long string of hilarious incidents of Napolini's arrival by train, negotiations in Hynkel' palace, a parade and arms display and the evening ball are sheer mad comedy based on the principles of start-stop, high-low, big-small, flip-flop. The routines of the American slapstick, even the classic pie-throwing sequence are reworked in scenes of diplomatic settings. Napolini relents, only to be cheated by Hynkel. In effect, one dictator cheats the other. There is no statesmanship, no valour, only cunning and caprice.

The devices of advantage seeking are quite consciously applied and they flop when the other behaves quite unpredictably. There are five such efforts and misfires. They are also repeated in the so-called process of negotiation. From words to fist fight and from mincing words to twisting tails, it ends with the Dictator agreeing to sign the treaty first and Napolini agrees to withdraw his army next. But the path for invasion of Osterlich is now clear.

A funny breakaway comes when Hynkel asks lady Napolini for a dance, and she being a woman of some weight, carries him around for a while, when he leaves, complimenting her but exhausted.

Part 3 of the plot shows the invasion, during which Hynkel is mistaken for his lookalike and arrested by his own soldiers and the Jewish barber makes the anti-war speech from the war-victory podium.

Summing up

We have presented here a small segment from an extensive examination of the cinematic structure of *The Great Dictator*, limited to reveal how the thematic foundation of the film embodies an integrated humanist denial of violence, exemplified at the highest level by dictatorship and war. The entertainment value of its comic nature does not reduce the evocative power of the film to raise serious human issues. In actual fact, it is precisely the comic devices, which highlight the basic irrationality of anything, which supports violence. For example, humour is created by the manner of debunking the idea that human worth is equated to power position. Script events are often structured to show how mere signs and symbols of power attain unreasonably high value in public recognition. The facts of the matter are, however, quite different. Human beings have an intrinsic sense of value, which is the true source of awareness of differences in varied contexts of life and society. This awareness gives us the flexibility to handle issues in the practical business of everyday living. However, if differences were based on the hierarchy of worth, the situation would surely generate a wide range of fear, rage, hostility and anxiety about injustice, as also self-harm. If the idea of worth gets seeded, it will definitely yield a crop of unrest. If an already existing idea of worth is stimulated, it will invariably result in violence to others, as also to self. Power, dominance, victory and all these ideas originate from this fallacy about worth. Imagine a person who keeps on saying to himself and to the others: "I am what I possess, what I was born with or what I acquired", "I am superior because I am intrinsically better than the others", "I am in reality what others praise me about". If such ideas are whipped up they would well result in claims that the others have no right to be different, or even not have the right to live. Acts of violence can always be traced to originate in such background ideas. Evoke the idea of worth, and you will always provoke antagonism. This is the unfailing recipe for starting a riot.

All this may sound simplistic. In actual fact it is not so. Imagine any complex situation of conflict. Next, try removing from the situation this element of worth, and you will find that the complexity of the situation has vanished. This idea may appear abstract, even deterministic. However, it works all the time. Biological formulations, theories of natural selection, and other concepts of worth have been used all the time to justify violence as a logical method of annihilation of one species by another, one race by another, one religious or communal group by another. It is a recurrent story in human history.

Acts of violence involve angry rhetoric or brutal action, which, in their nature, are irrational. Think carefully about the following questions, which elaborate this idea.

"Why do I have to attack this person who calls me by a nickname given me by some other persons, some other time?" "Do I sincerely believe that I am what I have been called in abuse?" "Why do I have to flare up in anger when somebody is adjudged better than myself?" "Do I really regard myself the equivalent of the various insignia and symbols which I possess?" In actual life, everyone will laugh at me if I declare that all those who do not agree with me are bad or are mad, or that they deserve to be dead. The numerous comic events in the film bring out precisely such irrational aspects of violent behaviour.

Every human being needs to be happy. Hence, a major task of development is to discover ways of living, which maximise happiness. This would, in effect, subsume all individual and group efforts, goals and achievements. In contrast, a desire to cut off a slice from the other man's land always triggers off the process of conflict. Any act of aggression invariably challenges the very concept of justice. Human beings are capable of surviving without greed. It is more important to search for ways of living together rather than seek ways of taking advantage. The predominance of seeking advantage has created a cultural crisis in societies in transition.

Chaplin draws pointed attention to the function of machinery in society. Violence can be avoided if we keep our technologies man-centered. Violence is inevitable if greed cannot be avoided. We know that no individual human being is self-sufficient, or even aspires to be so. We have to live through mutual help. This is not a species issue or a territorial issue. Nor is it an issue of ensuring continuity of industrial production by feeding the war machines. Chaplin makes us think of the avoidable character of violence. Recall that Hynkel laments when his friend Schultz deserts him. The dictator, however great, is actually scared of the suggestion that he could be God, and everyone else could be looking up to him. The source of the scare is the deep realisation of one's fallibility. The dictator is certainly disappointed when the balloon bursts.

Human beings have a mix of the rational and the irrational in the guiding principles of living. We have a fair chance of a happier world if the irrational can be identified and controlled. Human beings can create their own chance of happiness. The choices that will open this opportunity are clearly expressed in the film. Presence of such a cinematic image in human cultural heritage is a strong source of reinforcement of conscious choice of simplicity over unnecessary complexity, of denial of terrorist rhetoric over fundamentalism, and choice of co-existence over advantage seeking.

15

Power Rangers
Violent Media and Violent Children

ANSHU KAUSHAL

On December 16, 1997, more than six hundred Japanese children had to be hospitalised as all of them were afflicted by sudden epileptic seizures. It was neither an accident nor a coincidence of fate. The epidemic that caused this emergency was a cartoon show by the name Pokemon, a roman contraction meaning pocket monster. The episode displayed bright explosions with swiftly changing blue and red colour patterns which caused epileptic seizures in children, even though most of them did not have any previous history of this stigmatised disease.[1]

This incidence is an eloquent commentary on the emotional and physical effect video games can have on children, whatever the opinion of market wizards on the issue.

The study of a child's developmental process reveals that mass media plays an indispensable role in his or her physical, emotional, cognitive and social development. Children are information seekers and today's electronic world provides them unlimited and sometimes unwelcome opportunities to access information by simply clicking a button. The right to information in the UN Convention of the Rights of the Child stresses on the positive role of the mass media which includes conveying appropriate information, supporting educational programmes and promoting the cultural heritage of the child. However, the heightened powers of the media which serve to enhance access to information also pose inherent dangers and make children vulnerable to multifarious risks.

In times of cut-throat competition, single-minded self-centeredness and over weening ambition, the "education of the character" (Hunt, 28) envisaged by the CRC for the mass media remains a far cry. Media has lagged behind in providing positive guidance and training to children and develop in them qualities that are indispensable for making them responsible adult citizens of the world. Most of the programmes shown on television are not in accordance with the spirit of education as they do not nurture high human values among children. In a society driven by technology where children can access desired and undesired information from diverse national and international sources, violence portrayed in different forms of mass media has become a great threat. It has left a painful scar on the delicate psyche of children by percolating into their innocent world and blemishing their minds with its corrupting influence.[2]

The nature and concept of childhood has undergone various changes at different periods of history. Contemporary childhood has metamorphosed from an ideal state of innocence and fun under various cultural, social and moral upheavals that rocked human civilisation in the preceding centuries. The process has been gradual and can be attributed to various factors. In the Indian context, the joint family system, which hitherto was the "psycho – social matrix of childhood" (Kakar, 113), has shrunk drastically to give rise to smaller units popularly known as nuclear families. This entails an early separation of the child from the secure fold of a large family heightening his/her psychological stress and inner conflict. It may cause mental disturbances in the child, instigating him/her to act violently. In some cases it may manifest as an unnatural fascination with watching violent acts.

Psychologists have looked far and wide to find out the causes that prompt children to act violently. Violence among the youth is a complex problem and is caused by an interplay of many factors like domestic violence, poverty, drug abuse, racism, peer pressure and inefficient parenting to name a few. However, the role of television in this process is underestimated as much confusion has been caused due to conflicting opinions on this issue. Since the time it was introduced, to the present day, television has carved a niche for itself in our homes. Captivating the senses with its swirling images and flickering contrasts, television has entranced both young and old. Children of the twenty-first century are immersed in the excitement and happiness that television promises to offer. Under the garb of entertainment, media has also come to reflect the all-pervading violence of modern society through images that hit the television screen every second. Television programmes, especially those catering to children make use of violence for entertainment which, to a great extent, shapes the world they live in. Studies have indicated that violence on the small screen can have debilitating effects on the behaviour pattern of children in general.[3]

In an era when child welfare receives much scholarly and media attention, it sounds ironical to talk about a sharp rise in acts of violence committed by children. The Civil Rights Movement, which emphasised upon the education and welfare of children also brought into focus the dignity and rights to which children are entitled. It emphasised that all humans, including children, are endowed with the faculty of reason and hence should be given freedom to think and act independently. This movement led to the democratisation of childhood and generated a consciousness among people that children are participants in society and their civil, cultural and moral rights must be respected. Children should be treated as individuals and not sub-persons, their needs and desires should be catered to as seriously as their adult counterparts. This theory, coupled with the approach of psychoanalysts world over that childhood plays an important part in shaping the personality of the adult, led to a sudden glorification of childhood. The consumer goods industry exploited this sentiment to target children as their prime consumers, flooding the market with special toys, books, magazines, foods, accessories, video games, television channels etc. designed exclusively for children.

Internet, television, i-pods, video games, computer games and play stations – violence has become an inescapable reality for all forms of electronic media which are easily available to children these days. The impact of violence depicted in media has been the subject of debate among child advocacy groups for decades. Although studies have not been able to prove conclusively that violence on television has a negative impact on children, it has been regarded as the most notorious source causing aggressive behaviour among children. Television has become a pervasive feature of a majority of households and therefore a powerful force in the social, cultural and moral upbringing of children across the globe. Most children are exposed to it for an average of two to three hours daily. With such an extensive exposure, media becomes an effective tool in shaping the perception and attitudes of tender minds.

In such a context, the content of television programmes aired exclusively for children has come under scrutiny. Research has shown that violence on television for children has been rising steadily over the years. The social learning theory propounded by Dr Albert Bandura establishes that children learn by emulating or through 'modelling'. According to the principle of observational learning, "Models can be physical, involving real people, or symbolic, involving verbal, audio, or visual representations, or combinations of these. Modeling is recognised as one of the most powerful means of transmitting values, attitudes, and patterns of thought and behaviour" ("Children and Media Violence"). Television is influential and can be an effective tool in instructing and inspiring children but when it portrays violence, the outcome can be devastating.

A mounting body of socio-scientific evidence suggests a negative effect of the electronic media environment on children. A vast body of psychiatric reconstruction studies establish a causal link between viewing violence on television and causing children, who are frequent viewers of these violent episodes, to act violently. Ironically, cartoons contain a level of violence which would not be acceptable in real life. Violent incidents are highest in cartoon programmes which are considered appropriate and entertaining for children by their parents. Physical violence is a recurrent motif in shows like *Tom and Jerry* and *Looney Tunes* where characters are thrashed, stabbed, pushed down a cliff or run over only to reappear on the screen in a moment's time. In a real life incident, a nine year old boy pushed his little sister off a cliff causing her to die instantly.

On being asked by his parents why he did it, the child replied innocently that it was nothing and his sister would very soon spring back to life as cartoon characters always did in his favourite television show. It cannot be denied that the feedback that children get from these shows is that violence is funny and harmless and they start mimicking acts of aggression as a pleasurable activity.

Another category of programmes portrays violence as a means of eliminating the villains and is extensively used by the heroes against the evil doers. Action cartoons like *He-Man, Spiderman, Batman* and *Power Rangers* depict the aggressors as attractive and powerful. The behaviour of these larger than life heroes may well be designated as socially deviant but it is viewed sympathetically for it puts an end to evil and evil doers. These characters are showered with accolades at the end of each episode which translates in real life into a justified action entailing neither punishment nor remorse. Assaults by children instigated by copying cartoon violence led to shows like *Mighty Morphin Power Rangers* being taken off air in several countries. The child viewers emulate the mannerisms of the iconic super heroes and utilise violence as a way to settle conflicts in real life or as a means of retaliation against their so called victimisers.

On-screen violence, shown as a normal part of presentations for children, can have complex psychological effects on their impressionable minds. It inculcates aggressive behaviour and belligerent attitude among children who are exposed uninterruptedly to violence in media. Psychologists state unequivocally that viewing violence in screen has taught children to tease others and become vengeful. Acquired at a young age, such habits can become lifelong. They can encourage anti-social behaviour like bullying, gang fights or homicidal tendencies among adolescents and domestic violence, rape or murder among adults. Prolonged viewing of violence on media leads to emotional desensitisation of children towards the effects of violence. Children identify with the acts of the perpetrator (hero) in the action cartoons which seldom show the suffering of the victim (villain), causing their empathy with the victim to diminish. Violence thus becomes an accepted way of life for children who start looking towards violence not as the last but the first resort in solving problems. Osofsky and Osofsky warn that exposing children to violence determines how children process their life experiences, how they behave in diverse situations and how they react to provocation. Violence shown on media is often disconnected from real consequences. By portraying violent acts, media strikes at the very foundation of our moral values toppling the social structure of a civilised society. Superheroes may possess good values and their message may be pro social but the way in which it is conveyed justifies violence. Children absorb unlimited pathological themes in their long hours of television viewing and even if they take them with some seriousness, children cannot fail to affect developing attitudes toward violence, sex and social restraint.

Television, like literature, attempts to prepare children to enter the adult world by familiarising them with its modus operandi. It paves the way for a child's social behaviour and instructs him/her to move along that very path in real life. Constant depiction of violence on television affirms the view that violence is an accepted way of life. The children begin to nurture the belief that the world is a violent and mean place and there are only two ways of dealing with it – fight or flight. Children may start mistrusting others and resort to real life violence as a means of self defence or they may forever be scared of becoming victims of violence. Constant pelting of the television screen with violent images reinforces real life experiences of children living in a violent environment. For those not living in such environments, television certainly makes violence appear thrilling.

Children of different age groups view and understand television in different ways. Their response to television programmes is based on variables like hours of viewing, attention span, age, capability of processing the content viewed and real life experiences. No study has found the effect of television on infants conclusively but evidence suggests that they can imitate what they see on screen. In an internet version of an interview printed in *The Executive Intelligence Review*, the co-author of the book *Stop Teaching Our Kids to Kill: A Call to Action against TV, Movie & Video Game Violence* Lt. Col. David Grossman states "the written word can't be processed until age 8, and it is filtered through the rational mind. The spoken word can't be processed until age 4, and it, too, has to be filtered in the forebrain before it trickles down to the emotional centre. But, these violent visual images: At the age of 18 months, a child is fully capable of perceiving and imitating what they see. And, at the age of 18 months, these violent visual images, whether they be television, movies, or video games, go straight into the eyes, and straight into the emotional center" ("Interview with David Grossman: Giving Children the Skill and the Will to Kill"). Late George Gerbner, founder of Cultural Indicators Project and Professor of Communication of the Annenberg School of Communication, Philadelphia, says that when violent imagery is repeated continuously on the television screen, it creates a sense of reality among children. Media makes violence appear so commonplace in today's world that moral solutions seem unlikely.

Viewing violent programmes can also cause sleep disorders, irritation and anxiety among infants. Children of preschool age watch television with the intent of exploration and search for meaning in what is shown on screen. However, their ability to analyse the motive and consequences of violence is limited and they are unable to put violence in the right context. This makes them particularly vulnerable to such content displayed frequently on their television screens. Children of this age group have been found to act more aggressively than usual while playing after being exposed to graphic on screen violence. Violence is doled out to children in attractive packages of vivid production features like rapid character movement, scenic locations and unusual sights and sounds which makes them soft targets of media violence at a very tender age. The screen images are manipulated in such a way by television producers that the show turns violent scenes into a powerfully addictive substance for a child from which he or she just cannot turn away.

The age that follows preschool is critical in understanding the effects of violence on the psyche of children. Between the age of six and eleven, children develop enhanced cognitive abilities and their attention span also increases. They are able to follow plot movement and can draw inferences about implicit content shown on television. The mental effort that children put into viewing a certain programme determines their reaction to it. For example, if a child views violence casually, he will react to it in a superficial way, whereas if the mental effort in viewing television is serious, the impact of violence can be profound. If a violent act is shown to produce pain and suffering and is disapproved on screen as evil, children refrain from taking part in such an activity. On the other hand, if violent acts are presented in a positive light, children may identify with it and make it an important ingredient of their own life. Children, especially boys, identify with the acts of electronic superheroes like Spiderman or even their favourite WWF stars and emulate their actions in real life developing in them the propensity to act aggressively.

As children step on the threshold of adolescence, the pattern of their life changes completely. They spend less time at home and do not watch as much television as they did earlier. They develop abstract thinking abilities which equip them to question the reality of what is shown on television and their tendency to identify with televised characters decreases. A small percentage of children, however, continue to live in the reality of television and fantasise about superheroes. Most psychological establishments consider adolescence to be the most turbulent period of one's life, a time when anxiety, carelessness and risk taking behaviour is at its peak. If these adolescents are continuously exposed to violence and crime, they become susceptible to imitating these actions and applying them to real life situations. This kind of content may have an immediate or "sleeper effect" in normalising violence and making it appear completely acceptable. Some psychologists warn that young children, particularly boys, may be attracted to violent programmes precisely because access to such programmes is restricted by their parents. A liking for such programmes may be a form of assertion of their independence or a test to diagnose their ability to handle such content. Aggressive adolescents are at a greater risk of turning into aggressive adults which makes it imperative for us to understand early factors that determine what might happen later.

Violence is not a new phenomenon for children. They have been exposed to violence well before television arrived. Immortal children's stories like Little Red Riding Hood or Hansel and Gretel contain acts too gruesome for children to read. For long, the western world has kept its children bereft of the Indian mythological stories citing violence as a cause. Violence, however, has acquired a dangerous magnitude and has snowballed into a serious problem in the contemporary world. Aided by novel scientific inventions and driven by a materialistic culture, violence is thriving among humans. We need only glance at the rising number of incidents school shooting, homicide, suicide, rape and kidnapping perpetrated by youths to understand the extent of this sinister trend. Television and movies normalise acts like carrying a gun and glamorise the use of deadly weapons as a source of personal power. Simply copying what is shown on media is one of the means by which violence creates unhealthy outcome among youth. When some children open fire at their own classmates or a child kills a sibling because he does not want to share his toys, it certainly points towards the moral vacuum that televised violence has created in the minds of today's youth by legitimising it on screen. Social commentators attribute the rising trend of violence among youth to the exposure of youngsters to violence and lack of positive values in media content.

It is well known that technological advancement has brought about changed relations between men and between groups. The media has acquired importance as a vital agent of social stimuli and replaced many functions of personal contact. Mass media communicates information to millions of people simultaneously in an astonishingly brief time but the presentation is not through personal contact. In the present day world of instant gratification, socialisation has given way to social networking where one can dispose a relationship at a click of a mouse or change one's profile in a jiffy to make it more desirable. This has led to an upheaval in the interaction processes and values in the tech savvy youth. The absorption of people in different forms of mass media results in far less time for intimate social connectedness, which is evident not only in homes but also in broader patterns of community vitality. Watching television has drawn flak for causing positive civic participation to deteriorate, indicating an unhealthy trend in social connectedness. Watching television removes us from the physical reality of our current lives for long periods of time. When we watch television, our social interaction stops altogether, conversation becomes partial and it takes away from us an opportunity to build collective perspectives by sharing and learning through verbal interaction. A breakdown in normal patterns of social interaction and other socialisation experiences is one of the causes of aggressive behaviour among children. The socialisation process involves a set of mutually related practices that direct the individual's goals, motives and behavioural habits toward conformity to the conventions of the society that he/she lives in. Behavioural deviations that are especially dangerous to society take place through failures of socialisation which result in anti-social behaviour among the youth and produce internal conflicts within them. The deviations from social conventions are threatening to the stability of society as anti-social elements cannot assimilate smoothly into society. Idols serve as agents of socialisation by providing models for behaviour which influence the youngsters. When the behaviour of these models is inappropriate, the resulting social learning may prove to be not at all adaptive, making it difficult for the child to assimilate into mature society.

People have always had a penchant for violent spectacles. Ancient Roman rulers organised gladiatorial combats where slaves and prisoners were forced to fight ferocious beasts to death. It was a part of their public policy, for such fights kept the citizens entertained, but distracted from key political issues. William Shakespeare deviated from classical playwrights in that his plays carried the depiction of gruesome violence on stage. The Elizabethan audience flocked to see murder, beheadings and bloodshed on stage and perhaps felt a sense of gratification to see characters suffer like themselves. Death and violence fascinated the Elizabethan audience. Social critics in the eighteenth century expressed concern over the tendency of juveniles to mimick the bloody actions reported in newspapers. In the twentieth century, there was a growing concern among people about the blatant display of violence and lawlessness in an otherwise popular media – the film. Modern man does not kill people within public eye like the Romans did, but by providing easy access to fantasy slaughter, he contributes extensively to the growth of violence in contemporary society.

Violent movies or television programmes are not the only anti-social forces at work. However, on screen violence is certainly a contributing factor and has a negative impact on the beliefs, behaviour and values of growing children. The entire world was shocked after a wave of school killings engulfed America some years ago. High school and middle school students went on a shooting spree, taking the lives of their classmates and teachers and in some cases, their own lives as well. The world was forced to think as to what could have caused these youngsters to carry out such cold blooded killings. Attention soon turned to the kind of entertainment that they were obsessed with. It included violent song lyrics, first person shooter video games and movies glorifying violence. There is, of course, no substantial evidence that violent entertainment caused these children to become killers, but the effect of being raised in a violent media environment could not have been healthy. Televised violence is a preparatory school for criminal and anti-social behaviour among children. India too has not remained untouched by the onslaught of television. There has been a steady rise in juvenile crimes like killing schoolmates, abducting and molesting girls and kidnapping and assaulting classmates particularly in the metropolitan cities of India. Research proves that emotionally immature individuals can be seriously affected by fighting or brutality shown in films and video games and disturbed young people can be led into the habit of expressing their aggressive energies by actions that are socially destructive.

Home video game industry is almost fifty years old. The content and role of video games has changed greatly since they first appeared in the 1970s. Technology advanced at a geometric rate and so did the quality of video games, with more compelling and lifelike portrayal being easily available to children. Initially designed as teachers, arcade games, console games and computer games invaded numerous homes. Playing video games became a visual feast to be gorged upon by children and youngsters. Video games are natural teachers. Children find them extremely motivating since they are highly interactive and can engage the attention of children for long hours. Driven by modern technology, the content of video games became more graphically violent. It came to glorify gang culture, celebrate cruelty, reward murder, acknowledge theft and trivialise violence toward women. As the popularity of video games grew rapidly so did the level of public concern about the deleterious impact of these games. The world of video games marketed for children is a dark, frightening and gory place, especially in the action and adventure genres. Ironically, these ultra violent video games became top sellers in the gaming industry. Playing these games involves a different dimension of cognitive and emotional engagement. Unhealthy level of preoccupation with these devices is sure to have profound and lasting effects on the behaviour of children.

The teenagers of today are the most technology driven as compared to the bygone generations. Their sense of identity, family, community, friendship and morality is shaped by the virtual world. When children and young adults spend a huge chunk of their time in the company of violent media, there are bound to be adverse effects. The lovable gaming characters like Mario and Luigi have been replaced by ones who kill for thrill. Games like the *Grand Theft Auto*, *Mortal Kombat* and *Doom* award the players for unlawful acts like murder, traffic violation, arson and theft. To quote an example, the first assignment of the player of *Grand Theft Auto III* is to secure large amounts of cocaine to lure gangsters on to him. As an investigator, he can gain success only by becoming one of them. In his pursuit to bust these gangs the player indulges in unlawful and anti-social activities like demolishing buildings, taking down a bank, diving out of moving vehicles, ramming his car into others' and even running an adult film studio. His motive may be noble but it is achieved through ways that society does not sanction. It is not difficult to guess what message it carries for its young players. Apart from employing cutting edge scientific technology to enhance the presentation of the game, companies that manufacture these games have added a surprising amount of variety in the gameplay by backing it up with a compelling plot quite akin to real life situations. Violent games are teaching children of all ages to practise anti-social activities though it be in the virtual world. Lt. Col. David Grossman in his article "Trained to Kill" determines that the conditioning reflex and motor skills that children practise in these games are applied by them in real life. The electronic exercises that these games offer are similar to those taught to combating soldiers in a training camp. As a result, repeated exposure to these exercises conditions the brains of children to kill or at least become insensitive to violence being committed around them.

This debate raises a very vital question – Why are children attracted to violence? Two world reputed newspapers, the *New York Times* and the *London Times* have irrefutably recognised the claims of studies which show that viewing violence has a detrimental effect on tender minds. The attention has thus shifted from underlying sources of violence to effects of televised violence on young children. Technology has assumed a position of autonomy above society in the children's innocent world. In times of instant gratification and high end consumerism, these hi tech gizmos replace the real world with a virtual one, and thrill the person wired to them by allowing him to do what he cannot do in real life. Media has become a rite of passage among adolescent subcultures. To be a part of the digital generation, it is imperative for youngsters to be charged up and always connected. Gaming offers young children new feelings and experiences and in their unquenchable desire for sensation seeking, they are willing to take big risks. Most of the video games require the players to accomplish a challenging task. As the level of the game rises the tasks become more and more difficult to accomplish. Youngsters who are able to complete these challenging tasks, derive a sense of achievement from playing these games and scoring high in them becomes a rewarding experience. Games also provide a means of escaping the tension and stress of everyday life and offer an interesting way to counter boredom. Video games give free rein to fantasies of power, glory and freedom in a realistic environment, giving respite from mundane lives to most children. These games cater to the risk taking and novelty seeking instincts and are particularly popular among adolescent boys. In fact, an entire culture dedicated to violent gaming has been created in this age and this culture has changed people's personalities and value system for the worse.

The pervasiveness of violence in media has raised some potent questions on its role in shaping the norms and attitudes of the upcoming generations. The oft repeated accusation against violent electronic media is that it does not teach moral consequences of a violent act to its users. According to the American Psychological Association, violence portrayed in video games subtly encourages children to use aggressive language and view even more aggressive images. It triggers anxiety in youngsters thereby decreasing their ability to control anger. As a result they tend to resolve anxiety and anger inappropriately by externalising it. They can attack something, kick a wall or be mean to a pet. Children resort to violent acts instead of taking recourse to traditional ways of relieving anxiety like soothing themselves, talking about it or even expressing it through crying. When children spend most of their free time with violence simulators like these games, they develop a violent mindset which they carry with them into adulthood. According to the of eminent psychologist and popular talk show host, Dr Phil Mc Graw, children spend a lot of time playing violent games at precisely the age when they should be learning positive ways to relate to other people and resolve conflicts peacefully. Understanding the message given by video games is an important first step in understanding the effects of these games on children.

Technological changes have brought about changes in human relationships and changes in human consciousness. Across decades and modes of presentation, violent entertainment has been viewed as an evil influence on youth. It has given rise to a culture of disrespect in which children get the message that it is acceptable to treat each other rudely or aggressively. Technology is changing the rules of social engagement. It has brought with it a steady decline in social etiquette of the younger generation. The addiction to hi tech gadgets is so great that the youngsters are unable to differentiate between private and public space. Advances in technology have opened new venues for social interaction in which youth can be easily victimised. These new venues lure the young users out of the secure boundaries of a family or neighbourhood or community into a mysterious world which may be wrought with unknown dangers. The culture of violence values competition and individuality over cooperation and community feeling and deters society from bonding cohesively. Violence in media can be easily labelled as a threat to public health. It causes video induced seizures, attention disorders, obesity, postural, muscular, and skeletal disorders among children. What use is a medium which is popular but does not nourish human spirit or help develop personal and human potential? With our upcoming generations virtually at the mercy of mass media, a conscious approach to the question of means of communication is the need of the hour.

Endnotes

1. Condensed and re-worded from internet source: http://www/forteantimes.com/features/articles266/pockemon_panic.html
2. An article published in *The Hindustan Times*, 27 July 2009 mentions that a video game *Prototype* has a protagonist, Alex Mercer who runs through New York spraying bullets and killing people. He also happens to pick up passers-by and 'consume' them to 'improve' his health. The writer rues the fact that the makers of such gory games as *GTA: Vice City, Prototype, GTA IV* care about nothing but the profits while children and society suffer (see Gopal Sathe, "No Child's Play." *The Hindustan Times*, 27 July 2009, p. 11).
3. See John McCarthy, "Television is making torture acceptable." *The Tribune*, 4 May 2007. McCarthy says that "the biggest lie that has gained currency through television is that torture is an acceptable weapon for the 'good guys' to use if the stakes are high enough."

Works Cited

"Children and Media Violence." *Encyclopedia of Death and Dying*. Web. 8 June 2010.

Jeffery Steinberg and Dennis Speed. "Interview with David Grossman: Giving Children the Skill and the Will to Kill". *The Executive Intelligence Review*. Web. 19 September 2010.

Hunt, Peter. Ed. *Critical Concepts in Literary and Cultural Studies*. 4 vols. London: Routledge, 2006.

Kakar, Sudhir. *The Indian Psyche*. Delhi: OUP, 1996.

Contributors

T.S. Anand has had an eventful teaching career spanning over 36 years at PG and UG levels. Author of 14 books of creative literature and criticism and Honorary Editor, *Literary Voice,* a journal for English Studies, he is also a winner of Olive I. Reddick Prize for Best Research Paper.

Usha Bande, former Fellow, Indian Institute of Advanced Study, Shimla, and retired Principal, was earlier on the Faculty of English Literature. She has worked extensively in the field of Women's Studies, has authored several books and is Guest Faculty at various institutions of repute like Vishwa Bharati University, Shanti Niketan and many others.

Shibani Basu Dubey is on the faculty of English at Mata Gujri Mahila College, Jabalpur, Madhya Pradesh. She has worked for her doctorate on the plays of Girish Karnad.

Anshu Kaushal, a young scholar teaching in R.K.M.V., Shimla is working for her doctorate on children's literature.

Jasbir Jain, Director IRIS and formerly Sahitya Akademi Writer in Residence (2009), Emeritus Fellow (2002–2004), is recipient of the 2008 SALA Award for Distinguished Scholarship as well as IACS 2003 Award for contribution to Canadian Studies. Her recent publications are: *The Writer as Critic* and *Indigenous Roots for Feminism: Culture, Subjectivity and Agency*, both in 2011.

P.K. Kalyani is Associate Professor, Department of English, M.S. University, Tirunelveli, Tamil Nadu. She has to her credit a book entitled *Translation Studies* and a large number of research papers. Dr Kalyani was awarded SAARC Fellowship in 2009 and currently she is working on a major UGC research project. She is Chair, Women's Welfare Committee of her University.

Josè Sol Lucia holds a Doctorate in Theology (Centre Sèvres, Paris, France). He is the Director of the Chair in Ethics and Christian Thought at "Institut Quìmic de Sarrià" (IQS), Ramon Llull University, Barcelona, Spain.

Manjinder Kaur is based in Ludhiana and is currently teaching English. She has recently completed her M.Phil and is pursuing doctoral research.

Silky Anand Khullar teaches English in Master Tara Singh Memorial College for Women, Ludhiana and is engaged in research.

Seema Malik is Chairperson, Department of English, Mohanlal Sukhadia University, Udaipur. Her main area of interest is women's studies specially women's autobiography. Her two recent publications are *Ethics and Aesthetics: Essays in Literature* and *Partition Fiction*. She has completed two UGC research projects and has a number of research papers to her credit.

Veena Poonacha is Director, Research Centre for Women's Studies, Hon. Director, Centre for Rural Development, and Project Director for the Avabai Wadia Archives for Women in SNDT Women's University, Mumbai. She has undertaken research across India (particularly Gujarat, Maharashtra and Karnataka) for national/international agencies to investigate state/community responses to domestic violence and other related issues. Her current research project for the Department of Minorities Development, Government of Maharashtra, seeks to examine development deficits in two minority-dominated urban slums in Mumbai.

Vineeta Kaur Saluja is the founder Principal, Mata Gujri Mahila Mahavidyalaya, Jabalpur. She has fifteen years of administrative experience and has several books as well as a large number of papers to her credit.

Contributors

Rajesh K. Sharma is on the Faculty of English, Punjabi University, Patiala. He has as vast research experience and has authored many book.

Avadesh K. Singh is at present Convener, Knowledge Consortium of Gujarat. Earlier he was Vice-Chancellor, Babasaheb Ambedkar Open University, Ahmedabad (2006–2009). He has been the Coordinator, the University Grants Commission (UGC) Special Assistance Programme (SAP DRS) on "Indian Renaissance Literature". Author of 15 books, he has published more than 130 papers. His book *Literature, Criticism and Aesthetics in India* is under publication. Since 1994, Dr Singh has been Editor, *Critical Practice*.

Jyoti K. Singh is a Lecturer based in Chandigarh. She has worked in the field of Indian women's novels, interpreting these from the psychological angle using new women's psychology. She has published a book entitled *Indian Women Novelists*.

Shyamala Vanarase is a psychologist by training and profession as well as a social worker based in Pune. She has taught at Pune University and also at SNDT, Pune and headed the Psychology Department. She is also a UNICEF consultant for Development of Master's Programme in Communication Media for Children. Since 1979, she has set up the Centre for Psychological Services along with Dr Sudheer Vanarase.

Index

Abraham, Francis, 81, 94
al Qaeda, 77
Anil's Ghost (2000)
   by Michael Ondaatje, 18, 23–26

Barthes, Roland, 33
Beauvouir, Simon de, 126
Beteille, Andre, 85
Blackmur, R.P., 37
Bond, Edward, 1
Breast War, 84, 85
Byrne, Donne, 177

caste violence, 83, 90
childhood
   concept of, changes in, 204
collective violence, 120
conflict(s), 89
   positive role of, 93
   types of, 89: realistic, 89;
      non-realistic, 89–90
Coser, Lewis, 89–90
Cry, the Peacock (1963)
   by Anita Desai, 149
Currinbhoy, Asif, 118

Dahiya, Bhim S., 114, 184
Dahrendorf, Ralph, 81
Das, Veena, 141
democracy, 76
   schizophrenic nature of, 76, and
      violence, 76–77
Derrida, Jacques, 34
Desai, Anita, 155
Deshpande, Shashi, 116, 130, 151
Devi, Jyotirmoyee, 138, 139, 143, 144, 145, 146, 147, 148
Dodiya, J.K., 178–79

Index

domestic violence, 50, 98, 120
  in Kiran Desai's *The Inheritance of Loss,* 120–23
  strategies to deal with, 54–57, at state level, 57–61; at community level, 61–65
dowry death(s), 116

Eliot, T.S., 34, 37
Ellacuria, I., 69
ethnic cleansing
  in Bosnia, 68

false divinities, 72
  in the 20th century, 72: Liberalism, 72; Communism, 72; Fascism, 72
Fanon, Frantz, 85
Fessard, Gaston, 72, 77
Francisco, Joson, 147
Friday, Nancy, 130
Fromm, Eric, 5–6

Galtung, Johan, 69
Gandhi, Mahatma, 6
gender violence, 50
  forms of, 50; in India, 50, 126–27
genocide, 77
  as the ultimate degree of violence, 77–78
Gilligan, Corol, 127
Golding, William, 5, 11–12
Goldman, Emma, 3

Hardt, Michael and Negri, Antonio, 43
Harney, W.H., 9

Haynes, Douglas and Prakash, Gyan, 174
Horney, Karen, 151, 155
humanity, 72
  division of, 72–73
Hunt, Peter, 104

India's Bandit Queen (1991) by Mala Sen, 18, 20–22
Indian English
  literature/playwrights, 114
  'violence' in, 117–19
Indian society, 126
  gendered violence in, 126–27
Indra, 126
interpersonal violence, 119–20

Jain, Jasbir, 157, 162
Jogi, Ajit, 171
Jordan, Judith V., 127

Kakar, Sudhir, 204
Kar, P.K., 120
Karat, Brinda, 52
Karnad, Girish, 178
  plays of, 178, power–violence nexus in, 178–84
Keane, J., 66, 68
Krishnamurti, J., 4

literature–society relationship, 119

Mackenzie, W.J.M., 82
manifested violence, 82
Mannes, Marya, 131
Mannoni, O., 3
Maslow, Abraham, 7

media, 204
  role of, in perpetuating violence among children, 206–16
Mehta, Dina, 116
Menon, Ritu and Bhasin, Kamla, 139, 140, 142
Mukherjee, Bharati, 154, 157

Nahal, Chaman, 115
nationalism, 72
  and violence, relationship between, 73–74
  concept of, 72, as the worst form of violence,, 72
  forms of, 72–73
non-realistic conflict, 89
Noor (2003)
  by Sorayya Khan, 18, 26–29

Pandey, Gyanendra, 138, 141
Paris, B.J., 5
partition literature, 116
  violence as depicted in, 116
partition violence, 138
partition
  of India, 138, 140
Patel, Vibhuti, 175
physical violence, 82
Plath, Sylvia, 151
power elite, 3
power
  Foucault's concept/analysis of, 4
power–violence nexus, 178
Prasad, Madhusudan and Kumar, Alok, 115
Pritam, Amrita, 143
psychological violence, 82, 98

Queen of Dreams (2000)
  by Chitra Banerjee, 98, portrayal of terrorist violence in, 98

realistic conflict, 89
regional terrorism/violence, 97, 107
Richard, I.A., 36
Riches, David, 48
Rosenthal, M.L., 151
Russell, Bertrand, 177–78

Sankaranarayanan, Vasanthi, 169
Sarabhai, Mallika, 2
Satchidanandan, K., 116–17
Scott, James, 174
self-inflicted violence, 119
Sharma, Kalpana, 52
Shiva, Vandana, 7
Sidhwa, Bapsi, 115–16
Simmel, Georg, 93
Singh, D.P., 105
Singh, Manjit and Singh, D.P., 96–97
Singh, R.K., 116
social exclusion, 75
  as a form of violence, 75–76
socio-economic injustice, 70
Spivak, G., 152, 153, 164
Stevens, Wallace, 38
Strathern, Andrew and Steward, P.J., 48
symbolic violence, 45

terrorism, 77, 97, 106
  forms of, 97

terrorist violence, 97
The Dark Holds No Terrors (1980)
by Shashi Deshpande, 125, nuances of gendered violence as shown in, 127–37
The Great Dictator
as film of Charlie Chaplin, 186, expression of violence in, 186
The House of Blue Mangoes (2002)
by David Davidar, 82, caste violence as portrayed in, 83
The Inheritance of Loss (2006)
by Kiran Desai, 98, 105, regional terrorist violence as depicted in, 106–13; domestic violence in, 120–23
The River Churning
by Jyotirmoyee Devi, 139, partition violence in, 144–48
triangle of violence, 48

violence against women, 50
violence, 1, 4, 17, 18, 81, 85, 96, 107, 125
among children, 205
among the youth, 204
as a matter of discourse, 42–43
as entertainment, 67
functions of, 82–83
in creative and critical acts, 33
in Indian English literature, 114–16
in the 20th century, 66–67, 185
in the historical process, 4–7
in tribal/dalit writing, 165–75
main manifestations of, 70: socio-economic, 70–72; nationalism, 72–74; social exclusion, 75–76; genocide, 77–78
methods of, 18
necessity of, for the continuation of civilisation and culture, 17–20; as expressed in the subcontinental literature, 20–29
need for re-defining, 43–47, 82
role of mass media in perpetuating, 205
the singular nature of the phenomenon of, 68–70
types/forms of, 2, 70–78, 82, 97, 114, 119, 125
violent women
in fiction, 149–62

Weber, Max, 85
Westkott, Marcia, 151, 174
WHO, 44, 119
Wife (1976)
by Bharati Mukherjee, 149

Yeats, W.B., 6